D1137338

BISMA

'It is good to have so accessible a biography of Bismarck in one volume. Feuchtwanger takes account of much of the recent writing on the history of the period. Especially valuable is the highlighting of connections between Bismarck's domestic and foreign policies.'

John Breuilly, University of Birmingham

Bismarck was arguably the most important figure in nineteenth-century European history after 1815. In this new biography, Edgar Feuchtwanger reassesses Bismarck's significance as a historical figure. He traces his development from a typical *Junker*, a reactionary and conservative, into the white revolutionary who recast European affairs more drastically than anyone since Napoleon. Feuchtwanger's lucid account demythologizes the German leader without demonizing him. This book leaves the reader with a strongly-etched portrait of one of the decisive makers of the modern world.

Edgar Feuchtwanger studied history at Cambridge, taught British and German history at the University of Southampton and has been visiting professor at the University of Frankfurt. His major publications include *From Weimar to Hitler* (1995), *Disraeli* (2000) and *Imperial Germany 1850–1918* (Routledge, 2001).

ROUTLEDGE HISTORICAL BIOGRAPHIES

SERIES EDITOR: ROBERT PEARCE

Routledge Historical Biographies provide engaging, readable and academically credible biographies written from an explicitly historical perspective. These concise and accessible accounts will bring important historical figures to life for students and general readers alike.

In the same series:

BISMARCK

Edgar Feuchtwanger

LONDON AND NEW YORK

First published 2002
by Routledge
11 New Fetter Lane, London EC4P 4EE

Simultaneously published in the USA and Canada
by Routledge
29 West 35th Street, New York, NY 10001

Routledge is an imprint of the Taylor & Francis Group

Typeset in Garamond and Scala by Keystroke, Jacaranda Lodge,
Wolverhampton
Printed and bound in Great Britain by TJ International Ltd, Padstow,
Cornwall

British Library Cataloguing in Publication Data
A catalogue record for this book is available from the British Library

Library of Congress Cataloging in Publication Data
Feuchtwanger, E. J.
  Bismarck / Edgar Feuchtwanger.
  p. cm.
  Includes bibliographical references and index.
  1. Bismarck, Otto, Fèrst von, 1815–1898. 2. Statesmen–Germany–
  Biography. 3. Prussia (Germany)–Politics and government–1815–1870.
  4. Germany–Politics and government–1871–1888. I. Title.

  DD218 .F48 2002
  943.08′092–dc21
  [B]   2002024909

ISBN 0–415–21614–1 (pbk)
ISBN 0–415–21613–3 (hbk)

CONTENTS

PLATES

CHRONOLOGY

	Personal	Political	General
1815	birth, 1 April	Battle of Waterloo, 18 June	German Confederation established
1832	enters University of Göttingen	Hambach student festival	first British Reform Act passed
1839	returns to Pomerania to manage estates		
1840		Frederick William IV becomes king	
1847	marriage, 28 July	United Prussian Diet meets	Offenburg meeting issues radical programme
1848	becomes known as ultra-conservative, writes in *Kreuzzeitung*	United Prussian Diet meets, April; Prussian constitution promulgated, December	outbreak of revolution, February–March
1849	elected to Prussian parliament	Frederick William IV refuses German crown, 3 April	revolution crushed in Germany and Austria
1850	makes important speech on Olmütz agreement, 3 December	three-tier electoral law introduced in Prussia	Erfurt union, promoted by Radowitz, fails
1851	appointed Prussian envoy to Diet of German Confederation in Frankfurt, 8 May	Otto v. Manteuffel is Prussian prime minister	German Confederation re-established by Schwarzenberg
1855	defeats Austrian request for mobilization of	Prussia remains neutral in Crimean War (1853–6)	fall of Sevastopol, 8 September

	Personal	Political	General
	German forces; January, visits Paris, August		
1859	transferred to St. Petersburg, March	'New Era' in Prussia	Italian war between, Austria, France and Piedmont
1862	becomes Prussian ambassador in Paris, May; Prussian prime minister, 23 September	large liberal majority in Prussian elections, May	Prussia rejects Austrian proposals to reform German Confederation
1863	negotiates Alvensleben convention, February; prevents king from attending Congress of German Princes, August	crown prince protests against suppression of press freedom, June	accession of Christian IX of Denmark, November, precipitates Schleswig-Holstein crisis
1864	initiates joint action with Austria against Denmark	Prussian victory at Düppel (Dybbøl), April	Denmark cedes Schleswig-Holstein to Austria and Prussia, October
1865	does not recommend immediate war against Austria at crown council, 29 May; given title of count (Graf), September	Gastein convention, 20 August, divides administration of Schleswig and Holstein between Prussia and Austria	Frankfurt diet votes to back Augustenburg as duke of Schleswig-Holstein, 6 April
1866	proposes elected parliament for German Confederation, April; escapes assassination attempt, 7 May	battle of Königgrätz (Sadowa) 3 July	indemnity law passed by Prussian parliament, September
1867	acquires estate at Varzin	North German Confederation established	Luxemburg crisis, May
1868	warns against expectations of early completion of German unity	elections to Zollparlament fail to produce pro-Prussian majority, February;	Cretan revolt against Turkey

	Personal	Political	General
1870	encourages Hohenzollern candidature for Spanish throne	Franco-Prussian War, 19 July; German victory at Sedan, 2 September	Russia abrogates Black Sea clauses of treaty of Paris
1871	receives Sachsenwald estate with Friedrichsruh; given title of prince	proclamation of German empire at Versailles, 18 January	treaty of Frankfurt ends Franco-Prussian war, 10 May
1872	intensifies Kulturkampf	appointment of Falk as Prussian minister of culture, January	emperors of Germany, Austria and Russia meet in Berlin, September
1873	temporarily cedes Prussian premiership to Roon	May Laws against Catholic church	stock market crashes start, May; Three Emperors' League, October
1874	escapes assassination attempt at Kissingen, 13 July	National Liberal strength peaks in Reichstag elections, January	French indemnity payments completed
1875	withdraws to Varzin, June–November	Era Bleichröder-Delbrück-Camphausen articles, June–July;	'war in sight' crisis, April–May
1876		German-Conservative party founded	Balkans crisis
1877	on sick leave, May to February1878; Kissingen memorandum, June	negotiations with Bennigsen about National Liberal entry into government	Russo-Turkish war breaks out, April
1878	takes first steps towards protection	assassination attempts on emperor; anti-socialist law	Congress of Berlin, June–July
1879	meets Windthorst at parliamentary soirée, May	tariff law passed, July	dual alliance between Germany and Austria signed, October

	Personal	Political	General
1881	prevents marriage of Herbert to Elisabeth v. Carolath	first accident insurance proposal	Three Emperors' League renewed, 18 June
1882		Reichstag rejects tobacco monopoly proposal, June	Triple Alliance between Germany, Austria and Italy signed, May
1883	Dr Schweninger takes over as doctor	health insurance bill passed;	further alleviation of Kulturkampf laws;
1884		third accident insurance proposal accepted	letters of protection for Angra Pequena (Lüderitz Bay, South-West Africa) issued, March
1885		expulsions of Poles and Jews from eastern provinces begin	crisis over Bulgaria flares up, September
1886	Herbert becomes state secretary for foreign affairs, May	tension with France over General Boulanger	new septennial law proposed
1887		cartel elections, January	reinsurance treaty with Russia, June
1888		year of the three emperors: death of William I, 9 March; death of Frederick III and accession of Willliam II, 15 June	Mediterranean agreement between Britain, Austria and Italy, February–March
1889	in Friedrichsruh and Varzin, with brief breaks, June to January 1890	miners' strikes in the Ruhr; old age pensions law passed	proposal of alliance with Britain
1890	resignation, 18 March	large socialist gains in Reichstag elections, 20 February	reinsurance treaty with Russia not renewed

	Personal	*Political*	*General*
1892	journey to Vienna for Herbert's wedding, July		
1894	conciliation visit to Berlin, 26 January; death of Johanna, 27 November	Caprivi resigns, October	Franco-Russian military convention, January
1896	reinsurance treaty with Russia revealed, October	Kaiser's Kruger telegramme, January	
1898	death, 30 July	first German navy law	

INTRODUCTION

Bismarck dominated Germany and Europe in the second half of the nineteenth century. In creating a unified German state he carried out a revolution from above comparable in historical importance to the French Revolution. His stature was, for many contemporaries and for the generations immediately following, that of a hero who had won legendary triumphs and achieved sensational successes. The German empire of 1871 proved, however, a short-lived construction and survived for only twenty years beyond Bismarck's own life. By 1918 the Hohenzollern monarchy he had fought to preserve was no more. The powerful position he had established for Germany in Europe had vanished. What followed thereafter was even more unstable and catastrophic. By 1945 hardly anything of his legacy was left. Prussia, to the aggrandisement of which he had devoted his life, had ceased to exist. Eastern Pomerania, where he grew up, became part of Poland, the nation whose revival he had always feared as a mortal threat to the Prussian state. Varzin, the estate in eastern Pomerania which he bought in 1867 with the money given to him by a grateful nation and from where he controlled the affairs of Prussia, Germany and Europe for many a long month, is no longer German soil. When Schönhausen, his family's ancestral home on the east bank of Elbe, 50 miles west of Berlin, was about to be occupied by Russian troops in 1945, his niece Sibylle, who had married his younger son Bill, her cousin, shot herself.

BISMARCK – IMAGE, MYTH AND REALITY

Such drastic reversals of fortune have brought about equally drastic reassessments in the historiography of modern Germany as a whole and of Bismarck's place within it. The interpretation of Bismarck's role has veered from unashamed triumphalism to outright condemnation. There was a gap between Bismarck the mythical figure – half Wotan, half Siegfried, as many Germans saw him – and the real man. Physically he was a big man, who towered over most of his contemporaries, given to corpulence in later life, brought on by immoderate eating and drinking. As chancellor he more often than not appeared in uniform, but though his political triumphs gave him the rank of general some of his bitterest battles were fought against his own generals and the horrors of war genuinely shocked him. The public image of Bismarck, the giant with sword sheathed but ready for battle, was a mask. The impression of stolidity was false, for he was a man of extraordinary passion, which he had to struggle to keep under control. For most of his life the passion was consumed by politics and left room for little else. He lay awake at night hating his enemies. He became a pure politician, who subjected everything, situations, countries, personalities, to a friend–foe calculus. Those who opposed him he hammered into the ground. He was incapable of magnanimity to his foes and could not recognize that they might be motivated by principles. He was a supreme realist, to the point of cynicism, he suspected idealism, had little sense of justice or feeling for freedom as a general good. His realism was grounded in pessimism, and even at moments of the greatest triumph he was not tempted by hubris. His pessimism extended to human nature and often reached the point of misanthropy. He preferred his dogs, the large German mastiffs that added to the monumental image the public had of him. To a visitor, who saw him in August 1878, when he was about to make a crucial political turn, he said 'three times, he cared nothing for political parties, conservative or liberal, they were all the same to him; he was going on his way, he who went with him was his friend, he who was against him was his enemy – to the point of annihilation.'[1] It was an attitude that deformed German political culture.

There was another, softer side to him, an almost poetic quality that made him a wizard with words and a brilliant and fascinating conversationalist. When he spoke his voice was high and thin, almost feminine, and his personal charm, when he chose to turn it on, was great. Diplomats were seduced by it, when they ought to have known better. As a public speaker he was not stentorian or a demagogue, rather a man who weighed his words carefully, delighting in sarcasm and irony, a parliamentary polemicist who hardly ever used a script and whose speeches still read well. To his family, his wife and three children, he was totally devoted, but he expected their complete submission to his needs. His enemies were their enemies and their task was to form a phalanx around him against the hostile outer world. Rarely were so many contrasting qualities concentrated in such profusion in a single individual. Genius is more difficult to define in politics than in art. Bismarck claimed that politics was an art, and if there is such a quality as political genius then he had it. But opinions diverge diametrically when it comes to deciding whether his was a genius that produced beneficent results.

BISMARCK'S CAREER

We can now see that Bismarck's extraordinarily powerful impact owed much to the fact that he was a man who could thrive in the halfway house between absolute monarchy and parliamentary institutions that existed in Prussia after the revolution of 1848. He entered politics as a conservative Prussian *Junker* in 1847. The Junkers, the name customarily given to the landed aristocracy in the Prussian provinces east of the Elbe, were regarded by most of the world as reactionary backwoodsmen. Bismarck came to early prominence because, unlike most politically active members of his class, he was able to master the techniques required in a parliamentary assembly. He was on a steep learning curve and soon realized the maintenance of the conservative order required more than a dogmatic adherence to monarchical legitimism. His performance as a spokesman for the conservatives in the period after the failure of the revolution gave him the reputation that enabled him to leapfrog into a key diplomatic position in 1851, at the age of 36. He was appointed the Prussian envoy to the diet of the German Confederation at Frankfurt. It was a capital vantage point for observing what was going on within and between the nearly forty German states that made up the Confederation.

The relations between the two major German powers, Austria and Prussia, were naturally the main preoccupation of the Prussian envoy. Beyond the German Confederation there was the European power system, of which Bismarck gained an intimate knowledge from his position at Frankfurt. Like the domestic politics of Prussia and many other European countries, this system was also at a halfway stage, between the cabinet diplomacy of an earlier period and the entry of public opinion and eventually of the masses into politics. Bismarck developed above all into a master of diplomacy and the conduct of foreign policy was his main preoccupation for the rest of his life. But he realized that diplomacy could no longer be conducted in a vacuum, if indeed that had ever been the case. Social, economic and ideological forces exerted increasing pressure: that was precisely the reality of the halfway house.

Bismarck's appointment as Prussian envoy in Frankfurt lasted nearly eight years, until the spring of 1859. It is a very richly documented period of his life and has therefore influenced the writing of his biography very considerably. He was not a leading actor, as he became in the 1860s, and could therefore express himself mainly through the advice he gave. The stream of letters and memoranda he unleashed upon his nominal superiors in Berlin enable one to trace the evolution of the ideas which he could put into practice in the following decade. He keeps on reiterating his conclusion that Prussia could only survive and prosper through a showdown with Austria about the respective position of the two countries in German affairs. In such a confrontation Prussia would need all the allies she could get, including France, ruled by Napoleon III. The prospect of an alliance with a Bonapartist regime was abhorrent to the Prussian conservatives who had sent Bismarck to Frankfurt. He was, however, not a man who allowed ideologies, programmes, or preconceived ideas to inhibit his ruthlessly realistic assessment of the immediate situation. His strength was that he could gauge the immensely complex web of forces that were operating at any given moment and that he had, once in power, the enormous mental energy to manipulate them in his own interest. He was no mere opportunist, but he was intensely suspicious of all idealism and all idealists. The outlook upon European affairs he developed in the 1850s was therefore not a blueprint for what he was going to do in the following decade, but more of a thorough mapping of the diplomatic scene, an approach to problems and a methodology for solving them. He knew he could not make events, merely use them. He liked to quote the Latin tag 'unda fert nec regitur': one cannot make a wave, only ride it.

Bismarck became prime minister and minister of foreign affairs in Prussia in September 1862. The following eight years, until the proclamation of the German empire in January 1871, are the heroic period of his life. From inauspicious beginnings he went on to transform Germany and

Europe. The unification of Germany was accomplished by the Prussian monarchical regime and its armies, but his was the direction. The national-liberal movement played the subordinate role he allotted it, when once it had been expected to play the leading part. The Habsburg empire, the other leading player in Germany, was excluded. These were the far-reaching consequences of Bismarck's work. There was about Bismarck in his heyday something of the gambler, not in the reckless way of Hitler, but as a man prepared to take high risks at the margins of possibility, but with alternative fall-back positions always at the ready. Another Latin tag he liked to quote was 'flectere si nequeo superos, acheronta movebo' (If I cannot move the Gods, I will turn to the Devil). At key moments in his career, he was prepared to use all means available to achieve the success he judged to be within his grasp. Therefore both contemporaries as well as posterity have seen him as a man of revolutionary temperament. In 1866, for example, in what may be called the hinge of fate of his public life, he risked war with Austria, lining up for the struggle all available auxiliaries, including Hungarian revolutionaries, in order to achieve the supremacy of Prussia in Germany. Yet his fundamental purpose was to keep revolution, the kind of upheaval that had threatened Europe from time to time since 1789, at bay. He was not a red, but a 'white revolutionary'. Better to make a revolution than to suffer one, he said. Not unnaturally, many of his conservative friends and party colleagues felt that his means were in danger of overwhelming his ends. He had always been supremely self-confident; and, as he moved from one sensational success to another, his belief in his own superiority became unshakeable.

After 1871 there was no more scope or need for revolution. In foreign affairs, the area which Bismarck still thought of as his preferred sphere of activity, his aim was to maintain the status quo and the security of the new state he had created. War was the godfather of revolution and to be avoided, but it was not a case of maintaining peace at all costs, for war remained an instrument of policy for cabinet politicians of Bismarck's generation. He was not above using the threat of it and when he did so it usually also had a domestic purpose. It is, however, the impact of Bismarck's prolonged tenure of power on Germany's internal affairs that has chiefly exercised revisionist and post-revisionist historians. The essence of the German semi-constitutional system had been created by Bismarck in 1866 and maintained by him against those who wanted to move towards a fully fledged parliamentary system on the western model. This system of skirted decisions, as Wolfgang Mommsen, a leading contemporary German historian,[2] calls it, was perpetuated and it formed German political attitudes for the rest of the imperial period. Germans believed that the state existed above politics, but this left no room for the deeply divisive conflicts of a rapidly industrializing and modernizing society to express themselves in a politically legitimate form. Bismarck's presence was so overwhelming, his mythical stature so deeply embedded, that he could manipulate or ignore these conflicts. His successors could not break the mould and in the Wilhelmine age after 1890 the German scene was like a high-pressure cooker waiting to explode. Even after the collapse of the German empire in 1918 the attitudes and patterns of behaviour formed in the Bismarck period continued to affect German politics profoundly.

BISMARCK AND THE HISTORIANS

Until 1945, or at least until 1918, the writing of German history was dominated by the national-liberal school of historians. They saw in the rise of the Second Reich, principally the work of Bismarck, the natural culmination of German history. The existence of such a view among leading nineteenth-century German historians was itself a factor in easing Bismarck's task. Protestant Prussia was seen by these historians as the appropriate focus for a revival of German unity, which had been lost in the later Middle Ages, in the wars of religion of the sixteenth and seventeenth centuries and finally in the upheavals of the French Revolution and the Napoleonic age. It was Bismarck, the historical giant, who turned this vision into reality. Alternatives, such as a more loosely constructed Central Europe including the German-speaking subjects of the Habsburgs, *Grossdeutschland* as opposed to the Prussian-led *Kleindeutschland*, fell by the wayside. When Bismarck achieved the unification by Prussia of the states comprising the German Confederation of 1815, leaving the Habsburg empire outside, he advanced to heroic status as the founder of the Reich, the *Reichsgründer*. Heinrich von Sybel was a leading member of the national-liberal school of historians and also a liberal member of the Prussian parliament. In January 1871, when William I was proclaimed German emperor at Versailles, Sybel wrote to his colleague Hermann Baumgarten: 'How has one deserved the mercy of God, to live through such great and mighty events? And how will one live afterwards? What has been for twenty years the content of all one's desires and strivings, has now been accomplished in such boundlessly magnificent manner! Where shall one find, at my time of life, a new meaning for the future?'³ Sybel and Baumgarten were both liberals, who only a few years previously had been bitter opponents of the repressive regime which Bismarck had set up in Prussia when he took office as prime minister in September 1862. Now he was their hero and that of the German nation.

The Bismarck cult was at its peak in the twenty years between his death and Germany's defeat in 1918. Bismarck monuments sprang up all over Germany and his name was invoked on innumerable occasions when Germans gathered to celebrate the greatness, power and future destiny of their nation. To mark the centenary of the birth of the Reich's founder on 1 April 1915, eight months into a world war against a hostile coalition that Bismarck had always prevented from coalescing, the historian Friedrich Meinecke wrote: 'It is the spirit of Bismarck, which forbids us to sacrifice our vital interests and has forced us to the heroic decision to take up the prodigious struggle against East and West, to speak with Bismarck: "like a strong fellow, who has two good fists at his disposal, one for each opponent."' Meinecke was by no means an extremist among nationalist historians. Born in the year Bismarck came to power he lived long enough to fall foul of the Nazis and to experience the total collapse of Germany in 1945. His book *The German Catastrophe*, published in German in 1946, is a poignant attempt to come to terms with what had gone wrong. He was far too subtle a historian to have portrayed Bismarck, even in 1915, as a hero without fear and reproach. He had to admit that Bismarck had been more successful in establishing the external than the internal unity of the Reich. Albeit in muted form he foreshadowed what another forty or fifty years on became the nub of the case against Bismarck, that he treated whole sections of his own nation, first the Catholics, then the workers, as enemies, as *Reichsfeinde*: 'He divided the parties into either supporters or enemies of the state and treated them accordingly.' In Meinecke's eulogy of Bismarck as the forger of German power there was, even in 1915, thinly veiled criticism of his successors: 'Bismarck would have been horrified, if he had thought of the possibility of the world-wide hostility of today, he would at first sight have believed in the irresponsible levity, or the limitless incompetence of our statesmen.'⁴ Bismarck himself had helped to fan this criticism after his fall in 1890 and it swelled into a chorus after the German defeat in 1918. Bismarck's genius now shone all the more brightly in comparison with the disastrous record of his successors, who had ruined his inheritance. It became possible after 1918 to document the inside story of the Bismarck years much more fully than had been possible while the Hohenzollerns were still on the throne. Two volumes of Bismarck's memoirs had been published immediately after his death but now the third volume, giving his side of the story of his fall, was made public. It contained his far from flattering characterization of the kaiser before and after his accession.

Neither the domestic nor the foreign political situation of the Weimar years was conducive to a critical reappraisal of Bismarck. The energies of the German historical profession were concentrated on rebutting what was called the war guilt lie, the clause in the treaty of Versailles pinning responsibility for the outbreak of the First World War on Germany. There was no room for a fundamental questioning of the historical justification for Bismarck's life work nor of the methods he used. Historians who did question, for example Johannes Ziekursch and Eckhart Kehr, were professional outsiders.[5] The Nazis used Bismarck for their own purposes. In 1933, when Hitler wanted to hide his revolutionary purpose from the German middle classes, he portrayed himself as the last link in a Prussian tradition reaching from Frederick the Great through Bismarck and Hindenburg to himself. Posters and postcards showing the profiles of the men announced: 'What the king conquered, the prince formed, the marshal defended, was saved and united by the soldier.' The Nazis could not pay homage to Bismarck without reservations. To their regret he had not aimed at including all Germans in his Reich. He had been backward in failing to recognize the crucial role of the biological factor of race in history. He had not based his policies on the supremacy of the German master race, nor had he stopped the Jews from undermining it. It was left to Hitler and his movement to carry out the racial revolution which would be the ultimate culmination of German history. When in March 1938 the Austrian *Anschluss* occurred, it was said that Hitler had accomplished, without firing a shot, what even Bismarck had failed to do. The iron chancellor was a precursor, but even he could not compare with the Führer, who had now united all the German countries into one Reich. 'Ein Volk, ein Reich, ein Führer' was the slogan shouted by the masses acclaiming Hitler.

After 1945 a reassessment of Bismarck and of modern German history in general was slow in coming. The generation of German historians that had lived through the two world wars preferred to hark back to Bismarck's greatness to show up the depth of failure among his successors. Conservative and nationalist, but anti-Nazi historians like Gerhard Ritter in the postwar era drew a sharp contrast between Bismarck's carefully calculated policies directed towards limited and realistic objectives, and Hitler the gambler risking all in a utopian drive for world domination. It was part of a tendency to see the morally and materially destructive Third Reich as a deviation from the normal course of German history, due to exceptionally adverse circumstances and to the incursion of the masses into a political process previously dominated by elites. Hitler was the demagogue who had succeeded in temporarily mesmerizing the stirred-up masses, but he was otherwise an alien intruder into the traditional norms of German political behaviour. German historians were reacting against the hostile view of their history and identity that two world wars had engendered in the outside world. For non-Germans Bismarck usually held a prominent place in the gallery of German villains. He was the Prussian Junker who unified Germany by blood and iron, ditched the liberals and foisted Prussian militarism on the whole of Germany. In his widely read *History of the Third Reich* the American journalist William Shirer draws such a picture, in the few pages he devotes to Bismarck in his chapter on the roots of the Third Reich. A.J.P. Taylor was far too good and sophisticated a historian to portray Bismarck in such a simplistic way in his short biography published in 1955 and sees him perhaps too much as man moved by short-term calculations. But he does not doubt that excess of militarism and deficit of liberalism came in the wake of Bismarck.[6]

The generation of German historians who opposed the Versailles treaty in the 1920s and were still around after 1945 felt the need to defend the rise of the German nation state and Bismarck's role in it. The exception was again a man who stood outside the ranks of the academic historical profession. Erich Eyck wrote the first major Bismarck biography following the rise of Hitler, a three-volume work, on which he was working before and during the Second World War. Eyck was a liberal who had to go into exile after the rise of Hitler. He writes in the tradition of the great liberal opponents of Bismarck, men like Eduard Lasker or Ludwig Bamberger, who in their writings and speeches attacked the domination of the iron chancellor and lamented the devastation he was inflicting upon German political culture. Eyck does not belittle Bismarck's genius, but agrees with Bamberger's description of him as 'un barbare de génie'. A review of Eyck's third volume in *The Times Literary Supplement* at the end of the war says that the book reveals 'much of the evil of Hitlerite Germany as an inheritance from Bismarck'. Eyck as a German conveys something of the distaste that anyone brought up in the Anglo-Saxon liberal tradition experiences when confronted by many aspects of Bismarck in word and deed. This distaste was already experienced in the chancellor's lifetime and permeates the correspondence of Vicky, crown princess of Prussia and empress of Germany, with her mother, Queen Victoria. It surfaces again in Otto Pflanze's three volumes on *Bismarck and the Development of Germany*, the major recent American work on the subject, and is even more evident in Edward Crankshaw's biography, published in 1981. At the end of his book Crankshaw writes:

> To say that Bismarck was a precursor of Hitler is evidently untrue; but it is not untrue, I think, to say that those aspects of the German character which made it possible for Bismarck to rule for just on thirty years were those same aspects that made it too easy for Hitler to take power and to keep it.[7]

In the 1960s German assessments of Bismarck and of modern German history began to change. A book published in German in 1961 by the Hamburg historian Fritz Fischer, *Germany's Aims in the First World War*, is generally credited with having broken the mould. It contradicted much of the work done in Germany on the war guilt question and caused great controversy. A younger generation of academic historians welcomed Fischer's evidence that there was in Germany before 1914 a strong tide of opinion flowing in favour of expansion, if necessary by war. How far this influenced official policy remained in dispute. Soon other work was published, reassessing the politics of imperial Germany, and therefore Bismarck's place in it. Students of Bismarck had hitherto celebrated him as above all a genius in the conduct of foreign policy and contrasted his skill and moderation with the lack of these qualities in his successors. German historiography had always assumed the primacy of foreign policy, that the destiny of a country was mainly determined by its situation within the international system. A country like Germany, in the centre of Europe, could only survive with strong government and this was what Bismarck had provided. It was the reason why the constitution of imperial Germany, in essence drawn up by him, did not establish a fully parliamentary regime. It had been an article of faith for generations of Germans that this was suitable and necessary for their country. German historians working on Bismarck after 1960 all but reversed this principle. They examined his foreign policy and that of his successors from the point of view of domestic politics and often assumed the primacy of domestic politics. The concept of social imperialism became important. This was the idea that expansion abroad, imperialism, colonialism and their concomitants were the result of domestic circumstances. Their prime purpose was to divert public attention from problems at home, to reduce the pressure for change and to safeguard the privileges of existing elites. Thus Bismarck's excursion into colonial expansion in the 1880s was seen as being motivated not so much by considerations of diplomacy as by electoral and political necessities within Germany. A seminal work of this kind was H.-U. Wehler's *Bismarck und der Imperialismus* (Bismarck and Imperialism), published in 1969.[8] The process of unification in the 1860s was interpreted as largely predetermined by economic forces in Herbert Böhme's *Deutschland's Weg zur Großmacht* (Germany's Path to Great Power Status), published in 1967. In these and other works the previous preoccupation of German historiography with the strictly political and with single important actors was discarded in favour of preoccupation with social and economic factors. It was an aspect of the westernization of West German culture. History, in common with other branches of knowledge, was adopting methods that had long been accepted in the western democracies.

Primacy of domestic politics and emphasis on social and economic forces produced a much more negative interpretation of Bismarck. He could no longer be seen as the great man who almost single-handed brought about the establishment of the modern German nation state. If he was largely the servant of impersonal forces, then the use he made of them could not be regarded as beneficial. After the disasters of the first half of the twentieth century many features of the Reich established by Bismarck could no longer be seen in a positive light. It was through him that the Prussian monarchy and its armies became the unifiers of Germany, while the liberal movement, previously the main protagonist of the German national idea, was at best allowed to play an ancillary role. The essentials of the political system of imperial Germany were shaped by him and designed to suit the retention of power by him. The custom and practice of operating this system were established in the twenty years Bismarck remained in office after 1870. His was a charismatic rule, preserved through manipulation of opinion, instrumentalization of political and societal forces for his own ends, and through the use of Bonapartist devices, such as turning elections into plebiscitary acclamations. Revisionist historians of the 1960s and 1970s postulated a German *Sonderweg* (separate path), a deviation from the liberal parliamentary democracy that was the norm in the West. It soon became a matter for debate whether there was a *Sonderweg*, but whatever the problems of the concept, it is hardly disputed that imperial Germany was a more authoritarian and less liberal society than those of western Europe, Scandinavia and North America. Bismarck's influence on the origins and the further development of modern Germany was so great that a good deal of the responsibility for these shortcomings, as they were regarded by the revisionists, was his.

Revisionism provokes further revision. In the 1980s West Germany experienced a conservative turn in its political culture and the reunification of Germany in 1990 changed the perspective on Bismarck once more. Major contributions to the interpretations of the Bismarck period and of imperial Germany by German historians, such as the Bismarck biographies of Lothar Gall in West Germany and Ernst Engelberg in East Germany, the writings of Michael Stürmer, the histories of Thomas Nipperdey and H.-U. Wehler, can hardly be said to represent a return to the national-liberal school.[9] In varying degrees they emphasize that in Bismarck's heroic period, in the years of unification, he was aligned with powerful ideological and material forces and was therefore able to have a revolutionary impact. He carried out a revolution from above and Germany continued to bear the marks of a country where revolution had been made from above and not from below. Post-revisionist historians concede that in the last twenty years of his time in power there was more of a sense of stagnation about Bismarck, and Gall gives this section of his biography the title 'The sorcerer's apprentice', who used the spell he learnt to bring forth the flood but forgot the magic formula to call it off. Nipperdey, whose underlying theme is the legitimacy of the modern German nation state, cannot avoid castigating some of Bismarck's methods of governing. Wehler, the doyen of revisionists, modifies the *Sonderweg* concept, but continues to interpret Bismarck's rule as charismatic. The charismatic ruler has to keep on replenishing his charisma through success and once he fails to do so starts losing control. After 1870 the scope for sensational successes diminished for Bismarck and his charisma became less compelling. He was incapable of giving up power gracefully and condemned himself to an increasingly sterile battle to keep control. In 1890 the brash young Kaiser William II had little difficulty in forcing his resignation. It was, however, not the end of the story, for soon the myth of the legendary founder of the Reich revived with redoubled force. Germans still find it a struggle to come to terms with the myth, but the Anglo-Saxon reader has the great advantage of being able to approach Bismarck without such mental baggage.

1

EARLY DAYS

Prussia was Bismarck's country and it was he who transformed it into the German Reich. Prussia was a country that had no geographical or ethnic identity and its shape and the composition of its population changed over the course of time. For a short period at the end of the eighteenth century it contained almost as many Polish speakers as German speakers. What gave it shape and identity was its ruling dynasty, the Hohenzollerns. They came from South Germany and their rule in what later became Prussia began in the march of Brandenburg in 1415. The Hohenzollerns established in the territories they acquired an ethos that impressed itself upon the peoples they ruled. It was this ethos more than anything else that constituted the Prussian identity. Three great Hohenzollern rulers following each other with hardly a break in the seventeenth and eighteenth century put Prussia on the map as a major European power. They were the Great Elector, who ruled from 1640 to 1688, Frederick William I, the soldier king, who ruled from 1713 to 1740, and, most famous of all, his son Frederick the Great, whose reign extended from 1740 to 1786.

There followed a period of decline, which ended in almost complete annihilation at the hands of Napoleon, in the battle of Jena in 1806. Prussia recovered from this low point largely through the work of some notable civil and military reformers, most of whom came from outside the country, men like Stein, Scharnhorst and Gneisenau. 'Travailler pour le roi de Prusse' was an old saying, indicating that the Hohenzollern rulers had always known how to attract hardworking military and civilian officials for little material reward, often from other parts of German-speaking Central Europe. They had also offered refuge to Huguenot exiles driven from their native country by the revocation of the Edict of Nantes in 1685. French names became common in the Prussian aristocracy. This was what the Prussian ethos was all about: hard work for the common good, efficient, incorrupt administration and religious toleration, which was necessary in territories where there were Lutherans, Calvinists and Catholics. The dynasty itself was Calvinist. These were some of the positive aspects of Prussianism, but there were also plenty of negative ones. It was a military state and much of what was produced went to the maintenance of the army, with the aim of enabling the country 'to punch above its weight'. The people were treated as a means to this end; they were, in Frederick the Great's phrase, 'the infilling substance of the state'. Such a state, even if ruled by an enlightened despot like Frederick, was no match for the highly motivated soldiers of the French Revolution. After the defeat of 1806 the reformers tried to remedy some of these shortcomings, by bringing in a greater measure of self-government and by replacing the mercenary army with a citizen army.

When Bismarck was born on 1 April 1815 the Prussian reform era was ending, with most of the reforms left unfinished. The Junkers, the aristocracy to which the Bismarck family belonged, had resisted them to the best of their ability. But the battle of Waterloo, in which the Prussian armies were to play a considerable role, was only weeks away and Prussia was on the side of the victors. As a result she was to undergo yet another transformation, giving her control of large and potentially valuable territories in the Rhineland and in northern Saxony. In the late eighteenth century Prussia had almost more Polish than German subjects. After 1815 she became a mainly German power, the second European great power in the German Confederation that replaced the defunct Holy Roman empire. It was on these foundations that Bismarck, half a century later, established the Second German Reich.

*

Otto von Bismarck-Schönhausen was the offspring of a marriage between a typical Prussian country Junker father and a mother who came from a non-Prussian family of academics. Otto's maternal grandfather had opted to work for the king of Prussia as an official, had been a cabinet secretary to Frederick the Great and an influential cabinet counsellor under his two successors, Frederick William II and III. He had been a servant of monarchical absolutism, but he was influenced by the ideas of the Enlightenment. The Bismarck family had been landowners in the march of Brandenburg since at least the fourteenth century. At a moment in the Franco-Prussian War in 1870, when his king caused him particular annoyance, Otto recalled how the Suabian Hohenzollerns had made his sixteenth-century ancestors move from Burgstall, north of Magdeburg and west of the Elbe, to Schönhausen, for no other reason than that they liked to hunt around Burgstall. But the Bismarcks were not rebellious and service in the Prussian armies became normal for them by the eighteenth century, as it did for many Junker families. Frederick William I, the soldier king, in an instruction to his successor, mentioned the Bismarcks among others as a family that he had found disobedient. Bismarck was always very conscious that he belonged to a class that had lorded it over the peasants since time immemorial and that the state building of the Hohenzollerns had to rest on a compromise with the interests of his class. The nobility in the old provinces of Prussia were the irreducible building blocks of the Prussian state. The Hohenzollerns had the knack, nevertheless, of turning the narrow and selfish concerns of their landowning class into loyalty to themselves and to the state they were building up. The Junkers turned into a service aristocracy, the backbone of the Prussian military state. Otto's great-grandfather and grandfather fought for Frederick the Great. His father Ferdinand did not serve long in the army and returned to manage his estates. Besides Schönhausen, on the Elbe, they had three estates in Pomerania, in the area north-east of Stettin (now Szczecin) known in German as Hinterpommern, the Pomerania of the back of beyond, and generally considered the most backward region of the old Prussian provinces.

Otto's mother Wilhelmine Mencken married into this archetypal squirearchical family at the age of seventeen, in 1806. Her father had died five years earlier, but she remained linked to the court and was a playmate of the later Frederick William IV. Coming from an influential family at the hub of affairs, she resented being buried away in the country. Her husband was amiable and easy-going and prepared to take her advice on important family decisions, though in dealing with his peasants he behaved like a mini-king. She was intensely ambitious for her two surviving sons and determined that they should not lead the undistinguished lives of country squires. Reform of the school and university system was a central feature of the Prussian renaissance after Jena. In 1810 Wilhelm von Humboldt had founded the new University of Berlin and thereby took a big step towards making the Prussian and German university system prestigious throughout the world. Wilhelmine Mencken wanted her sons to be highly educated and follow in the footsteps of her distinguished family of academics and public servants. She was a bluestocking and somewhat lacking in maternal warmth. Thus it came about that both her sons were sent away to school, Otto, the younger, at the early age of six, when it would have been more usual to have them privately educated by a tutor in preparation for joining the public education system at a later stage. Otto, like his elder brother Bernhard, was sent to the Plamann Institute in Berlin, a school once dedicated to the progressive principles of Johann Heinrich Pestalozzi, but by the time the young Bismarck went there, it hardly deviated from the conventional groove of authoritarian learning and discipline. In adult life Bismarck often compared it to a penal institution, but this was an exaggeration. He claimed that he resented the fate his mother had imposed on him, and that even in the holidays she was often not there to look after him because she was taking the waters for her weak health. In pursuit of dry learning she had deprived him of the joys of a childhood spent in the countryside. Looking out of a window of the Plamann Institute, he found that the sight of a team of oxen ploughing made him weep with longing, so he claimed, for Kniephof, the Bismarck estate in Pomerania, the paradise from which he had been separated.

When he was the all-powerful chancellor it became a habit for Bismarck to spend long periods on the country estates a grateful nation had provided for him and to absent himself, sometimes for diplomatic reasons, from Berlin. He enjoyed flirting with the idea that he might retire to the simple life of a country gentleman, to which he had been born. Yet it would never have suited him, and when for a time in his mid- and late twenties he did manage the Bismarck estates he grew restless. His mother may have occasioned him much unhappiness in his youth, but by the course she marked out for him she steeled his ambition to impose himself upon the world. In an often-quoted remark he once said he wanted to 'make his own music, as he saw fit, or none'. He could not rest until he fulfilled this ambition and he could not desist from 'making his own music' until he died. After leaving the Plamann Institute he went from 1827 to 1832 to two well-known Berlin secondary schools. During this time he lived in the Berlin flat of his family, together with his uncle General Friedrich von Bismarck. As an adolescent he got to know life in socially and politically influential circles in the capital and heard the talk of people who were close to the centres of power.

*

Otto was too averse to discipline and conformity to have made a good pupil and student, despite his high intelligence. When at the age of seventeen the time had come for him to go to university he first went to Göttingen, which lay outside Prussia in Hanover, still linked to the British crown, and later to Berlin. Göttingen and Berlin had distinguished professors, whose names are still remembered, for instance Dahlmann, one of the Göttingen Seven, who were to be dismissed in 1837 by the newly enthroned king of Hanover for their loyalty to the constitution. In Berlin there was the famous jurist Friedrich Carl von Savigny, and Hegel had taught there up to his death in 1831. Bismarck, who, because a career in the public service was intended for him, studied law, made scarcely any use of the available opportunities. The only professor whose lectures he attended with some regularity in Göttingen was Arnold Heeren, then a widely renowned historian. Heeren made much of the influence of material conditions, the processes of wealth creation, in all periods of history, and stressed the influence of trade and economic considerations on the relations between states. This made a lasting impact on Bismarck and may have helped him later to appreciate the importance of economic forces and of economically rising social classes.

Otherwise Bismarck led the life of a heavy-drinking, hard-fighting, whoring young nobleman let off the leash. He was tall and physically imposing, dressed extravagantly and went around with a large dog. He did not join a *Burschenschaft*, one of the politically active student associations, which were a major factor in keeping German national consciousness alive after 1815. The *Burschenschaften* were about to come together in the Hambach meeting of 1832, one of the landmarks in the liberal, national struggle against the conservative regime associated with the Holy Alliance and Metternich. The *Burschenschaften* did not allow duelling and it would not have sat well with Bismarck's aristocratic self-consciousness to have joined them. In the *Corps Hannovera*, which he did join, he fought twenty-five duels in the space of three terms. In letters to a student friend, Scharlach, he affects a cynical, hardbitten, anti-intellectual tone: 'If you want to read this letter in the spirit in which it is written, you must drink a bottle of Madeira first. I would apologize for my long silence if you were not so well acquainted with my inborn repugnance to ink and if you did not know that in Göttingen I prefer to drink two bottles of hock rather than write a letter, and that the sight of a pen gives me convulsions.'[1]

This was not all there was to Bismarck even in his student days. His three closest friends were outsiders in this environment. They were the American John Lothrop Motley, later the distinguished historian of the Dutch Republic, and two brothers from the Baltic German aristocracy, Counts Hermann and Alexander von Keyserling. Alexander, whom he got to know in Berlin, was a scholarly figure, who, like Motley, remained a lifelong friend. From them we learn of a very different side of Bismarck, long discussions on religion, politics and literary explorations, Byron, Shakespeare, Heine and many others. Bismarck knew English well and often used English quotations and phrases in his correspondence and speeches. Heine's ironical, ambivalent writings were close to his own style of expression. He read widely, but not systematically. He dipped into books and more often than not cast them aside, if he failed to find what he wanted. To the world he might look like the typical Junker, but he wrote of the life of his social equals in the same sharply perceptive, cynical, witty tone that he affected in all his letters. Again to Scharlach he wrote in 1833 that should he visit him in Kniephof ten years hence he would find him as a reserve officer run to fat, who regards Jews and Frenchmen with repugnance and takes it out on his dogs and his servants when his wife becomes the domestic tyrant, and so on in similar vein. Alexander Keyserling remembers him as saying 'a constitution is inevitable, this is the way to external honours, inwardly one must be pious.'[2] A typical Junker backwoodsman would not have thought a constitution inevitable. He himself remembered in the 1860s a bet that there would be a united Germany in twenty years. No doubt he thought it would be under the king of Prussia, a very different expectation from that entertained by the *Burschenschaften*. Motley and Keyserling, from their very different backgrounds, were highly critical of the hidebound regimented atmosphere of Prussia and through them Bismarck must have learnt how Prussia was viewed by more liberal outsiders. Motley was a republican, and Bismarck professed to be republican, though in theory rather than practice. He was certainly an unbeliever and had given up saying his prayers at the age of sixteen. In 1839 Motley published a youthful novel, *Morton's Hope*, in which appears a young nobleman probably modelled on Bismarck: Otto von Rabenmark is an exuberant, daredevil young student seeking notoriety among his contemporaries. But at home he is rational, widely read, highly gifted, conscious that his public appearance is role-playing.

Bismarck passed the exams to become a Prussian official and spent a period as a young official in Aachen in the summer of 1836. It was a life he disliked from the beginning; 'the longest title and the most splendid decoration in Germany will not compensate me for the shrivelled outlook, which is the result of such a life', he wrote. Contempt for bureaucracy accompanied him all his life, though as the all-powerful minister he later knew well how to use it. The Junker in him had the same ambivalent feeling towards the bureaucratic Prussian state as he had to the ruling Hohenzollerns. He would have liked to become a diplomat, but when he told Ancillon, the Prussian foreign minister, of his ambition, he was informed that Prussian country Junkers lacked the wider horizons to do well in the diplomatic service. In Aachen he had little time for the native bourgeois elite – he called it 'the native Canaille' – and sought the company of the many foreign, mostly aristocratic and English visitors who came to this then fashionable spa. Thus he fell successively in love with two young Englishwomen, first a Miss Laura Russell, niece of the duke of Cleveland, and then more seriously with Isabella Loraine-Smith, the daughter of a well-connected and affluent Leicestershire parson.

From his correspondence with his brother Bernhard, some of it revealed only within the last thirty years, it appears that he was much pleased with his entrée into this aristocratic English circle. Its wider horizons enabled him to cast off his self-image of a Pomeranian backwoodsman. His boundless pride and highly vulnerable self-esteem took a knock when he heard rumours that the current duchess of Cleveland was, in a previous incarnation, a high-class prostitute and that Laura Russell might be the off-spring of one of her liaisons. He wrote to his brother that among the English party he might be pointed out through a looking glass: '. . . look there, that tall monster, that is the silly German baron, whom they have caught in the woods, with his pipe and his seal-ring'.[3] With Isabella Loraine-Smith it became an even more consuming passion and he followed her and her family around Europe for much of the year 1837, got engaged and piled up more debts. He extended his original leave of absence from his post in Aachen from a fortnight to many months. Finally it all broke up. In his usual ironical-cynical style he told his friend Scharlach, many years later in 1845: '. . . after two months' possession my conquest was taken from me by a colonel aged 50, with 4 horses and an income of 15,000 Reichsthaler. Poor in my purse, sick in my heart, I returned home to Pomerania.'[4] Isabella did not marry the colonel either, but a banker from

Harrow. It is intriguing to speculate what would have happened had she married Bismarck.

He never returned to his post in Aachen and obtained a transfer to Potsdam. His boss in Aachen, Count Arnim-Boitzenburg, later a minister, wrote to him welcoming his decision to return to 'more arduous official duties ... for which you strove in vain under the prevailing social circumstances in Aachen'.[5] He worked for five months in Potsdam, then reluctantly did his army service, having tried to avoid it by claiming a weakness in his right arm. Some years earlier, when his mother saw how little serious study agreed with him, she suggested a career in the army, but he found the idea abhorrent, strange for one who was to lead the Prussian military monarchy to a peak of power. But, as a young man, official service, civil or military, was clearly not for him. All the time he was seriously embarrassed by his debts. In the autumn of 1838 he decided to leave the public service and devote himself to the management of the family estates. He moved to Kniephof in the spring of 1839. He was barely twenty-four and there had already been many false starts in his life. It was perhaps fortunate that his mother died in January 1839, for she must have been severely disappointed in him. In an often quoted letter to a cousin, which was also intended for other members of the family, he justified his decision to give up a public career.[6] He makes much of the need to improve his financial situation and to do so by increasing the profitability of the family estates, which were not doing very well. But then he argues at length as to why the life of a Prussian public servant did not suit him, that it was his ambition to command rather than obey. There is the remark that he wishes 'to make his own music', for the Prussian official is like the individual player in an orchestra, he has to play his part without a view of or influence over the whole. In a state with a free constitution those concerned with affairs of state can bend their efforts towards ends of which they approve, but in Prussia you have to merge your individuality into the caste of officialdom and make its outlook your own.

*

Thus it came about that he spent the next eight years, till his entry into politics in 1847, as a country Junker. First the two brothers administered the three Pomeranian estates jointly, while the father ran Schönhausen. In 1841, when Bernhard was elected *Landrat*, he retained Jarchelin, while Otto ran Kniephof and Külz. The Landrat was the official administering a district on behalf of the central government and at this time the position was usually held by a local landowner. After the death of Ferdinand in 1845 Otto took over Schönhausen. The return to Pomerania was a retreat, but its main motivation was to preserve his own individuality. He was a Prussian Junker with deep roots in the countryside, yet a man conscious of possibilities within himself far transcending the narrowness of Junkerdom. For a while the life in the Pomeranian countryside seems to have satisfied him. He and his brother had some success in improving the financial situation of the estates and the double-entry booking keeping, about which he joked as usual, taught him something that was still useful when he later had to make economic judgments on a much larger scale.

Although strictly feudal ties no longer existed, there were not many independent farmers in that part of Pomerania. Most of Bismarck's workforce were tied to the estate by being provided with houses, primitive as they were, and having a share in the grain harvest, in return for their services. Money wages hardly existed. In any case the peasants were still subject to the jurisdiction and police power of the landowner, on whose estate they lived, and would have found it difficult to break away, had they wanted to. When he became politically active after 1847, Bismarck fought fiercely for the retention of these Junker privileges, which had become anachronistic even in the eyes of many estate owners. In his personal relations with his workforce Bismarck seems to have been jovial and easygoing and by no means a harsh disciplinarian. For all the survival of feudal features, most of the east Elbian estates, many of them now in the hands of 'new' middle-class families, were operating quite successfully in a commercial, capitalist, free-trading market. So were the Bismarck brothers. It was this that made the Junkers politically confident as a class and had enabled them to halt further reforms. It also enabled them to confront encroachment by the bureaucracy of the state. Bismarck himself managed to reduce the burden of personal debt that had been one of the factors inducing him to return to Pomerania. He began to enjoy a modest financial independence that proved of value at the beginning of his political career in the late 1840s.

He also shared fully in the life of his own class, their festivities, entertainments, hunts and balls. He now acquired the reputation of the 'mad Junker', *der tolle Bismarck*, the boisterous, hard-riding, sharp-shooting young man, who was reliving the carefree ways of his student days. There are many tales of his firing his revolver to announce his arrival, or indicating his impatience when waiting to depart with a friend. But a lot of it was role-playing, hiding emptiness and frustration, and there was now less of an audience for the other side of his nature, such as Motley or Keyserling had provided. He still read widely, if unsystematically, a lot of literature, some of the current works on agricultural economics, even some philosophy and theology, including the new biblical criticism, in which German authors such as David Friedrich Strauss were leaders. He was, as he himself recognized, still 'a child', searching for a meaning to his life. His sister, Malwine, known as Malle, twelve years his junior, became a trusted companion and remained so for the rest of his life. In 1844 she married one of the extensive Arnim clan. Yet at times he felt lonely and the urge to marry. He proposed to Ottilie von Puttkamer, daughter of another large Pomeranian clan. It was a severe blow to his self-esteem, when she turned him down in a hurtful way, prompted by her mother, who did not consider him good enough. After two years there were distinct signs that his idyll of the Pomeranian countryside was turning into 'blue mist', as he put it.

In the summer of 1842 he went on a journey for several months, to England, visiting York, Manchester, London and later going on to France, Switzerland and Italy. Among his impressions of England were the friendliness of the people, but the indifference of the food. He visited the House of Lords and saw peers roasting their steaks in front of the open chimney fire. He seems to have toyed with the idea of getting even further away by entering the British colonial service in India. He was restless, bored and 'drifting listlessly on the stream of life without any direction other than the mood of the moment, and it matters not to me where it lands me', as he wrote to his friend Scharlach in August 1844.[7] He still liked cutting a figure in aristocratic high society, as he did on a visit to the island of Norderney, where he moved in the circle round the blind Hanoverian crown prince. Some twenty years on Bismarck was to deprive him of his throne. He was so bored that he briefly returned to the public service in Potsdam, but it lasted only a few weeks. The 'ridiculous condescension of his superiors' seemed to him unbearable. We have from this period the draft of a newspaper article, in which he defends hunting against attacks which depicted it as an arrogant Junker pastime, damaging to the crops of hard-working farmers and reeking of Anglomania. Bismarck, for all his contempt for the narrowness of Pomeranian Junker life, is still the class-conscious nobleman, who makes no apologies for his life-style or his privileges.

*

Among his Junker neighbours in Pomerania there was a circle of pietists, not unlike the evangelicals to be found among the British aristocracy of this period. These 'awakened' Lutherans among the Prussian aristocracy were, like their English counterparts, reacting against the rationalism of official religion. In Prussia they were sometimes driven to defiance of what the church, closely tied to the state, imposed upon them and clashed with it. Most of them had fought in the Napoleonic wars, had come under the influence of the Romantic movement, and had ended up with an intensely personal religious faith as their refuge. In their country houses they held prayer meetings, listened to lay preachers, came together with their labourers in divine service. They believed that their faith offered solutions not only to the personal, but also to the social, perplexities of their time. Initially there was about this religiosity an ascetic tone, but by the 1840s it had become softer, and quiet enjoyment of social pleasures was no longer frowned upon. Bismarck's contact with this circle came mainly through the family von Thadden, known by the name of their estate as Thadden-Trieglaff. The two brothers Gerlach, Leopold and Ludwig, who were to play a major role in Bismarck's career, were related to Adolf von Thadden by marriage. The Gerlachs belonged to a group close to Frederick William IV, before and after he came to the throne in 1840. Their ideals and outlook had much in common with those of the king and he called Ludwig von Gerlach, the younger of the brothers, to a post in the Ministry for the Reform of Justice soon after his accession to work on a new divorce law. Leopold later became the king's influential adjutant.

Bismarck's friend from his schooldays, Moritz von Blanckenburg, became engaged to Thadden's daughter Marie. The 'mad Junker', who professed not to be a Christian, but was so obviously formidable, presented a challenge to the missionary zeal of his pietist friends. Blanckenburg tried to convert his friend, by word of mouth and by letter. He failed, but his wife-to-be made a much greater impression. Marie von Thadden was one of two or three women in Bismarck's life for whom he fell deeply, but whom the code of behaviour of his time put out of his ultimate reach. The two spent much time together in deep conversation, sometimes making tongues wag, but even Marie found Bismarck a hard nut to crack. In the winter of 1844–5, when she had already been married to Blanckenburg for a few months, she wrote to a friend: 'To see a man suffer so much from the coldness of unbelief as Otto Bismarck is very melancholy, to talk for hours, days about all the great holy truths and yet to find it impossible to give even a drop of that peace that comes from faith to a poor frozen heart is very painful.'[8] Marie was as much drawn to Otto, whom she calls 'the lower Pomeranian Phoenix, known as the last word in wildness and arrogance', as he was to her. He was so much more interesting than her 'good Moritz' and she was highly intelligent and passionate.

As it was, she could only leave him to her good friend Johanna von Puttkamer, a much less exciting girl, but eventually Bismarck's wife. They first met at the Blankenburg wedding in October 1844, without much mutual interest, but Marie did her best to bring them together. In November 1845 Bismarck's father died and Otto took the big decision to take over Schönhausen, but for a while he moved to and fro between the estate near the Elbe and Kniephof. In August 1846 Marie arranged for a party of Pomeranian friends to travel to the Harz mountains, the kind of convivial, gay occasion, lubricated by plenty of champagne and poetry reading, that Junker pietists were not too puritanical to spurn. It was meant to bring Otto and Johanna closer together, but what did so even more decisively was Marie's sudden death in November. She fell victim to an epidemic, to which her mother had also succumbed. Bismarck was deeply shaken and, as he told his future father-in-law in his letter asking for Johanna's hand only six weeks after Marie's death, for the first time he prayed again. Heinrich von Puttkamer, of Reinfeld, was also a pietist Junker, more quietly pious than the Thaddens, and he needed some convincing that the mad Bismarck was the right man for his daughter. Bismarck may well have painted his conversion in higher colours than it deserved, but there can be no doubt that he had moved from his earlier scepticism. He was never an atheist – Marie sometimes called him a pantheist – but all revealed, organized religion had for long been repugnant to him. Neither had he ever shared the optimism about the human condition of the Enlightenment; he was always highly aware of human weakness and of the need for society to be anchored in some faith in a divine order. The change that now came over him was not a Pauline conversion, but an acceptance that he could not live without some sheet anchor to give meaning to his life. Readings from the Bible and from Luther gave him comfort for the rest of his days. He knew that even he, great man as he became, was never the complete master of his destiny. But even in matters of religion he did not give up his individuality and he never pretended, even to his wife, that he fully shared the beliefs of her pietist family and circle. Total submission to the divine will, which they put at the forefront of their religion, was not for him; his recovered belief in the existence of God reinforced the sovereignty of his personality.

Johanna did, however, become his other sheet anchor by providing for him a secure, unquestioning domesticity in the titanic struggles of his life. She probably never fully fathomed the depths and the heights of his volcanic personality, nor could she follow him in what became the all-dominating passion of his life, politics. All she could do was to share to the full his hatred of his enemies and to make sure that they did not disturb his domestic peace. Nevertheless he could repose total trust in her, he shaped her to his needs and made her privy to his thoughts. In his letters to his fiancée and young bride Bismarck reveals a very different side of his personality to the supercilious, cynical arrogance mixed with self-irony that marks his other correspondence. He is warm, loving, full of empathy, going all-out to achieve that full understanding which his total commitment to her demands. When this correspondence was revealed after his death, many had difficulty in recognizing the domineering man of power with whom they had become familiar. When they were married in July 1847, Otto had already taken the first steps into his turbulent political life, and he had arranged his married and his religious life in such a way that they became a springboard for his public life.

2

ENTRY INTO POLITICS

In the days of his discontent, depression and boredom in Pomerania, the thought that politics might provide an outlet for him was never far from Bismarck's mind. His brother Bernhard was Landrat in the small town of Naugard, near the Bismarck estates in Pomerania, and Otto would have liked something similar for himself. The nearest he came to it was to become dyke warden at Schönhausen, responsible for preventing the Elbe from flooding the countryside, which it did in 1845, before Bismarck's arrival, lapping the steps of the terrace of the Bismarck castle. The transfer to Schönhausen after his father's death was at least partially motivated by the thought it would help him to find a public role. Various men of influence had kept an eye on him, as a potentially valuable recruit to Junker political activities. The most important was Ludwig von Gerlach, who in 1844 had become president of the *Oberlandesgericht*, the highest provincial court, in Magdeburg, not far from Schönhausen. Bismarck was in regular consultation with Gerlach, twenty years older than himself, and held him in high regard. It was this contact that helped him to get elected as representative of the Magdeburg estates to the united Prussian diet of 1847. The previous representative had had to retire for reasons of health, but Bismarck, although not on the list of alternatives and only recently returned to the province, was chosen. It gave him the opportunity for his political debut.

The demand for a national representative body had been alive in Prussia since the reform era. Frederick William III had promised a constitution in

1815, but it never came. Provincial estates were called into being in 1823, but their competence was extremely restricted. It was the need to raise a loan for the building of a railway from Berlin to Königsberg in East Prussia that forced Frederick William IV to call the united diet in February 1847, but in opening it the king declared that he would never allow a piece of paper, namely a constitution, to come between him and his people. But such a declaration merely gave further impetus to demands, which were stirring up Prussia and much of Germany. The repressive system of Metternich and the Holy Alliance was crumbling. In Prussia the Rhineland provinces were economically more advanced than any other region in Germany and a middle class based on commerce and developing industry was flexing its muscles. Even in the aristocracy there was an increasingly vocal liberal faction that wanted a national constitution. Further down the social scale, economic depression and poor harvests were stoking up the social pressures. Radicals and democrats stood ready to politicize economic hardship. The moderate liberals in the diet, led by men like David Hansemann, a Rhenish entrepreneur, were not willing to grant the government a loan without obtaining political concessions. This was the situation when Otto von Bismarck, aged thirty-two, made his appearance in the diet on 17 May 1847.

If Bismarck was to make his mark in this assembly, it would have to be as the spokesman of the ultra-conservative faction to which he was linked. He would have to oppose the reformist liberal constitutionalism that was the prevailing tendency even in a body very selectively chosen. It was a task to which his confrontational style and his forensic skill were eminently suited. For his adversaries he had nothing but contempt and his attacks were unrestrained by any feeling of respect for them. In the picturesque language he used in his letters to Johanna, he called the representatives of the Rhenish bourgeoisie 'wine salesmen' and those who talked of human rights, like the Westphalian liberal aristocrat Vincke, 'boring humanity blatherers'. In his first speech he was replying to an East Prussian liberal aristocrat, who argued, as many did in those days, that the Prussian people's fight in the wars of liberation against Napoleon now entitled them to renewal of the bond between crown and people. Bismarck, who had not even been born when the speaker was fighting against Napoleon, got up and declared that this historical construction was entirely mythical. The Prussian people had simply risen against foreign oppression and it was a libel to imply that expectations of reform had been necessary to spur them on. Bismarck's tone was deliberately offensive and when a storm of indignation arose against him in the assembly, he sat quietly reading a newspaper.

Later in the session he spoke against the admission of Jews to official positions, identifying himself with the doctrine of the Christian state to which the Gerlachs, Ludwig and his older brother Leopold, and the king himself were committed.[1] Curiously enough, it was a converted Bavarian Jew, Friedrich Julius Stahl, who had become the chief ideologue in Prussia of a conservatism founded on this theocratic concept of the state. It was equally curious that Bismarck, but recently a professed unbeliever, should now publicly espouse it. In this, and in some of his other speeches, he was sticking to the line suggested by the Gerlachs, but he was far too much his own man to adopt it without qualification. A more pragmatic approach and greater attention to material interests in the political process was already differentiating him from the strictly dogmatic adherence to principle taken especially by Ludwig von Gerlach. In the speech on the Jewish question there are signs that he was uncomfortable with too ideological a line of argument and that he preferred practicalities. He confessed that he had imbibed anti-Jewish prejudices with his mother's milk and that he would find it difficult to bend the knee before a Jewish official representing the majesty of the king. On the other hand he admitted that there were now many entirely respectable persons among the Jews in the larger Prussian cities. A state not founded on Christian principles would depend on the changing and vague ideals of humanity of those temporarily in control of it, and this might open the way to an attack on property rights, when for example some believed that theft was justified in order to restore the inherent equality of men. It was a vague reference to Proudhon's 'Property is theft', which Bismarck had no doubt heard of, and could be neatly turned against the liberal opposition, who were all men of property.

He was already highly skilled in advocating positions that were on the face of it incompatible. For example, he supported the liberals in their demand that the diet should meet at predetermined intervals. It hardly suited him to have the assembly, which had enabled him to make his political debut, quickly dissolved, as it was. He nevertheless declared that the king had total discretion over its meetings and that his will must in no way be subjected to limitations. Bismarck had prepared two more speeches unashamedly and brazenly defending Junker privileges, on hunting for game, a great grievance of the peasants, and on patrimonial jurisdiction, the landowner's right to administer justice on his estate. He was unable to deliver them before the diet was dissolved in June 1847, but he carefully preserved them among his papers. Bismarck had made his mark among the ultra-conservative court party and had shown himself more skilful as a speaker than some of their old stagers.

After the dissolution of the diet, Otto and Johanna got married, on 28 July 1847, and went for more than two months on a honeymoon journey that took them to Prague, Vienna, Venice and back via Switzerland. Johanna had never been so far afield and was overwhelmed by new impressions, while Otto took great delight in her enthusiasm. In Vienna they managed to penetrate into a small garden at the Schönbrunn Palace and took a walk there in the moonlight. Bismarck remembered the magic of it many years later, when as the powerful Prussian prime minister he saw the same spot again. In Venice he was invited to dinner by Frederick William IV, without Johanna and for a political discussion. Major von Roon, another friend of Bismarck's who held a position in the royal entourage and was to prove a powerful supporter in his later career, helped to secure him the invitation. In Berlin and in public the king had treated the son of his former playmate rather distantly, but it was clear that he fully approved the young man's forthright stance in the diet. Bismarck could hope that if circumstances favoured it a public position of influence and power might be his.

*

In February 1848 revolution in Paris toppled the throne of Louis Philippe. It provided the spark setting alight the already volatile situation in the German-speaking countries of Central Europe. Metternich had to flee Vienna on 13 March and five days later the barricades went up in Berlin. Frederick William IV decided to compromise, rode round his capital draped in the black-red-gold colours of the revolution and with his queen saluted those who had fallen fighting his troops. Bismarck's reaction, when he heard at Schönhausen of the fighting in Berlin, was quite different. Hotblooded, confrontational and politically inexperienced, he did what he could, from his relatively insignificant position, to engineer an immediate military suppression of the revolution. He tried to rally the peasants round Schönhausen for a march on Berlin, but quickly realized that this would be a quixotic undertaking. Instead he went himself to Potsdam and stayed with Roon. The king was still in Berlin and refused to move to Potsdam and give the order for a military suppression of the revolution. Bismarck played a subordinate role, acting more or less as a courier, in trying to obtain such an order from the king, failing that to bypass him and obtain the permission to act from elsewhere in the house of Hohenzollern. It hardly stopped short of deposing Frederick William IV. Bismarck failed to gain access to the king, but he saw Princess Augusta, the wife of Prince William, brother of the king, heir to the throne and later the first German emperor. Augusta was the granddaughter of the Grand Duke Carl August of Saxe-Weimar, for whom Goethe had worked for many years as chief minister. Augusta was a woman of vaguely liberal sympathies and this attempt to involve her in a counter-revolutionary plot, while her husband had fled to England, turned her into a life-long enemy of Bismarck.

For the moment Bismarck had misjudged the situation. The king's unwillingness to use force and his decision to make the two leaders of the Rhenish liberal opposition, Ludolf Camphausen and David Hansemann, his chief ministers was not just cowardice, as Bismarck thought, but proved a way of separating moderate liberals from more radical democrats. The willingness of Bismarck and his friends to bypass the king showed how conditional Junker loyalty to the Hohenzollerns really was. Then even Bismarck began to wobble. When the united diet reassembled in early April 1848 he declared in a speech that the past was buried and that it was more painful to him than to most that it could not be reawakened, 'when the crown itself had thrown earth on to the coffin'.[2] It did not go down well with the Gerlachs, who had already taken steps to form what they called a *ministère occulte* around the king, to advise and steady him. It became known as the court camarilla. It was a kitchen cabinet and had no formal existence. Besides the Gerlachs General von Rauch, Prussian military plenipotentiary with the tsar and adjutant to the king, and another officer and royal adjutant, Edwin von Manteuffel, who was to cross Bismarck's path for many years, were among those associated with it. The camarilla had considerable influence on events in 1848 and, mainly through the Gerlachs, Bismarck was on its fringes.

In May 1848 there followed the elections to the Prussian national assembly and to the Frankfurt parliament, both of them on the basis of universal male suffrage. modified by an indirect system. In indirect elections the voters do not themselves vote for the deputies, but for electors, who then in turn choose the parliamentary representatives. Bismarck was very eager to present himself for election to the Prussian assembly, but even on his own home ground of Schönhausen he could not get selected as a candidate. In the summer months of 1848 he was able to spend more time with Johanna, who was now pregnant with their first child. He helped to found a conservative newspaper, the *Neue Preussische Zeitung*, generally known as the *Kreuzzeitung*, because of the iron cross, dating back to the Wars of Liberation, that appeared on its masthead. He became a constant contributor, responsible for the acid, ironical style of polemics that marked its pages as it did his speeches. The editor was Hermann Wagener, another member of the Gerlach circle, who would attach himself to Bismarck for most of his career. The other major form of activity in which the conservatives now engaged, imitating their liberal opponents, was the promotion of a multitude of associations, using various names such as Prussian, veterans, or constitutional associations, to give organizational backbone to their cause. At the centre there was the *Verein für König und Vaterland* (Association for King and Country), in which Bismarck took an active part. He also played a leading role in organizing what came to be known as the *Junkerparlament*, a meeting of some 400 landowners in August 1848 protesting against the agrarian programme of the Hansemann government.

This type of political activity, which sought to mobilize a more popular constituency for the conservative cause, was viewed with some apprehension by the older leaders of the cause, but the younger generation of leading conservatives, among whom Bismarck was one, saw no alternative. They felt confident that the Junkers, together with many from other groups in society, small businessmen, artisans, farmers and peasants, could fully hold their own against the divided and incoherent forces that had made the revolution. As far as Bismarck was concerned, any differences of style or even fundamental outlook that may have divided him from the Gerlachs and other older men of influence mattered little at this stage, nor did he carry enough weight to be able to separate himself from his patrons. For them he was still an able and energetic adjutant to the cause, his usefulness only limited by the fact that his image as a reactionary hothead was so firmly established that for the time being he could not function in too public a position. Nevertheless, the king listened patiently to him even when he was by implication attacking the hesitant royal stance, no doubt seeing in this eloquent and forceful young member of the nobility a man with a future in his service.

By the summer of 1848 the forces of the counter-revolution were recouping their strength all over Europe. Paris had again set the signals when General Cavaignac had crushed a workers' uprising in June. In circles like the Prussian camarilla the verb *cavaignacen*, to do in Berlin what Cavaignac had done in Paris, came into use. Prussia refused to continue the fight on behalf of the Frankfurt parliament against Denmark over Schleswig-Holstein by concluding the Malmö armistice on 26 August. There was huge indignation among the nationally minded public throughout Germany at what was seen as a betrayal, which also showed up the essential impotence of the Frankfurt parliament. All the indications are that Bismarck cared little about what went on in Frankfurt or about Schleswig-Holstein and saw everything from an entirely Prussian perspective. He was entirely opposed to 'the German swindle in all its varieties', he told his friend Wagener. When he became the hero of German nationalism later on, German historians had a difficult task in scraping together the few remarks of his that might have shown some sympathy for German national aspirations at this stage of his career. The cultural and historical existence of Germany was naturally part of his identity, but his Prussianism had absolute priority. He was aware of the importance of German national feeling now and for the future, but German nationalism must not be a means of advancing the aims of liberals, let alone democrats, nor a smokescreen for them; it must be made subservient to the interests of the Prussian state. That was Bismarck's position.

The confidence of the Prussian conservatives was further boosted when on 31 October the revolution in Vienna was crushed by the troops of Marshal Windischgrätz. Frederick William IV was now ready to act. A vote in the Prussian national assembly to demand support for the revolutionaries in Vienna provided an excuse to move against it. A new ministry under Count Brandenburg, an illegitimate member of the house of Hohenzollern, was installed, troops under General Wrangel occupied Berlin without meeting much resistance and the national assembly was adjourned and moved from the capital. With his usual sarcasm Bismarck told his wife that the assembly's call for 'passive resistance' was what would in common parlance be called 'fright'. In his reminiscences Bismarck reports that when he was mentioned as a possible minister in the Brandenburg government, the King had written against his name 'only to be used when bayonets rule without restraint'.[3] At the end of 1848 the revolution had largely run out of steam, but even the camarilla accepted that one could not simply return to the status quo.

On 5 December the king imposed a constitution. It provided for a parliament, initially to be elected by a wide, though indirect franchise, soon narrowed to the three-tier franchise, which prevailed in Prussia until 1918. Under this franchise the voters were divided into three classes, each paying the same amount of tax and having the same voting power. The bulk of the population voted in the third class, while a small number of very rich men made up the first class. As wealth grew with industrialization, it became an increasingly plutocratic franchise, favouring, so Bismarck came to believe, the mainly liberal commercial and entrepreneurial classes. Stahl had advocated the idea that conservatives, although committed to a divine-right kingship with full executive powers, should go beyond the representation of estates and provide a forum for the nation as a whole, but with strictly limited powers. Bismarck had adopted Stahl's ideas in his extensive journalism, although his tendency to argue concretely rather than abstractly had taken the edge off the universalizing philosophical character of Stahl's own writings. To the king, to the Gerlachs and other old-style legitimists the idea of a constitution was repugnant, but they now accepted the necessity. Bismarck was no more enamoured of constitutions than they were and would have no truck with popular sovereignty, but the limited Prussian-German constitutionalism, which he did so much to maintain in the future, turned out to be the ideal arena for him. He was determined to be a candidate in the first elections, but realized himself that there was no chance of being adopted on his home ground around Schönhausen. In the public mind he figured as the blinkered, quixotic champion of the Junker backwoodsmen. It required considerable string-pulling, by a Jewish relation of Johanna's, among others, before he could find a constituency in Brandenburg, for which he was narrowly elected. In February 1849 he put Schönhausen out to rent and moved with his family to Berlin. He had become a professional politician, in the sense this term had now taken on in Prussia. He had enough financial independence, modest rather than ample, to enable him to make this choice. He could now expect that sooner or later an important public appointment would come his way.

In the first, short-lived *Landtag* (parliament), elected in February 1849, there was a sizeable conservative faction, over 50, when there had been virtually none in the assembly of 1848, showing that their propaganda and electoral activity had borne some fruit. Only a few had, like Bismarck, close links with the camarilla. The main issue before the Landtag was the German question. In Frankfurt the formation of a unified Germany under Prussia, Kleindeutschland, emerged as the only option left. In Vienna the preservation of the Habsburg empire had, after the defeat of the revolution, become the priority. The protagonist of centralizing this empire and throwing its full weight into the scales of German politics was Prince Felix Schwarzenberg. This left no room for the *grossdeutsch* solution, which the majority of the Frankfurt parliament originally wanted. In Schwarzenberg, had he lived, Bismarck might well have found his match. What he wanted for the Habsburg dominions was very similar to what Bismarck envisaged for the Hohenzollerns. The reorganization of German Central Europe would take place under Austrian leadership. The *kleindeutsch* imperial crown the Frankfurt liberals were now offering the king of Prussia as a second-best was bound to be opposed by Austria under Schwarzenberg, probably supported by Russia. Prussia might be fighting a war against the two conservative powers, when it had scarcely slain the dragon of revolution.

This alone would have made it very difficult for Frederick William IV to accept the crown formally offered him by a delegation from Frankfurt on 3 April 1849. It was also for him, and for all conservatives, a crown tainted by its emergence from revolution. In the Landtag a majority supported the acceptance of the Frankfurt constitution and crown, but Bismarck was naturally among those who opposed it. In his usually provocative way he declared that any monarch taking a crown from the hands of the Frankfurt parliament had effectively ceased to rule. In colourful language he expressed his opinion on the crown offered: 'The Frankfurt crown may shine brilliantly, but the gold which makes this brilliance real, is to be obtained by the melting down of the Prussian crown and I have no confidence that this recasting will succeed with this constitution.'

But German national aspirations were not so easily dismissed, especially as Frederick William was susceptible to their appeal. Moreover, just as in Prussian domestic affairs a constitution, however limited, was now required to create a new stability, so in Germany as a whole some greater unity needed to be established, to accompany the greater economic unity already being brought about by the customs union, the *Zollverein*. The king wanted in some way to revive the medieval German empire and he was naturally keen that Prussia's role in such a scheme should be great. Whatever was established must have the consent of the ruling princes, preserve the leading position of Austria and be in no way tainted with revolution. The man who became the Prussian king's chosen instrument for squaring this circle was Joseph Maria von Radowitz, a man who had entered the Prussian service from a Hungarian-Catholic background and with whom the king had had a close friendship for many years. A start was made in May 1849 on what became known as the union, later the Erfurt union, because of the meeting place of its parliament. It was based on an agreement between the three kingdoms of Prussia, Saxony and Hanover, but further progress depended on the adhesion of other rulers. Many did join it, but the two important states of Bavaria and Württemberg did not. The moderate liberals who had tried and failed to establish a Prussian-led Germany through the offer of the imperial crown to Frederick William IV threw their weight behind the union scheme as another second-best option. From their foundation meeting at Gotha they became known as the Gotha liberals.

In the summer of 1849 there were violent uprisings in many parts of Germany, including Saxony, where the Russian anarchist Bakunin and the composer Richard Wagner joined the barricades. The most serious of the risings was in Baden, where Prussian troops led by Prince William, returned from his English exile, crushed it ruthlessly, executing many of the insurgents. These risings were the last desperate attempt by the radical democrats to rescue something from the wreck of the revolution, which in their view had been betrayed by the princes and the moderate liberals. The role which Prussian troops played in the suppression of these final revolutionary spasms gave the union project enhanced attraction in the eyes of many German rulers and their governments, but their adherence was only a temporizing step until the revolutionary danger should be well and truly banished. At the end of August 1849 Schwarzenberg made it clear that Austria would not accept this Prussian-controlled union, even if it was loosely linked to the Habsburg empire, and that Vienna wanted to revive the German Confederation of 1815. The Austrian position had by this time been much strengthened by the crushing of the Hungarian revolution with Russian help. The tsar was also very suspicious of the Radowitz union plans, seeing in them a concession to revolution and a potential change in the European power balance.

*

This was the position when Bismarck spoke on 6 September 1849 in the Prussian Landtag in a debate on the government's union proposals.[4] It was the second Landtag elected under the imposed constitution of December 1848 and had the task of revising and restricting that constitution. Bismarck had again been narrowly elected. He and his friends on the extreme right disliked the union proposals and hated Radowitz, with his nebulous ideas that smelt of revolution and endangered Prussia. But for the moment they were the policy of the king and of the Brandenburg government and Bismarck had to step warily. He warned that the union should not become what the liberals wanted, a last-minute attempt to realize what had failed in Frankfurt and in Prussia. This movement that had failed was not primarily a national movement but a social one. Through false propaganda the envy of those without property had been aroused against the rich, at a time when years of free thought had undermined the ethical elements of resistance in men's hearts. Such a phenomenon, claiming to have the *Zeitgeist* on its side, could not be appeased. True conservatives, and after all the king and Radowitz claimed to be conservatives, had above all to safeguard the Prussian state, with its unique qualities, on which Frederick the Great had based his policies. For Frederick the Great, he speculated, it would have been either a question of coming together with Austria or using Prussian arms to impose himself on Germany, thereby giving Germany the position in Europe that was her due. Bismarck emphasized again that the loyalty of Prussians was to the state that the great king had served, and not to the black-red-gold flag, 'which had never been the colours of the German Reich, but for the last two years the colours of revolts and barricades'. With this speech Bismarck showed that he was not merely a champion of the extreme right in domestic politics, who had made his mark through provocation and controversy, but that he had something pertinent to say on Prussia's external position. Moreover, he could put it diplomatically, so that the many different factions that existed even among conservatives found something to agree with.

When the parliament of the proposed union was established in the spring of 1850 Bismarck was a member of it. Another member described him as 'a long, tense, slightly plump figure, with a blonde beard and thin hair on top, he does not speak fluently, but spits out his words, as if in suppressed rage about the Revolution and the revolutionary assembly.'[5] It was mainly a Prussian chamber elected on the three-tier franchise and on a very low turnout. The Gotha liberals formed the majority. Bismarck asked for a revision of the proposed constitution of the union, as it would subject the Prussians, 16 million out of 21 million, to the remaining 5 million. For him it was not a question of merging Prussia into Germany, but of submerging Germany in a Greater Prussia. By this time the union project was in deep trouble and Schwarzenberg was not prepared to leave the Prussians a face-saving way out of the impasse in which it had landed them.

Plate 1 Bismarck in 1874
Source: Bildarchiv Preussischer Kulturbesitz

Plate 2 Johanna von Bismarck-Schönhausen
Source: Courtesy of Hulton Archive

Plate 3 Bismarck with his family. Left to right: Oscar von Armin (brother-in-law), Malwine von Armin ('Malle, sister), Sibylle (niece, later wife of Wilhelm von Bismarck), Johanna, Bismarck, Wilhelm (son)
Source: Courtesy of Hulton Archive

Plate 4 Varzin: Wood Engraving of 1898
Source: Bildarchiv Preussischer Kulturbesitz

Plate 5 Walking the tightrope of constitutional conflict, cartoon in *Kladderadatsch*, 1866: Bismarck's performance compared to Blondin's tightrope crossing of the Niagara Falls between the United States and Canada
Source: Courtesy of Professor William Coupe

Plate 6 William I, king of Prussia and German emperor, in 1881
Source: Bildarchiv Preussischer Kulturbesitz

Plate 7 Crown Prince Frederick William (in 1888, Frederick III) in 1875
Source: Courtesy of Hulton Archive

Plate 8 Victoria (Vicky, daughter of Queen Victoria of Britain), Crown Princess Frederick William; in 1888, Empress Frederick III
Source: Bildarchiv Preussischer Kulturbesitz

Plate 9 The Kaiser, William II, visiting Bismarck at Friedrichsruh, 30 October 1888
Source: Courtesy of Hulton Archive

Plate 10 Frederick the Great, Bismarck, Hitler: on a postcard of 1933
Source: Bildarchiv Preussischer Kulturbesitz

The crunch came over Electoral Hesse, which straddled the lines of communication between the eastern and western provinces of Prussia. By restoring an absolutist regime the elector had become deeply unpopular and aroused widespread resistance. He banked on the support of Austria, while the opposition to him hoped to keep alive the Erfurt union and the possibility of Prussian intervention. War between Austria and Prussia threatened, when on 26 October Austrian troops, armed with the authority of the revived German Confederation, entered Hesse. Frederick William had just given Radowitz an official position by making him foreign minister. He was now faced with the dilemma of risking war in support of a revolt against a legitimate ruler, or bowing ignominiously to Austrian pressure by abandoning the whole union project. To go to war under these circumstances would have been foolhardy. The situation was similar to what it would have been had Frederick William accepted the imperial crown offered by Frankfurt six months earlier, but this time Prussian prestige and honour were more directly challenged. Even many conservatives were caught up in a wave of anti-Austrian emotion. Schwarzenberg's reconstitution of the 1815 Confederation, with Austria still holding the presidency, seemed a deliberate affront to Prussia.

Bismarck's reactions were initially ambivalent. He could not entirely escape the feeling of outraged patriotism which the Austrian actions provoked. Even as it became clear that for conservatives the need for anti-revolutionary solidarity must take priority, he was still writing in the *Kreuzzeitung* that war was inevitable if Austria was not prepared to concede full equality to Prussia in Germany. He seems to have been involved in heated arguments with Leopold von Gerlach, the less dogmatic of the two brothers, who was by this time the most influential member of the camarilla group. He had become adjutant-general to the king in April 1850 and saw him every morning when he was drinking coffee with the queen. However much Bismarck's Prussian pride was offended by humiliation at the hands of the Austrians, he had been bitterly opposed to the Radowitz project, even if he had trimmed his public utterances somewhat. His cool realism told him that the plans of the king and Radowitz were bound to fall between two stools and that such an ill-considered attempt to catch the wind of German national feeling, the swindle coming out of Frankfurt, was deeply damaging to the real interests of Prussia. When the king had dropped Radowitz on 2 November 1850 Bismarck had rejoiced. He had 'ridden round the table on his chair for joy' he wrote to Wagener, consuming many a bottle of champagne. 'You won't believe how strongly the German swindle and the rage against Austria has taken hold even in conservative circles,' he added.[6]

The *Punctation* of Olmütz, the treaty concluded between Austria and Prussia on 29 November 1850 at Olmütz in Bohemia, was the end of the union project. Prussia was to rejoin the German Confederation, on terms to be negotiated, but which in the event left Austria with the presidency. Prussia had to acknowledge the competence of the Confederation to restore the legal status quo in Electoral Hesse and Holstein. To contemporaries it looked like a total humiliation and was compared to the defeat at Jena in 1806, but it was not quite that. Schwarzenberg had not secured any advance towards his own long-term project, the formation of a 70-million bloc in Central Europe. The Zollverein, of which Austria was not a member, still stood in the way. Nevertheless the task of making Olmütz look like anything other than a defeat was not easy. It fell to Otto von Manteuffel, who had taken over the negotiations with Schwarzenberg after the sudden death of Brandenburg and was to hold the offices of prime minister and foreign minister for the next eight years. It was significant that the Gerlachs picked on Bismarck to support the Olmütz agreement when Manteuffel presented it to the Landtag. Despite the disagreements that had arisen between them and him from time to time, they regarded him as their most skilled and articulate parliamentarian.

The speech Bismarck made on 3 December 1850 about Olmütz became a milestone in his career.[7] The spokesmen of liberals in the assembly had expressed their indignation about the disaster and had called for an end to the political system that had produced it. Bismarck now accused them of wishing to unleash a great war, with hundreds of thousands of dead and devasted provinces, for which the real interests of the state provided no justification. They were using talk of Prussian honour in order to send into the field a Prussian army for the same principles, against which that army had fought in the streets of Berlin. In arguing in this way Bismarck was not only attacking the opposition but appealing to those in the army, including Prince William, the heir to the throne, who were smarting under the humiliation of having had to withdraw in face of the Austrian threat. He was telling them they would not have been fighting for Prussia, but for the party of revolution. Bismarck reverted to this core of his argument throughout his speech, always finding fresh, colourful and polemically effective ways of turning it. In his deliberately provocative way he characterized the possible intervention in Hesse as an attempt to involve Prussia in a quixotic undertaking on behalf of 'offended small-town celebrities who think their local constitution is endangered'. War would only be justified if Prussia did not attain equality with Austria in all questions affecting Central Europe, but for such a war the time was not ripe. 'I seek Prussian honour in keeping Prussia above all away from any shameful connection with democracy, that Prussia should in this as in all other questions never allow anything to happen in Germany without Prussia's consent, that what Prussia and Austria together in their independent judgment consider rational and politically justified should be put into operation by the common action of the two protective powers of Germany.' In this way he glossed over the fundamental dilemma that a choice had to be made between fighting revolution and asserting the Prussian national interest against Austria and that in the present situation fighting revolution had to be the priority. He was arguing in a way that showed his mentality far removed from those like the Gerlachs, who were wholly committed to legitimist principles and would always put conservative solidarity first. Bismarck was turning into an exponent of *Realpolitik*, a word that was becoming popular as the clashes of the revolutionary years died down. *Realpolitik* meant that the age of ideology was ending and that politics would henceforth be dominated by material considerations and national interest rather than by abstract ideals.

The Manteuffel regime was a bureaucratic regime, in general committed to the maintenance of the status quo, but tempered by the perception that the maintenance of Junker privileges in all circumstances could not always ensure stability and social peace. Not all of the privileges abolished during the revolution were restored. Bismarck had often cursed bureaucracy up hill and down dale, but it was to the bureaucratic state he now had to turn to satisfy his expectation of employment. His Olmütz speech, in its subtle appeal to all shades of conservative opinion, was designed to show that he was well qualified for high office. Some months were still to elapse before a suitable position materialized, during which he continued to make himself useful to the government as a parliamentary spokesman. There was briefly the possibility that he might become the chief minister of Anhalt-Bernburg, one of the dwarf states surrounded by Prussia, where, as he put it, the duke was an idiot and the minister was the duke. But then the much more influential position of Prussian envoy to the newly reconstituted German Confederation came up. It was a crucial appointment, for the negotiations about the terms on which Prussia was to rejoin it were still in progress and the post-Olmütz relationship between Austria and Prussia needed to be defined. Someone was required who could hold the fine line between cooperation with Austria while maintaining the Prussian interest. For Bismarck it was a remarkable advancement, for, as was widely noticed, his previous appearances in the public service had always ended prematurely and ingloriously. He owed it in large measure to Leopold von Gerlach, who persuaded the king. Frederick William did not need much persuading, as he was undoubtedly pleased with the young deputy's performance in the Landtag. When the king in his farewell audience on 8 May 1851 congratulated him rather wryly on his courage in taking an office so 'strange' to him, he replied 'Courage is entirely on the side of Your Majesty in entrusting me with such an office, but Your Majesty is not bound to maintain the appointment, should it not prove satisfactory.'[8]

Johanna was less pleased. She had lived with him in Berlin only for a few months and had then returned to her parents' home at Reinfeld in Pomerania, where their second child, Herbert, was born in December 1849. Otto appeared at Reinfeld as far as his increasingly absorbing political activities allowed. Johanna was never keen on life in society, which for Otto's political standing became a necessity. In Berlin he frequently appeared in society with his sister Malle von Arnim, who was striking looking and through her marriage very wealthy. Johanna never liked her. In the early months of 1851 Otto lived a bachelor existence in Berlin with his friend, relative and colleague Hans von Kleist-Retzow. He was also a member of the pietist Pomeranian aristocracy and had become as prominent as Bismarck as one of the younger spokesmen of the conservative party. To many he seemed more trustworthy than Bismarck, who could never quite shake off his reputation as a maverick. Kleist-Retzow's reward was to become *Oberpräsident* (provincial president) of the Rhine Province and his appointment must have made the transfer to Frankfurt more palatable to Johanna. She could not see her Otto advancing less rapidly than his peers. In convincing Johanna that they had to go to Frankfurt Otto used all the diplomatic skills for which he became famous. He continually harped on the fact that he had not sought this position, but that it was God's will and that he was God's soldier. He knew that her pietist convictions were much stronger than his own.

His letters to her amount almost to a second courtship and he even managed to convince her, who dreaded the prospect of socializing in the great world of Frankfurt, that she had to improve her French. There is, however, no reason to doubt his devotion to her or his need for the love and warm domesticity she gave him. To his request that she practise her French he added: 'You are my wife and not married to the diplomats, who can learn to speak German as well you can learn French. I married you to love you in God and according to the needs of my heart and in order to have in the foreign world a place for my heart, which all its dry winds will not cool. . . .'[9] While he was alone in Frankfurt, before her arrival with the children, he felt lonely: 'I felt homesick all day,' he wrote to her six weeks after his move to the city, '. . . then I sat in the window and in the summer air of roses and shrubs in the garden, when I heard from a window opposite, played by unknown hand on the piano, one [of] your beloved Beethoven pieces, only distantly and with interruptions, but for me it sounded more beautiful than any concert.' He needed her to keep his demons at bay, as he wrote to his friend Kleist-Retzow: 'The handle that the Evil One has on me is not love of external splendour, but a brutal sensuousness, which leads me near to the gravest sins, so that I despair of the grace of God and feel certain the seed of the divine word has not found fertile soil in my heart, grown savage since my young days.'[10] Kleist-Retzow had warned him that his appointment in Frankfurt might not last, but when, in reply, he says that he would prefer to return with Johanna to Schönhausen or Reinfeld and become a Landrat, one can be less sure that he means it; but fortunately for him the occasion did not arise. He was beginning a career that took him to vertiginous heights.

3

DIPLOMAT WITH A DIFFERENCE

The German Confederation, established in 1815 and now revived, was a union of sovereign princes with an identity in international law. Its sovereign members were represented by envoys in the diet in Frankfurt. The only feature the diet had in common with a parliament was its name, for the struggle against the idea of popular representation was its very essence. The envoys acted on the instructions of their separate governments, which were often slow in coming. The states represented at Frankfurt varied greatly in size and importance, ranging from small principalities like Waldeck or those of the Thuringian region to the two major European powers, Austria and Prussia. A large part of the Habsburg empire lay outside the Confederation, as did the Prussian provinces of Posen and West Prussia. During the revolution these provinces had been made part of the Confederation, but after its reconstitution the Prussian government hastened to take them out again, to emphasize the fact that, like the Habsburg empire, it was a European as well as a German power. The main organ of the diet was the inner council (*engerer Rat*), in which the eleven larger states had one vote each, while the remainder had six votes between them. In the plenary session of the diet, which met only rarely, the two largest states had four votes each. Austria held the presidency, which also gave it a casting vote.

Bismarck arrived in Frankfurt as the choice of those in Prussia whose priority was the fight against revolution. Before 1848 the Confederation had been the principal instrument for keeping all liberal constitutional, let alone democratic, aspirations at bay in Central Europe and it had discharged this role on the basis of close collaboration between Austria and Prussia. It was entirely natural that Vienna took the lead in this relationship and Berlin followed. The Habsburg empire was the older but also the greater power. It had scarcely been noticed yet that the settlement of 1815, by allocating the Rhine provinces to Prussia, had made this upstart, the least of the major powers, more German than Austrian and potentially more advanced economically. The move towards the formation of customs unions, culminating in the formation of the German Zollverein in 1834, had given a foretaste of this, but before 1848 it was neither sufficiently significant nor sufficiently complete to disturb seriously the political cooperation between Vienna and Berlin. The aftermath of the revolution, the Erfurt union and its demise at Olmütz, had, however, put a serious question mark over the conservative solidarity between Vienna and Berlin.

When he arrived in Frankfurt Bismarck had no preconceived notion of how to cope with the dilemma between cooperation and confrontation with Austria. On the one hand, he could not fully share the rigid ideological stance of some of the ultra-conservatives. It would have prevented him from making any serious challenge to the Austrian position in the Confederation. On the other hand, he was far too perceptive and analytical to be satisfied with the pragmatic approach that often characterized Manteuffel, who as foreign minister was his superior. Manteuffel often failed to see how Austria was seeking to use the Confederation to strengthen her pre-eminence in Germany. Circumstances quickly made the problem of maintaining the Prussian position against Austria the overriding day-to-day problem for Bismarck. At the personal level he was in Frankfurt diplomatic society something of an outsider; the modest scale on which the parsimonious Prussian state maintained its representatives, as well as his limited personal wealth, made it difficult to compete with someone like Count Thun, the Austrian envoy, a member of the very grand Bohemian high aristocracy. The Bismarck household in Frankfurt was easy-going and informal, as his old friend Motley reported after a visit:

> In their house everyone can do as he pleases . . . everything that goes on this earth in food and drink is on offer, port, soda water, beer, champagne, burgundy, red wine, everything is simultaneously at hand and the best Havanna cigars are smoked.[1]

In his private letters Bismarck wrote about the Frankfurt diplomatic community in the same irreverent, ironical manner that he had earlier applied to the Junker society in Pomerania. Immediately after his arrival he wrote to Johanna:

> I never doubted that all their cookery was done with water; but such thin, simple watery soup, in which one can't see a single trace of fatty pork floating, has surprised me. . . . Nobody, not the most malignant doubter of a democrat, can believe the amount of charlatanism and self-importance there is in this diplomatic game.[2]

The battle and intrigues of the diplomatic ladies make perfect material for his caustic pen. One of them tries to introduce an alcoholic, down-at-heel English milady into the circle, against the fierce resistance of others. Lady Rollington is forced on Bismarck at a ball, he is 'quite taken aback by this apparition, disfigured by a rash, reeking of cognac, her fleshly protrusions spilling to an indecent extent out of her opulent get-up'.[3]

His contempt for the whole machinery of the diet, in which the envoys of insignificant dwarf states strut the stage, is reflected in an early letter to Wagener: 'Those from the small states are caricatures of pigtailed diplomats, who immediately put on their "official report" face when I ask them for a light for my cigar. . . .'[4] Bismarck, never one to offer the other cheek, therefore felt compelled to assert himself in great as well as in small matters. He let no occasion pass to claim equality with the Austrian delegate, taking his coat off when Thun appeared informally dressed, and smoking in official meetings, hitherto a privilege claimed by the Austrian presidency. It became very characteristic of his work in Frankfurt that in his reports home he voiced his opinion on a wide range of topics, especially on the great strategic questions, which would normally have been dealt with by a foreign minister rather than by one of his representatives. Over the next few years Bismarck unleashed a stream of letters and memoranda on all important questions of the day upon Leopold von Gerlach and Manteuffel. He allowed most of these documents to be published during his lifetime, presumably to show the consistency of his outlook over a long period. What is consistent is his conviction that Austria and Prussia had to arrive at some definition of their respective spheres of influence in Central Europe. Bismarck did not abate one jot his uncompromising hostility to revolution, democracy, liberalism and all its works, but he realized that conservative solidarity with Austria, which he had never greatly believed in, was now a chimera. Under Schwarzenberg Austria was on the offensive and Thun was a faithful executant of this policy. In the Habsburg empire Schwarzenberg was pursuing a centralizing and Germanizing policy. It was an essential concomitant of this policy that Austria should maintain and further enhance her position as the leading German power. 'The present Austrian system of germanizing centralization requires for a solution of its task a closer organic connection and a tighter hegemony in Germany', Bismarck wrote to Manteuffel in July 1854, by which time Schwarzenberg himself had left the scene. With the suspicion of the papacy and ultramontane Catholicism that was deeply rooted in him as a Prussian Protestant he added: 'The aims of the Ultramontanes go for the moment hand in glove with those of the ambitious men in Vienna. For both of them it is Prussia's power in Germany that is hardest and most difficult to swallow.'[5]

In November 1851 Bismarck had a conversation with Thun, which, if we are to believe the report he made of it to Manteuffel, was conducted in the light-hearted way of two gentlemen engaging in word-play, but was full of underlying menace. Bismarck complained of the aggressive Austrian policy against the Zollverein. Thun replied that he was sorry to see that Prussia wanted to reduce the Confederation to 'a police and military institution' and that the predominant influence of Austria in Germany 'lay in the nature of things'. When Thun produced a lot of '*grossdeutsch* fantasies' Bismarck helped him along by saying that Prussia and the Reformation were regrettable facts which neither of them could change. He added that a Prussia which renounced the heritage of Frederick the Great in order to become the hereditary *Reichchamberlain* was not a reality and he could not advise his masters to pursue such a policy until the guns had spoken.[6] Soon after this conversation Louis Napoleon carried out the coup d'état which made him dictator and then emperor of France. After initial anxiety about the significance of this event, Bismarck, with his unflinching realism, saw that the likelihood of renewed revolution had further receded and that the diplomatic options for Prussia had greatly widened. It was a view of Bonapartism that soon created a major difference of opinion between him and the Gerlachs. They could see in Napoleon III only a revolutionary usurper, an alliance with whom would be immoral.

The Zollverein and its further development was the chief obstacle to the vision, pursued by Schwarzenberg and his trade minister Bruck, of an Austrian dominated Central Europe with 70 million inhabitants. The

Austrians had, in spite of Olmütz, failed to secure changes to their advantage in the constitution of the Confederation and when Prussia adhered to it the original form was left unchanged. Even before Bismarck had been sent to Frankfurt there was no disposition in Berlin to make any concessions to Austria on the Zollverein and it was a major coup for the Prussians when, in September 1851, they secured the adherence to the customs union of a smaller union comprising Hanover, Electoral Hesse and some lesser states. This rounding off was of particular importance to Prussia, as these territories straddled the gap between its western and eastern provinces. At Frankfurt these matters were dealt with in a committee attended by Rudolf Delbrück, an official Prussian finance expert, who was to play a major role under Bismarck twenty years later in the economic unification of Germany. Bismarck fought every inch of the way to prevent Austria from making the Zollverein an integral part of the constitution of the Confederation and thus gaining an entry into it. When the Hanoverian estates applied to the diet for a revision of the constitution of their country in a counter-revolutionary sense, Bismarck could have been expected to agree with these endeavours. But since there was a danger that a revision of the Hanoverian constitution might bring a more pro-Austrian government to power in Hanover, thus putting the customs union treaty of September 1851 in jeopardy, Bismarck did not hesitate to oppose the Hanoverian constitutional revision. He wrote to Manteuffel that Prussian needs had to take precedence over those of Hanover, even if it meant sacrificing the counter-revolutionary cause there. Within weeks of arriving in Frankfurt he had convinced himself that a Prussian counterattack was the answer to Schwarzenberg's offensive.

Schwarzenberg died suddenly in April 1852 at the age of fifty-two and Austrian designs in Central Europe were not thereafter pursued with the same energy. Vienna could not force its way into the Zollverein and agreed to a renewal of the Zollverein treaty for twelve years from January 1854, after which the question of Austrian adhesion would come up for reconsideration. In fact the economic exclusion of the Habsburg empire from Kleindeutschland had become a fact. It did not end the struggle between Berlin and Vienna over many other matters and left plenty of scope for Bismarck. The thrust of his endeavours always was not to allow Austria to enhance the importance of the Confederation in its own interests. It mattered little to him if in the process the concerns of Germany as a whole were neglected, provided those of Prussia were satisfied.

The future of the German fleet was another issue on which Austria and Prussia clashed. The establishment of this fleet had been a matter of great pride to the German national movement in 1848, but now its continued existence became the subject of a bitter legal and financial wrangle at Frankfurt. Prussia had paid the lion's share of the expenditure on the fleet. Bismarck was determined not to allow the diet to take decisions on the fleet by a majority against the interests of Prussia and insisted that it was a matter in which the unanimity rule applied. Changes to the constitution of the Confederation could only be made by unanimous vote. Bismarck displayed great legal ingenuity on this and many subsequent occasions, his training in the law standing him in good stead. The quarrel became so bitter that the tsar intervened. Bismarck, with the support of his superiors, had hinted at a Prussian withdrawal from Frankfurt, a threat that was to re-emerge at intervals during the next few years. Even if this threat was only bluff at this stage, the tsar feared that the conservative solidarity, which he had helped to reestablish at Olmütz, was again in jeopardy. Gorchakov, his envoy to Württemberg and representative at the diet, was sent to mediate between the Prussian and Austrian envoys in Frankfurt. It was the first time that Bismarck met the Russian, who was to become a major sparring partner for the next thirty years. A few years later he gave this acid verdict on Gorchakov, in a letter to Leopold von Gerlach: 'G is a solemn, uncouth tom fool, a fox in wooden clogs, when he tries to be clever.'[7] The upshot of the long wrangle about the German fleet was that it was auctioned off, yet another bitter blow for German national sentiment in its time of humiliation. But Bismarck had made the Prussian interest prevail against Austria.

One incident in the fleet controversy was that the Confederation took up a loan with the Rothschilds in order to pay the officers and men of the navy, but without Prussian consent. In protest Bismarck withdrew the business of the Prussian legation from the Rothschild bank temporarily, but kept his own account with the bank. It was through the Rothschild bank that some years later he established contact with Gerson Bleichröder, who became his personal financial adviser and a conduit for confidential information. Soon after taking up his post at the diet Bismarck met the old Amschel Mayer Rothschild, eldest of the five sons of the original Rothschild and, at nearly eighty, still head of the Frankfurt branch. He took to him, and praised him to Johanna for his lack of pretence, in spite of his enormous wealth and great influence: 'he is entirely the old bargaining Jew and does not want to pretend anything else, a strongly orthodox Jew with it, who does not touch anything at his great dinners and eats only kosher.'[8] He then reproduced for Johanna the German-Jewish dialect in which Amschel Mayer spoke, telling his servant to take some bread for the deer in his park and offering Bismarck a valuable plant in his garden, that had cost him, 'on his honour,' 2,000 gulden, for a thousand, no, for nothing, 'I really esteem you, Herr Baron, you are a fine, a decent man.' The Baron's comments were nearly always caustic, about nearly everybody, but in this case they were softer and more sympathetic, as he describes the grizzled little old man, 'a poor man in his palace, childless, widowed, deceived by his own men and badly treated by his frenchified and anglicized nephews and nieces, who will inherit his treasures, without gratitude or love.'

Benevolence was not a quality that Bismarck could afford to cultivate in the intrigue-laden atmosphere of Frankfurt and Berlin. Since the volume and range of his official correspondence from Frankfurt much exceeded what would have been normal from a mere envoy, it fed the suspicion, especially in the mind of a bureaucrat like Manteuffel, that Bismarck had higher ambitions. He, in common with the Gerlachs and others of the legitimist faction, were fundamentally opposed to the bureaucratic absolutism, of which Manteuffel was now the most prominent representative. In the correspondence between Leopold von Gerlach and Bismarck he is usually referred to under the Shakespearean codename Fra Diavolo, or just FD. When in May 1852 the king chose Bismarck for a special mission to Vienna, where the Prussian ambassador had fallen ill, it exposed him to the crossfire of conflicting groups and viewpoints in Berlin. The king still hankered after a restoration of conservative solidarity. A restoration of the Holy Roman empire would have made him happy. In the letter he gave Bismarck to deliver to the Emperor Francis Joseph he described his envoy as a man 'who in our country is revered by many but also hated by some for his knightly and free obedience and his irreconcilable front against revolution to its very roots'. Others in Prussia, notably the heir to the throne, the prince of Prussia, and his circle, were still smarting under the humiliation of Olmütz and put it about that Bismarck had been too accommodating in Vienna. By this time a new grouping was emerging among Prussian conservatives, led by Moritz von Bethmann Hollweg, grandfather of the later chancellor, which, from the newspaper that they launched in late 1851, became known as the *Wochenblattpartei*. Bethmann Hollweg came from the Frankfurt patriciate and he and his supporters had their base among the aristocracy and the upper bourgeoisie of Prussia's western provinces and in Silesia. Their prescription for moving forward in the post-revolutionary situation was a renewed push towards Kleindeutschland under Prussian leadership, a policy with clear anti-Austrian implications.

There were thus at least three factions among Prussian conservatives, between whom little love was lost. There were the legitimist ultra-conservatives, uneasily yoked with Junkers concerned for their material position and remaining legal privileges; there was the bureaucratic, governmental world of Manteuffel; and there was the more liberal *Wochenblatt* faction, whose main support came from the prince of Prussia and his wife Augusta, who held court in Koblenz, a focus of opposition to the king's own court. Prince William had moved from the position that had compelled him to flee to England in 1848 and had earned him the name *Kartätschenprinz* (the grapeshot prince). His English exile and his wife had turned him into a liberal conservative, seeing himself and his associates playing a role in Prussia similar to that of the Whigs in England. He was also primarily a military man, who saw Olmütz as a humiliation that needed to be avenged.

Bismarck did not wholly share the outlook of any of these groups within Prussian conservatism, though his ideas overlapped with many of theirs. Ambitious as he was, it did not appeal to him to become a minister at the mercy of the vacillating and unstable king, with whose romantic Germanism he did not sympathize. About the Wochenblattpartei he had written to Manteuffel:

> A conservative opposition can only be conducted with and through the king, in that the interest of HM is enlisted against his own ministers, not through the public prints, but through personal influence at court; anything else has no basis with us or must become radical. . . . Even Junkerdom, which through its ramifications in landownership, in the army, in the bureaucracy is much more powerful than this Rhenish-conservative opposition, which can be successful against a determined ministry only if it has the support of the King.[9]

At Koblenz he was an object of suspicion. Augusta had not forgotten the incident of March 1848, when Bismarck had tried to involve her in treason, as she saw it. He had for a long time been more aware of his differences with his patrons, the Gerlachs, than they themselves were, but he was still seen as the camarilla's man and could not afford to detach himself openly. It was fortunate for him that his position in Frankfurt enabled him to put some distance between himself and the intrigues of Berlin. In the autumn of 1852 he gave up his seat in the Prussian chamber, having previously fought a duel with the leading liberal deputy, Vincke, brought on by a moment of excess in his normally confrontational style. Nobody was hurt. Bismarck may well have thought it prudent to be less closely involved with domestic Prussian politics for the moment and to stay out of the fierce infighting of the various conservative factions.

*

Bismarck's formidable energies were thus focused on foreign affairs and they remained his predominant interest for the rest of his life. Not that he ever believed that foreign and domestic affairs could be separated or that his powerful antennae did not stay attuned to domestic developments in his own and other countries, but in foreign affairs there was more scope for individual action and for the impact of a single powerful personality. For the moment, however, he could only report, comment and persuade, and his stream of communications with the men of power and influence in Berlin was a substitute for the direct action which was only to a limited extent open to him. A more critical phase in the affairs of Europe began with the Crimean War, which cast its shadow ahead with the opening of hostilities between Russia and Turkey in the summer of 1853. The dilemmas with which Bismarck had wrestled at Frankfurt and about which he had tried to impress his views on the various parties in Berlin now became more acute. Broadly speaking, the Wochenblattpartei wanted a western orientation and saw an opportunity for a renewed push towards Kleindeutschland under Prussian aegis, ending the Austrian influence in Germany. The camarilla on the other hand could not contemplate anything that might involve hostilities against Russia.

Initially the king leaned more towards the western orientation, especially as public opinion in Germany was clearly anti-Russian, and the Manteuffel government appeared to be following that line. But the king could not bring himself to risk war with Russia and abruptly switched back to neutrality. The leading advocates of the western alliance, including Bunsen, the Prussian ambassador in London, were dismissed. Another of the 'Koblenz malcontents' now sidelined was Count Pourtalès, a native of Neuchâtel (Neuenburg), which was then under the Prussian crown, between whom and Bismarck there was mutual contempt. Pourtalès described Bismarck as a Judas in knight's armour, while Bismarck characterized Pourtalès as 'blasé, with a light colouring of church, salon, learning and bordello'.[10] Other diplomats linked to the Wochenblattpartei, for example Robert von der Goltz and Guido von Usedom, were marked down by Bismarck as rivals, against whom he pursued henceforth an unrelenting vendetta. Bismarck had a hand in the fall of Bunsen, Pourtalès and other '*Bethmänner*', as the associates of Bethmann Hollweg were often called by their opponents. A little later the Prussian minister of war, Bonin, a pro-westerner, was also dismissed and a severe crisis ensued between the king and his brother, the prince of Prussia. Bismarck was asked to mediate, an indication how central a figure he had become among the Prussian ruling elite and how much he was in the confidence of the royal house. A visit by Bismarck to Prince William at Baden-Baden at the end of May helped to restore relations between the two brothers at least on a formal level.

But Bismarck was by no means an unqualified supporter of the pro-Russian orientation of his camarilla friends. At the centre of his calculations was still the rivalry between Prussia and Austria in Germany. He wanted to use the upheaval in European power relations caused by the crisis in the Balkans to enhance the power of Prussia in Germany at the expense of Austria. He therefore shared the aims of the Bethmänner to a large extent, but did not for a moment believe that they could be achieved by Prussia making a foursome with Austria and the western powers, nor did he consider it in Prussia's interest to incur greater hostility from Russia than was absolutely necessary. What was needed was a confident and if necessary aggressive neutrality, not a neutrality based on vacillation, such as the king's chronic indecision and the infighting of factions imposed on Berlin. He wrote to Manteuffel:

> Great crises make the weather favourable to Prussia's expansion, if we exploit them fearlessly and perhaps ruthlessly; if we want to go on growing, then we must not be afraid to stand alone with 400,000 soldiers, especially as long as the others are fighting and we can by allying with everyone of them still do better business than through a premature and unconditional alliance with so weak and dishonest a confederate as Austria.[11]

In the meantime Bismarck's Austrian opposite number at Frankfurt, Thun, had been replaced by Baron Prokesch von Osten. He was a man of middle-class origin, who enjoyed a wide reputation as a scholar and expert on oriental affairs. In Bismarck's view Thun became in retrospect decent and honest in comparison with Prokesch, whom he called a liar, an intriguer, a 'mousetrap grocer' lacking the manners normal in civilized society. Prokesch reinforced at a personal level Bismarck's deep distrust of Austrian policies and motives. He was therefore less than delighted with the next major step taken by his masters in Berlin, the offensive-defensive alliance (*Schutz-und Trutzbündnis*) between Prussia and Austria of 20 April 1854. All the other members of the Confederation were invited to support the treaty and finally did so, the Confederation declaring its adherence in July 1854. The aims of Austria and Prussia were very different in signing this treaty and no one was more determined than Bismarck to turn it to Prussia's advantage at the expense of Austria. When awaiting with growing uneasiness the signature of the treaty he had written to Gerlach:

> The sentiment of all my colleagues here, and as far as I can see of all the governments of the middle states [i.e. the members of the Confederation other than Austria and Prussia] is one of deepest concern, that the war policy of Vienna should sweep us into an engagement against Russia.[12]

What Austria wanted was to get the support of the Confederation in forcing the Russians out of the Danube principalities, Wallachia and Moldavia, what later became Romania. The occupation of these principalities by Russian troops in 1853 had been the opening of hostilities between Russia and Turkey in the summer of 1853. An additional clause in the defensive alliance between Austria and Prussia of April 1854 appeared to commit the partners, and other later adherents to the alliance, to support Austria in applying pressure on Russia. Bismarck used all means available to him both in Frankfurt and in Berlin to prevent such an interpretation and use of the alliance by the politicians in Vienna, among whom the Austrian foreign minister Count Buol was the most prominent.

Bismarck was assiduous in building on the fear of the middle states of being dragged into war against Russia and being left exposed to the designs of France and to the pressure of German nationalism. He had no illusions about their German patriotism, which figured in their rhetoric and in the press, but knew that the one thing that really mattered to them was the security of their thrones and their territories. In these circumstances it was hardly worth disguising 'our Prussian and egotistical policy' with the 'moth-eaten ermine of German patriotism'. When Bismarck tried to persuade his own king to use Prussian armed strength to make all sides pay Prussia the attention that was her due, the king smiled and replied in Berlin dialect: 'Luvvie, that is all very fine, but a man like Napoleon can make such gestures, not me.' The middle states wanted in fact to play neither the Austrian nor the Prussian game. There was a third Germany, led by Bavaria and Saxony, represented at this time by two energetic figures, von der Pfordten and Beust. They would cross Bismarck's path at intervals during the next decade.

For a time the Austrians were riding high, forcing the Russians out of the Danube principalities and having considerable success in dragging the German Confederation and its members in their wake. Bismarck could make little impression on the divided decision-makers in Berlin and felt increasingly marginalized. His letters to Leopold von Gerlach become rather defensive, for he knew that the man who remained for him an essential advocate at the centre of power, did not agree with his recommendation that Prussia should in its turn create a fright, among the middle states and even in Vienna, by threatening a link with Paris.

> Please don't take me for a Bonapartist, only for a very ambitious Prussian. From this point of view I consider it as impolitic to allow Austria to believe that we would never seek a separate understanding with the West, as to ram it down Western throats that we would never tie ourselves to Russia,[13]

he wrote to Gerlach in January 1855. In the autumn of 1854 the king had appointed Bismarck a member of the first chamber of the Prussian parliament, which had been reconstructed as a house of peers as part of the steady erosion of all liberal features in the Prussian constitution in these years of reaction. It scarcely lessened his isolation and there was no longer much likelihood of his becoming a minister in the foreseeable future. To his friend Kleist-Retzow he wrote in December 1854: 'Our foreign policy is bad, for it is driven by fear. I have had nothing to do with it since September and appear to have fallen a bit into disgrace, at least I have become rather dispensable.'[14]

This was just after Austria had concluded a convention with the western powers, in which Austria undertook to defend the Danube principalities against a return of Russian troops, while the western powers undertook to support Austria in case of an outbreak of hostilities with Russia. In a later secret agreement France guaranteed Austria the maintenance of the status quo in Italy. The Prussians were left in the cold. In a letter to Manteuffel Bismarck wrote prophetically; 'Even if the position of Austria was as rosy as Herr von Prokesch paints it, this Jewish mixture of cowardice, greed and impudence which characterizes present Austrian policy will, when sobriety returns, bring the imperial state severe misery'.[15] In fact Bismarck was now able to play one of his early masterstrokes, a foretaste of the humiliation he was eventually to inflict upon the Habsburg empire. He managed to rouse the fear of the middle German states of a war with Russia, or of being left at the mercy of France, to a sufficient extent to gain a majority in the Frankfurt diet against the Austrian request for a federal mobilization. The German states were not prepared to expose themselves for the sake of Austrian ambitions in the Balkans and for the first time Austria was put in a minority on a major issue.

The fact was that Vienna suffered as much from divided counsel as Berlin. Austria had gone with the West and by the presence of its troops on the Danube brought much help to the Franco-British invasion of the Crimea. But it did not go the whole hog and failed to enter the war on the western side. The chronic state of Austrian finances, always near bankruptcy, was one of the reasons. Austria earned only limited gratitude in Paris and London and only three years later found herself under attack from France in Italy. But at the same time the Holy Alliance was shattered for good and the Austrians had exchanged Russian support for hostility. As Schwarzenberg had predicted after Olmütz, Austria would astonish the world by her ingratitude towards Russia. Vienna could afford indecision between east and west even less than Berlin, for the Habsburg empire was exposed on too many fronts, in the Balkans, in Italy and in Germany. The constellation of powers was appearing upon the horizon, which would within a decade enable Bismarck to transform Europe.

For the moment the prospects did not look too good either for Prussia as a country or for Bismarck himself. After the fall of Sevastopol in September 1855 Russia was ready for peace and the Paris peace congress met in February 1856. The British wanted to exclude Prussia from the congress, her neutrality having caused resentment in London, but she was in the end admitted after pressure from Austria and France. At Frankfurt Prokesch had been replaced by Rechberg, with whom Bismarck was to cross swords frequently for the next few years. Rechberg was a smooth South German aristocrat of ancient lineage, a staunch Catholic, more conciliatory in manner and tactics than his predecessor. Bismarck thought him pedantic, like a minor judge, and as an enemy he preferred Prokesch. He told Gerlach that Berlin's conciliatory stance *vis-à-vis* Austria over the peace congress made him vomit. More than ever Prussia looked like the least great of the European great powers.

The dominant continental power was France and Napoleon III was the arbiter of Europe. Bismarck had taken the opportunity of the world exhibition of 1855 to visit Paris in August of that year and stayed with Count Hatzfeld, the Prussian ambassador. He was the brother of the unconventional Sophie von Hatzfeld, the friend of the socialist leader Ferdinand Lassalle, with whom Bismarck later had a significant encounter. He was introduced to the French emperor and also to Queen Victoria, who was on a state visit to Paris. He noticed little enthusiasm for the English queen among the French crowds. Bismarck felt that he had to apologize for his visit to 'Babylon' to Leopold von Gerlach, but told him that he thought Louis Napoleon was firmly in the saddle. As a person he found Louis Napoleon fascinating, perhaps recognizing a kindred spirit in a loner performing a high-wire act in front of a large audience. To his own king he described the French emperor as more good-natured and less clever than the world sees him. To his brother he wrote: 'He looks frightened, like the frontal view of a rat'.[16] Bismarck was now in his early forties, the vault at Schönhausen was, as he told his brother, coming closer, his ambition as burning as ever, but his future uncertain. He had risen as an ultra-conservative and as the protégé of the camarilla, but he cannot have thought that the long-term prospects of either the Prussian conservative party or of the camarilla were good.

*

In the next two years he wrote reports and letters to Manteuffel and Gerlach, which, even for him, were exceptionally substantial. It was as if against the odds he was trying to impose his own stamp upon Prussian policy. One of these extensive pieces from his pen is his assessment of the European situation after the conclusion of the Treaty of Paris; this letter to Manteuffel, dated 26 April 1856, has become known as the 'splendid report' (*Prachtbericht*).[17] He sees an alliance between France and Russia as likely. He does not see the rotten German Confederation as a match for such a combination. He warns against an alliance with Austria, which would tie Prussia to an inherently weak and untrustworthy ally. The Habsburg empire could collapse like a house of cards, but even apart from this danger, an Austrian-Prussian alliance would be the opposite of everything that gives strength to an alliance. 'Mutual political mistrust, military and political jealousy, the fear of the one that the other would in case of success prevent the enlargement of the other, in case of defeat would try to save his own bacon'. The lesser German princes would think only of saving themselves and their subjects from hardship and privation. An armed confrontation with Austria may not be imminent, but 'I must declare my conviction that in the not too distant future we will have to fight against Austria for our very existence.' If the Prussians did remain victorious against a Franco-Russian alliance, they would merely have fought for an Austrian preponderance in Germany. The time of anti-revolutionary monarchical solidarity is gone and would only recur if the French empire was overthrown by revolution. For the moment it is not a fight against democrats, but a matter of cabinet policy and in this our interests do not coincide with Austria. Half jocularly, Bismarck ends this report with the remark that 'your Excellency may regard it as lucky that the departure of the post forces me to end this immodestly long letter.' In his correspondence with Manteuffel Bismarck adopts the formalities appropriate to a subordinate writing to his superior, but in substance the tone is that of a lesson read to a pupil, albeit one couched in caustic wit and full of brilliantly conceived allusions. No wonder Manteuffel was wary of Bismarck as a potential rival and supplanter.

The personal and political bonds between Bismarck and the Gerlachs remained close, but it had been evident ever since he went to Frankfurt that there was a growing divergence of approach even with the less doctrinaire brother Leopold. Later there was great bitterness between Bismarck and Ludwig von Gerlach, the brother who survived to witness the former's rise to power and eminence. This may have led Bismarck to exaggerate the extent of the breach in the middle 1850s when he wrote his reminiscences in the 1890s. At least up to the time when in the autumn of 1857 the prince of Prussia began to act as regent for his mentally ill brother, Bismarck could hardly afford to lose the goodwill of Leopold von Gerlach. This is very evident from the tone of the lengthy letters the two exchanged in May 1857.[18] The correspondence with Gerlach kept reverting to France and to the nature of Bonapartism. Gerlach sees Napoleon III as the revolution incarnate, because his rule is based on the consent of the masses, on popular sovereignty. When he pursues French interests in Germany and Italy it must forward the cause of revolution. But in the end Gerlach agrees that one must deal with Napoleon, must not needlessly offend him, only bear in mind the danger he represents. He and Bismarck appeared to have reached agreement pragmatically, but events were to show that they were far apart.

In all the copious documents of his Frankfurt years there is little about the great strategic questions that were changing society rapidly in most European countries: the advance of industrialization, the growing importance of the middle classes connected with this process, the rise of an industrial proletariat. Such developments were not at the forefront of Bismarck's mind, but in a cosmopolitan, commercial centre like Frankfurt he was well aware of them. Much as he disliked the Gotha liberals, he could see that even in the revolution of 1848 they feared the masses more than their nominal enemies, monarchy and aristocracy. This clearly opened the way to novel alliances, to taking the bourgeoisie in the rear, to forcing into the open the basic identity of interest between bourgeoisie, monarchy and the feudal classes in face of the threat from the masses. Every now and then there is evidence in Bismarck's correspondence and reports that he was thinking along those lines. Writing to a friend in 1854 he remarks that the supporters of the three-tier system have not yet learnt that 'the bourgeoisie was ever the nurse of Revolution', while the *Volk* below three thaler consists '9/10 of royalists'.[19] Exponent of *Realpolitik* as he now is in foreign affairs, he sees domestic politics from the same perspective. For him the liberal bourgeoisie is entirely an interest to be manipulated and he has no sense that they, or indeed anybody, might cherish individual or national liberty as ideals for their own sake. The personal freedom that he cherished so much and that made bureaucratic routine intolerable to him was a privilege that he did not concede to others.

In a long memorandum he wrote for the prince of Prussia in September 1853 he goes at length into the question why Prussia cannot be compared with England. It is a recurring theme with him and he is always contemptuous of those who would hold up English liberalism as an example to be followed. 'No way did Prussia become great through liberalism and free thought, only through a series of strong, decisive and wise rulers,' he writes. When in April 1856 Gerlach asks him what he thinks of the English marriage of the Prince Frederick William, the future Prussian crown prince and eventual emperor, to Vicky, Queen Victoria's eldest daughter, he replies: 'I don't like the English aspect of the marriage, even if the marriage may be fine. . . . If the princess succeeds in leaving the Englishwoman behind and becoming a Prussian, then she may be a blessing for the land.'[20] For the rest of his life he destested Vicky, the English-Coburg princess, almost but not quite as much as her mother-in-law Augusta, the Weimar princess. Liberalism at this time still went hand in hand with German nationalism and Bismarck had no more sympathy for the latter than for the former. He was therefore entirely honest when he tells Leopold von Gerlach that he was still the man that stood 'on the same ground with him and nurtured the same plants on it', but he no doubt also agreed with Gerlach when the latter admitted 'that in my differences with you the thought frequently occurs to me that my views are out of date.' Bismarck's willingness to try anything that promised success was bound to separate him from the Gerlachs and many Prussian conservatives. His means became ends. Instead of being the victim of a revolution from below, he carried out a revolution from above, but a revolution it still was. Against this he would always argue that he was not making the wave, merely riding it. His religion, such as it now was, told him that the divine purpose was inscrutable and that no one could tell whither it would carry them. But in whatever direction it would go, he personally was determined to stay on top of the game.

The arrival of the prince of Prussia, first as temporary then, in October 1858, as permanent regent, in place of his incapacitated brother, was likely to make this difficult. The defeat of the liberals in 1849 had been the loss of a battle, but was not seen by most of them as the loss of the war. The change at the top in Prussia aroused great expectations and the regent was bound to go some way to meet them. Even before he had assumed the full powers of the crown, the minister of the interior Westphalen was dismissed. He had been associated with the repressive regime of the previous few years, but oddly enough was the brother-in-law of Karl Marx. Then the regent decided to replace the whole Manteuffel cabinet. Leopold von Gerlach, who had tried to prolong the temporary regency as long as possible, lost his job. It was the beginning of the 'New Era' and it looked as if the hour of the Wochenblattpartei had struck. In the new liberal-conservative cabinet of Prince Anton von Hohenzollern-Sigmaringen, Count Schleinitz, a confidant of the regent and particularly of his wife, and once a supporter of the Erfurt union, became foreign minister and therefore Bismarck's new chief. The cabinet included Auerswald, a member of the liberal cabinet of 1848, and Bethmann Hollweg. In addressing this new cabinet the regent said, with reference to Prussia's policy in Germany: 'In Germany Prussia must make moral conquests, through wise legislation at home, through a raising of all moral elements and through the pursuit of unification elements, such as the

Zollverband, which however requires reform. . . . The world must know that Prussia is everywhere prepared to protect the law.' Other passages, about religion, about the education system promoting intelligence, seemed to indicate that Prussia was turning its back on ultra-conservatism and repression. There was, however, also reference to the need for reforms in the army, so that Prussia could pull her due weight. There was a warning that the government could not allow itself to be driven by fashionable liberal ideas. Nevertheless, all over Germany public opinion now hoped that Prussia would resume the lead towards unification and moderate liberalization that she had given up nearly a decade earlier.

*

The New Era was not likely to be Bismarck's hour, even though his appointment to a ministerial post was still talked about. At the end of January 1859 his recall from Frankfurt and appointment as Prussian ambassador in St Petersburg was confirmed. He tried to persuade the regent that his unrivalled knowledge of the German courts would make him more valuable if he stayed in Frankfurt, but to no avail. On paper it was a promotion, as the regent told him: in fact it was a relegation. He had become attached, not only to the political side of his job in Frankfurt, but to the social life. It brought out the convivial side of him and gave scope to his witty, gregarious self. Even Johanna had made many friends there, though she still preferred domesticity to the social whirl. When his removal from Frankfurt was about to happen he told Johanna that he tried to prevent it 'if only to annoy that intriguing gossip, the female Usedom.' She was the English wife of Guido von Usedom, one of the diplomats around the Wochenblattpartei, who to his chagrin was about to succeed him as Prussian envoy to the diet. For years to come Usedom and his wife were to remain the objects of his vitriolic and petty hatred. For him it was to be 'cold storage by the Neva'. He was nearly forty-four and most of what was to guide him for the rest of his life was in place. But what sort of a future would he really have?

Whatever reputation as an ultra-conservative *Kreuzzeitung* figure and creature of the camarilla still clung to him, his views were not now far removed from those proclaimed by the regent to mark the New Era. His personal contact with the regent was good, if less close than it had been with his brother, though he had fewer friends at court and the regent's wife hated him. In March 1858 he had, at the regent's request, prepared a long confidential memorandum mainly about Prussia's position within the Confederation.[21] It contained all his usual observations about the rivalry with Austria, about the pro-Austrian position of most of the ruling elites in the other German states, the power of ultramontanism, the underhand machinations of Vienna and so on. In his recommendations on future policy, he made much of Prussia's advanced political development as compared with Austria. In 1848 this development had gone too fast and had therefore alarmed the other German states. But now the Prussian constitution was so firmly established that 'a degree of freer movement was permissible without damaging the authority of the government' than was possible elsewhere in Germany. 'The policy to be pursued within the Confederation specifically by Prussia can only gain in force by publicity and public discussion.' Nothing was more German than a policy firmly in the Prussian interest, he asserted. Even allowing for the fact that Bismarck was probably arguing along lines which the recipient would find congenial, he was envisaging something not too far removed from the 'moral conquests' of the regent's speech.

The regent had, without enthusiasm, taken the oath to the constitution and Bismarck himself now fully accepted the constitution. It was on this basis, should he ever become minister, that he would have to operate and his own position and power as minister would arise from a balance of forces. In foreign affairs it was no longer only the policy of cabinets that mattered. A wider public opinion and the media that both produce and reflect it had to be taken into account. In domestic affairs constitutions, parliaments, parties and again the press could not be wished away. Bismarck had come to terms with this transitional stage and realized that it offered him as much if not more of a chance than the world of undiluted monarchical power. As part of the New Era policy the Prussian parliament was dissolved and fresh elections were held. They produced a liberal landslide and a severe reduction in the number of conservatives. Bismarck had briefly toyed with the idea of returning to a parliamentary career and had written to his sister Malle after the announcement of the dissolution:

> After 30 years it matters nothing to me whether I play the diplomat or the Landjunker, and up to now the prospect of a brisk, honest fight, without official handcuffs, as it were in political swimming trunks, has had as much attraction for me as a continued regime of truffels, telegrams and grand crosses.[22]

With the conservatives decimated a return to a parliamentary career could offer him little.

The next three-and-a-half years were to prove very difficult for him. Too often it looked as if his modestly distinguished career had reached its limit and that neither his towering ambition nor his consciousness of exceptional ability could take him any further. When he now talked of giving it all up and returning to his country Junker roots it sometimes sounded as if he meant it. Three months after arriving in St Petersburg, in June 1859, before Johanna has been able to join him, he wrote to her:

> I feel most terribly homesick for you and everything . . . lying here so alone. . . . My thoughts have moved at the moment closer than ever to the possibility, when the occasion serves, of giving it all up. Who knows how long we shall live together in this world, and who knows what times we will see.[23]

He was seriously ill at the time, more seriously than he wanted his wife to know. He seems to have realized that his illness was partly psychosomatic and stopped the draconian regime of bleeding that the Russian doctors inflicted on him. He recovered, but, just as he was about to fetch his family from Pomerania, an injury below his knee, received while hunting in Sweden in 1857, blew up and was mistreated. A German doctor in St Petersburg, recommended to him by an old grand duchess of Baden, applied a poultice which ate deep into his muscles. After recovering from this in Germany in July 1859 he fell seriously ill again in November on his way back to St Petersburg. A thrombosis in his leg brought on pneumonia and he hovered on the brink of death. For three months he lay ill and convalescing at his friend Alexander von Below's estate at Hohendorf. He could not return to his post until the following June. In asking for an extension of leave from his chief Schleinitz in December 1859 he wrote:

> I see it all [his illness] as an explosion of all the aggravation which I accumulated for eight years in Frankfurt, about everything I saw and could do nothing about, without finding any hearing in Berlin, except from Herr von Manteuffel, who saw the situation clearly, but did not always find it expedient to act according to his insight.[24]

Another great European crisis, the Italian war, was demanding resolute action. What was happening confirmed the views that Bismarck had been forming for the past few years, but he was now even more distant, physically and metaphorically, from the process of decision-making. His reception in Russia had been good, the tsar himself treating him with greater intimacy than is usually accorded to an ambassador. He saw a great deal of the tsar's mother, who was the sister of the Prussian regent. Gorchakov was now foreign minister and Bismarck got on well with him. Later the Russian, a man of exceptional vanity, resented the overpowering position Bismarck had gained on the European stage. Bismarck owed his favourable reception to his well-known anti-Austrian reputation and he was pleased to find so much resentment against Austria. 'I am sorry for Karolyi [the Austrian special envoy]', he wrote to his sister,

> he goes around here like a leper; but the Viennese have behaved too stupidly; they always thought that Russia would good-manneredly sit still, when things get going in Italy; if the Austrians get beaten they will sit still; but if they are victorious, with or without us, there will for sure be an immediate attack on Hungary. . . .

Not everything in the Prussian embassy in the Russian capital was to Bismarck's liking. He complained about the first secretary, Kurd von Schlözer, whom the new chief tried to use as a cipher clerk, but who refused to be thus demeaned. Schlözer was an acute observer, Prussian envoy to the Vatican in his later career, who referred to Bismarck as 'the Pasha' in his private letters, 'a man such as I have never encountered before, who knows no consideration for anyone, a brute, always snatching at dramatic coups, out to impress, a know-all, without ever having seen it all'.[25] Bismarck did not often come across anyone prepared to stand up to his bullying and in due course the two learnt to respect each other. Bismarck saw a good deal of Russia and his descriptions, mostly in letters to his wife, are as vivid as ever. On a June night in St Petersburg:

> with these short nights even the dawn brings no real coolness, but the night air is sheer balsam, and in the secretive dusk, which hovers over the water at midnight, I could ride and drive around for hours, if the rising light did not remind me of the next day and its cares and work and if sleep did not demand its tribute.[26]

As had been the case in Frankfurt, he was accused, by those who did not wish him well and whom he suspected of Austrian machinations, of ignoring his official instructions and making his own policy and these accusations from time to time reached his superiors in Berlin. Although they must have suspected, to judge by the spate of unorthodox advice with which he habitually deluged them, that there was some truth in such imputations, he rebutted them in his usual confrontational style. It cost him a lot of nervous energy and contributed, as he himself admitted, to the breakdown in his health.

When Bismarck arrived in St Petersburg it was an accomplished fact that Russia would take the side of France in a Franco-Austrian conflict, something he had foreseen ever since the Crimea. A secret treaty of neutrality in the event of the expected war in Italy had been concluded between Paris and St Petersburg. Bismarck's recommendation to the Prussian policy-makers was not to allow Austria to use the machinery of the German Confederation to organize the forces of the German states in support of the Habsburg empire against France. Such a policy would reinforce the shackles which, as Bismarck had argued, day in, day out, the Confederation would place upon Prussia if the Austrians had their way. Instead he advocated a boldly offensive policy. To Alvensleben, who had taken Gerlach's place as the regent's adjutant, he wrote:

> The present situation [on 5 May 1859, a week after the outbreak of war, but seven weeks before the Austrian defeat at Solferino] offers us again the jackpot, if we allow Austria's war with France to fester, and then take the road with all our armies southward, with border posts in our knapsacks, which we can hammer back into the ground by Lake Constance or wherever the Protestant religion ceases to be in the majority.[27]

No doubt this was Bismarck's usual colourful language in a private letter, but as advice it could not be taken seriously. The regent and Schleinitz in Berlin did their best to extract what advantage they could by insisting that Prussia must have the command of any forces mobilized by the German Confederation. Bismarck's was envious that it was now Usedom who could play a strong hand at Frankfurt.

The reality, however, was that German opinion, even Prussian opinion, was deeply stirred and predominantly pro-Austrian. The Rhine would have to be defended on the Po, that was the widely heard slogan. Even the regent, while out to secure proper respect for Prussia and to avenge Olmütz, could not bring himself to go too far against the German brother nation and towards the hereditary enemy, as France was in many German eyes. To go as far as Bismarck advocated in exploiting Austria's hour of need, by breaking up the Confederation rather than seeking Prussian military command within it, could not be official policy. To the foreign minister Schleinitz Bismarck had written, in a private letter a week after the one to Alvensleben, that he would . . .

> prefer the word 'German' rather than 'Prussian' to be written on our flag only after we have been more closely and more usefully connected with our countrymen than hitherto; it will lose its magic, if one uses it now, in respect of the confederal connexion. . . . I see in our relationship with the Confederation a disease of Prussia which we must sooner or later cure *ferro et igni*.[28]

Iron and fire: three years later when he had become prime minister he was, famously, to talk of 'iron and blood'. For the moment he could do nothing and the torrent of words he unleashed from afar arose, as he put it to Alvensleben, from 'the need for a mental bowel movement'. He was aware, however, that those, other than his family, to whom he addressed them would file his views and forecasts for or against him, for future use. He had moved a long way from the views he once shared with the Gerlachs and other legitimist conservatives, who during the Italian war were solidly pro-Austrian. When his sister asked him, once the war had started, if he got to read the *Kreuzzeitung*, he replied 'yes the advertisements, all foreign affairs I havn't read for weeks, for this total rubbish wouldn't even be of interest to a medic.'[29]

The Italian war brought German national feeling once more powerfully into play. If the Italians could fight for their national unity, then the Germans must do it as well. What was to be done at this moment caused deep divisions and only a minority of Prussian liberals were prepared to go as far as Bismarck privately advocated. Some further to the left, like Ludwig Bamberger, 1848 democrat and later leading liberal, or the socialist Lassalle were also in favour of seizing the moment to establish a more united Germany under Prussian leadership, if necessary against Austria and with the help of France. Their agenda could hardly be Bismarck's. There was also a feeling in the air that what was needed was a German Cavour, a Caesarist figure who would cut the Gordian knot. In Bismarck's conversation and letters the thought increasingly surfaced that the German national movement, which in the past he had often contemptuously dismissed as 'nationality swindle', could now become an important ally for Prussia.

In July 1859, while he was lying ill with his damaged leg in a hotel in Berlin, Bismarck had a visit from Hans Viktor von Unruh whom he had known as the president of the Prussian national assembly in 1848.[30] He was the son of a Prussian general, but had become a typical representative of the entrepreneurial class, whose interests, Bismarck was beginning to see, might be harnessed to those of the Prussian monarchy and aristocracy. He became a leading figure in the German national movement. According to Unruh, who probably misdated the occasion to March 1859, Bismarck was reading the *Kreuzzeitung* and tossed it away with the remark that it lacked any spark of Prussian patriotism. For Prussia to support Austria in this war would be political suicide. Later in the conversation Bismarck said: 'There is only one possible ally for Prussia, if she knows how to acquire and deal with him.' When Unruh asked who this might be, Bismarck replied 'The German people.' When Unruh appeared puzzled, Bismarck said: 'I am still the same Junker you got to know in the chamber ten years ago, but I would lack any understanding or insight, if I didn't see this clearly.' Unruh said that if he saw Prussia's dangerous situation so clearly then he would prefer him to be foreign minister instead of Schleinitz. Within weeks of Unruh's encounter with Bismarck the *Nationalverein* (National Association) was founded, with a membership of influential men across Germany, with the aim of promoting Kleindeutschland under Prussian leadership. In September 1859 Unruh wrote to Bismarck urging a more energetic Prussian policy. But whatever hopes he might have roused in Unruh and his colleagues, his aims were not theirs. He wanted to exploit the German national movement to Prussia's advantage and above all to his own.

For the moment the cautious official policy pursued by the regent and Schleinitz, support for Austria at the price of Prussian command of the forces of the German Confederation, did not pay off. Austria and France did not fight it out to the finish, but initialled the peace of Villafranca a fortnight after the Austrian defeat at Solferino. Austria had preferred to cut her losses in Italy rather than surrender her position in Germany to Prussia. Napoleon preferred to make peace before the situation slid out of control and before German forces led by Prussia might challenge him on the Rhine. The chance that Prussia might appear as the saviour of Austria in Italy, while defending Germany on the Rhine, had not materialized. From the point of view of German nationalists neither Austria nor Prussia came well out of the affair. Such an outcome cannot have been entirely unwelcome to Bismarck, for it lent weight to the critical advice with which he had accompanied the course of events from a distance.

4

MINISTER IN WAITING

In the spring of 1860 Bismarck was sufficiently recovered from his illness to go to Berlin on political business. He attended meetings of the Prussian upper chamber, but more importantly, he was there at the request of the regent, who was contemplating a reconstruction of the ministry in a rightward direction, which might bring in Bismarck. The departure of Schleinitz from the foreign ministry was thought to be imminent, but in fact he hung on for another eighteen months and as minister for the royal house he remained a thorn in Bismarck's flesh for another twenty-five years. He was among those about whom he waxed vitriolic, calling him, with reference to the favour he enjoyed from the regent's wife, a 'harem minister', 'the mignon of the princess', who owed his career to petticoats. The moment was by no means favourable for the kind of bold, cliff-hanging policy that Bismarck envisaged, but had an offer been made to him he would probably have accepted. In May 1860 he wrote to his brother that he would have to be an ambitious fool to join that crew, but added: 'If the ministerial horse is paraded in front of me, I shall get on whatever the state of its legs.'[1] He was as fiercely ambitious as ever and the thought of allowing his chance to slip was torture to him. But the regent kept him hanging around in vain and eventually he returned to St Petersburg.

While he was in Berlin Schleinitz asked him to prepare a declaration to be made in Frankfurt about the reform of the Confederation. In submitting his draft Bismarck wondered if the issue of establishing an organ of popular representation within a reformed Confederation should be raised. It was a card he himself was to play at crucial junctures in the future. Already his tactical flexibility and willingness to face in different directions was creating mistrust. It was the reason why the regent, limited and lacking subtlety, was reluctant to make him a minister. In May 1860 in a last letter to Gerlach, who had not much longer to live, he once again defends himself against Bonapartism, admits that France might be a dubious ally, but concludes one must keep the possibility open, for one cannot play chess 'if 16 out 64 positions are out of bounds'.[2] He tries to explain his differences with his old friend and mentor by saying that he, Bismarck, never lived through the fight against the first Napoleon, 'revolution incarnate' to Gerlach.

As soon as he was back in St Petersburg in June 1860 he had further evidence of how widely his motives were now suspect. In the German press and among the leaders of the German national movement there were rumours that he was in favour of ceding the left bank of the Rhine to France in return for the annexation of Hanover, Electoral Hesse and Saxony, which would have brought about a territorial consolidation of Prussia. Bismarck was clearly much annoyed by these imputations and went to considerable lengths to rebut them. He wrote a long self-justificatory letter to Auerswald, who was probably the most liberal of the members of the New Era cabinet and whom he could hardly regard as a political friend.

> I have always had the courage of my convictions and if I considered the promotion of a Franco-Russian alliance and our adherence to it an advantage I would say so. The regent knows me and believes that I would honestly obey while I remained in his service, and if I could do so no longer, I would leave.[3]

What he said in this letter about his past attitude on Franco-Prussian-Russian relations was stretching the truth a little. He was out of sympathy with most of the manoeuvres of Prussian diplomacy at this time, such as the attempted reconciliation with Austria, when the regent met Francis Joseph at Teplitz at the end of July 1860. When the regent met Napoleon in Baden in June 1860, Bismarck thought it inappropriate that he allowed himself to be accompanied by most of the minor German rulers.

The diplomatic dovecotes were fluttered by the further moves towards Italian unification, especially Garibaldi's spectacular descent on the Kingdom of the Two Sicilies. Bismarck felt that a strong Italy was to Prussia's advantage and was not much bothered by the challenge to the principle of legitimacy posed by the dispossession of the minor Italian princes. He was, however, careful not to offend his superiors in Berlin in such matters. To Schleinitz he wrote privately:

> I endeavour in all my official duties . . . to exercise objectivity and correctness in the sense of our acknowledged policies; privately I cannot avoid confessing . . . that my views deviate a little from those approved in the all-highest quarter, and not in the direction of the *Kreuzzeitung*, but strangely towards the Italian side.[4]

But, leaving aside his close relations with the tsar and Gorchakov, which were valued in Berlin, the Wilhelmstrasse told him little of what was going on. The one major meeting he attended was that of the three rulers of Prussia, Russia and Austria in Warsaw from 25 to 27 October 1860, a vain attempt to revive the Holy Alliance. Shortly afterwards Schlözer described his mood thus:

> My Pasha is in a dreadful state of excitement . . . he thinks his moment has really come. There will be a heated session of the chamber, Schleinitz will leave in high dudgeon – and Pasha hopes to move in . . . nothing reaches him from the Wilhelmstrasse. They don't like him there. . . . He makes his own policy . . . he does not entertain here, complains it is too expensive, does not get up till eleven or half past in the morning, spends the day in his green dressing gown, takes no exercise, drinks a lot – and curses Austria.[5]

*

He had to wait nearly another two years for his moment, but events were taking shape in Berlin that would help to bring it on. A constitutional conflict over the organization and control of the army was in the offing and put an end to the liberal-conservative regime of the New Era. The Italian war and its repercussions in Germany had made it obvious right across the political spectrum how important an efficient army was for Prussia. In fact its recruitment and organization had hardly progressed from the state it had reached after the end of the Napoleonic wars. It had then been the concern of the military reformers, men like Scharnhorst, Gneisenau and Boyen, to turn the mercenary army that had failed to stand up to the soldiers of the

French Revolution into a citizen army based on the universal obligation of military service. In principle they had had established a service of three years, later in practice reduced to two, to be followed by two years in the reserve, and then service in the *Landwehr*, up to the age of thirty-two in the first levy, then in the second levy. This system had remained more or less in operation for over forty years. In the meantime the population of the country had greatly increased while the annual intake of recruits into the army itself remained at approximately 40,000. This meant that, for example in relation to the French army, the Prussian army was by the late 1850s only about a third as large. Another consequence was that only a proportion of the available age cohort had to serve, causing a sense of injustice.

While there was broad agreement that reform was necessary, the details immediately ran into ideological differences. The Prussian army had been used to defeat the revolution both at home and in other parts of Germany in 1848/9 and was seen by conservatives as the bedrock of the Prussian state. This view was particularly strongly held by the regent, himself a military man, who believed that the monarch's direct control of the army was the most essential part of kingship in Prussia. Against this, Prussian liberals felt that the concept of a citizen army, particularly as embodied in the Landwehr, was central to the idea of a more liberal Prussia, as envisaged by the revered reformers of the liberation wars against Napoleon. They were suspicious that a conscript army officered by the Junker aristocracy might again serve a reactionary political purpose. A compromise on the technical details, for example on the question of the length of service, would have been possible, especially as most of the liberals in the Landtag were only too anxious to reach an accommodation with the regent. 'Don't push him' was their slogan. They knew that in the regent's entourage there were men only too eager to use any liberal pressure, especially on the army question, to turn him back towards an absolutist royal regime. Two men were particularly influential in this respect. One was Edwin von Manteuffel, cousin of the former prime minister and chief of the king's military cabinet, through which the direct royal control of the army was exercised. The other was Albrecht von Roon, who became minister of war in late 1859. Manteuffel was a man of considerable stature, but a believer in a return to absolute government, ending the constitutional experiment and the existence of a national parliament. Roon was primarily a military administrator and technician, but his political views were also strongly conservative. Manteuffel had his own ambitions to become the leading man in Prussia.

Roon on the other hand became Bismarck's friend at court, in the way Leopold von Gerlach had been in earlier years. Roon introduced an army reorganization scheme in 1860 and put it into operation without regard for the Landtag budgetary powers. What the Landtag, reflecting the liberal desire to meet the regent more than halfway, had voted as temporary, was treated as irrevocable. Thus conflict became unavoidable.

In January 1861 Frederick William IV died and the regent became king as William I. In their efforts to bring the king over to their side the military party encouraged him in his view that at his coronation there should a traditional act of homage by the estates of the realm. This was incompatible with the sovereign's oath to the constitution and a deliberate affront to the concept of constitutional government. The liberal ministers of the New Era had to oppose such a highly symbolic act and it would have forced them out of office, the object of the military party. The growing tension was highlighted by a duel between Manteuffel and one of the leading liberal parliamentarians, Karl Twesten. Bismarck was not particularly interested in the army question in itself and says little about it in his correspondence. He was, however, well aware that an abrogation of the constitution, such as Manteuffel, Roon and *Kreuzzeitung* conservatives hoped for, would frustrate any active Prussian policy in Germany. Such an active policy, he was now arguing, would mobilize popular support for the government and enable it to resist the liberals in domestic affairs. Just he was about to return home for his summer leave in July 1861 the crisis reached a climax. Roon hoped that the king could be persuaded to reconstruct the ministry, getting rid of its more liberal members, and envisaged Bismarck as one who could take their place. Bismarck was as ever like a cat on hot bricks when the hope of ministerial office was dangled before him, but saw little prospect of longer-term success as the creature of a new camarilla.

Thirty years later he regarded his correspondence with Roon at this juncture as of sufficient importance to publish it in his reminiscences. 'The king cannot give way without ruining the crown for ever,' Roon wrote on 27 June 1861 and asked Bismarck if he would support him on the homage question.[6] The king was considering him as a successor to Schleinitz, who was leaving anyway, or as minister of the interior, more probably the latter. Bismarck had to be cautious in his reply, for he could not afford to offend Roon, but he did not regard the homage question as a good issue on which to make a stand. Again he harps on his view that a strong foreign policy is the best way out of the domestic impasse:

> It is my impression that the chief failure of our current policy lies in our having been liberal in Prussia and conservative abroad; we sold the rights of our own king cheap, those of foreign princes too dearly. . . . [For] fourteen years we have taught the nation a taste for politics, but not satisfied its appetite, and so it seeks fodder in the gutter. We are as vain as the French; if we can persuade ourselves that we have prestige abroad we can put up with a lot at home; if we have the feeling that every little Würzburger [a recent meeting of smaller German states was held at Würzburg] can tease us and hold us in contempt, because we hope a Confederation army will protect us from France, then we see something wrong in every corner at home, and every press reptile, who shoots off his mouth against the government, is applauded.

It is vintage Bismarck, written with typical verve and gusto, but highly diplomatic in its regard for the prejudices of its recipient.

As it was, before Bismarck reached Berlin the king had, to Roon's disgust, given way on the homage question, but the St Petersburg envoy was then called to see the king at Baden. He was asked to prepare a memorandum on the German question, again an important document illustrating Bismarck's views at this time.[7] In it he sets out the difficulties in reforming the German Confederation in a way acceptable to Prussia and then argues again for 'a national representation of the German people at the centre of the Confederation'. This would go some way to meet the dissatisfaction of the German population with the existing state of affairs. He does not think the establishment of such a representative body likely, as it would be opposed by Austria and the smaller German states. He suggests that the Zollverein might acquire a parliament, which might be developed into 'a body making agreements over a wider field'. Seven years later he established such a parliament. Bismarck revised this so-called Baden memorandum in the autumn and sent it to one of his conservative friends, Alexander von Below, with whom he had stayed during his illness the previous year. In his accompanying letter he warned his conservative party friends against 'the completely unhistorical, ungodly and illegal sovereignty swindle of the German princes, who would use our relationship to the Confederation as a pedestal, from which they can play the European power game'.[8] Clearly his contempt had been transferred from the 'nationality swindle' to the 'sovereignty swindle'. For Prussian conservatives to tie themselves to the latter was quixotic, he wrote:

I do not see why we should recoil so primly from the idea of a popular representation in the Confederation or the Zollverein. . . . On the national question quite moderate concessions might be received as valuable. One could a establish a quite conservative national assembly and still be thanked by the Liberals.

Bismarck was all the time arguing against the view, shared by every-body wedded to the existing social order, from the Prussian king downward, that movement on the German national question was synonymous with liberalism. His coming to power, at this moment still very uncertain, was to have the momentous consequence that nationalism and liberalism would become separated.

By the time the king received Bismarck at Baden the ministerial changes were virtually over and the hopes of the St Petersburg envoy were once again dashed. Roon put it all down to the petticoat machinations around the king, but there were other liberal influences at work in Baden as well. The Grand Duke Frederick I of Baden, King William's son-in-law, was making his country into the most liberal in Germany, and had just appointed Franz von Roggenbach, a liberal Catholic, his foreign minister. This Baden statesman was a liberal-national sympathizer who had his own ideas about reforming the German Confederation. His reactions to Bismarck's Baden memorandum were: 'An unprincipled Junker who wants to make a career through political blackguardism'.[9] Schleinitz now took on the royal house portfolio and was replaced as foreign minister by Count Bernstorff, hitherto ambassador in London. The conflict between the king and the parliamentary liberals was, however, still intensifying. When the session ended in June 1861 the Landtag was dissolved and new elections were held in December 1861. In the meantime the Progressive Party (*Deutsche Fortschrittspartei*) had been formed, out of the left-wing sections of the old liberals. It could be regarded as the executive committee of the Nationalverein (National Association) in Prussia and had equivalents in other German states. In the elections the Progressives obtained 104 seats, the various liberal factions together had about 250 out of 352 seats, while the conservatives were reduced to 14. The king had hoped that the elections would release him from the dilemma between surrendering the essence of his monarchical power or risking a civil war through a military *coup d'état*. Instead the conflict became fiercer than ever.

Bismarck returned to his post in St Petersburg in November 1861. He professed to be quite content there and his health was better than in the previous winter. He went hunting in the bracing Russian winter air, but there were days when it was so cold that 'the nocturnal sleigh ride would have been risky for my nose', as he told his sister. His children were, however, frequently ill in a house which even the strongest heating could not warm. Johanna would have liked a transfer to Paris, but London was also a possibility. To his sister he wrote in January 1862: 'Since my illness I have become mentally so tired, that I have not the energy for troubled conditions. Three years ago I would have made a useful minister, but now, when I think of it, I feel like a sick show rider who is still required to jump.'[10] Yet he cannot really have believed that he would see out a few more years in the diplomatic service and then retire to Kniephof or Schönhausen. He knew only too well that in Prussia politics were dangerously volatile and in his heart of hearts he must have hoped that the king might yet be forced to seek his help. The liberal majority elected in December 1861 was no longer in the mood to meet the government half way and to swallow the provocations of the military party. By a considerable majority the chamber voted for a proposal to split the military budget into specialized sub-heads, so that the government could no longer hide the on-going reorganization of the army within a broad item of defence expenditure. The king thereupon dissolved the chamber once more and dismissed the liberal New Era ministers, such as Auerswald and Bethmann Hollweg. Roon and Bernstorff remained in place. Elections held on 6 May 1862 saw a further shift to the left. The Progressives now held 133, the conservatives only 11, and the parties making a stand on the military question could command about 230 out of 352 seats.

*

Bismarck arrived in Berlin four days after these elections. His recall as envoy to Russia had been confirmed a few weeks previously, but his future had not been decided. The Prussian embassies in London and Paris were vacant and looked like probable destinations for him. But the possibility of ministerial office was once again real and he was to see the king in Berlin. William was more hemmed in than ever. In his own eyes a compromise with the chamber was impossible, because it would make the Prussian monarchy into a parliamentary one. The abrogation of the constitution, pressed on him by Manteuffel, Roon and others, was equally impossible. It might mean civil war. But in foreign policy the king was still not prepared to accept the recipe of Bismarck, to defy Austria and the other German princes, to set aside the Confederation and to do so with the support and possibly the alliance of France. In any case Bernstorff was for the moment not keen to give up the foreign ministry and return to London. Bismarck was reluctant to become prime minister without direct control of foreign policy. The king was racked by indecision and Bismarck was anathema to his family, to the queen, to the crown prince and his wife, and to his son-in-law in Baden. Augusta had told her husband passionately: 'For God's sake not this man as minister. It is a complete miscalculation to believe that a man like Bismarck can serve our country, who will certainly risk everything and who is everybody's terror, because he has no principles.'[11] After ten days of being kept hanging around Bismarck 'exploded'. He demanded to know his fate there and then and his appointment as ambassador to Paris was the result. Even now the King told him that it might be a temporary resting place and in fact his family never moved to Paris. It might well be that he himself thought it best to be out of the intrigue-laden atmosphere of Berlin for a while and, as he told all and sundry, to be kept waiting in a hotel for an appointment that never came was hardly dignified.

Soon after his arrival in Paris Bismarck had several meetings with Napoleon III. In a report to King William on his talk with the emperor on 6 June Bismarck took the opportunity to put some of his own views into the mouth of the French monarch. Napoleon is supposed to have said that in Prussia 'at the present moment only a government which gave hope to the national tendency in public opinion would be able to obtain a position in which it could dominate the domestic struggle with the parties' and 'if nothing was done in that direction, it was to be feared that Germany would move into ferment.'[12] At another meeting, on 27 June, the French emperor asked the envoy if he thought the Prussian king might be inclined to conclude an alliance with him. He then hinted that Austria and Russia were vying with each other to conclude an alliance with France. Bismarck, in his report to King William, gave his own view that there might be something in these hints. He again expressed his opinion that Austria would never allow a Prussian preponderance in Germany and would rather sacrifice Venetia or the left bank of the Rhine. This frankness can hardly have endeared him to the king, who must have been confirmed in his reluctance to entrust a man of such views with the conduct of Prussian foreign policy. Bismarck after his failure to gain office during his May visit to Berlin probably felt that he had little to lose by sticking to his guns. He hoped that the conflict between king and Landtag would develop in a such a way that he would be called to office able to pursue the policy he had long advocated.

In early July he paid a visit to London, with the permission of his superiors, still preparing himself for taking office. He found Palmerston as prime minister and Russell as foreign secretary better informed on Japan and China than on the domestic situation in Prussia. They thought that a Prussian government would have to be formed on the basis of the liberal parliamentary majority. Bismarck explained to them that such a government would carry out the programme of the Progressive Party and this would lead to initiatives on the German question which must lead to a breach with Austria and the other German states. It would therefore go right against what Palmerston thought desirable in Central Europe, namely peaceful coexistence of Austria, Prussia and the other German states within the constitution of the German Confederation. In reporting this to the king Bismarck could not resist a plug for his own prescription:

> Lord Palmerston . . . considered it a falsification of the fact, which, in his opinion, I had permitted myself in the interests of my reactionary party views, when I maintained that the resistance of the majority on the military question would vanish . . . if Your Majesty was prepared to use the army for a policy in the sense of the Nationalverein.[13]

During his London visit Bismarck also talked to Disraeli as leader of the opposition. According to the Saxon envoy in London, a friend of Disraeli's, writing in his memoirs many years later, he was supposed to have said that 'he would seize the first best pretext to declare war on Austria, dissolve the German diet, subdue the minor states, and give national unity to Germany under Prussian leadership.'[14] Disraeli's reaction was said to have been 'take care of that man, he means what he says.' Whatever Bismarck did say, he was confirmed in his view that Britain, seen by so many liberal Germans as a potential ally, would stay out of the German imbroglio, provided her interests were not disturbed. He did find that there was support for the Danish position in Schleswig-Holstein.

On returning to Paris Bismarck seems to have concluded that for the moment there would be no resolution of his undecided future. Queen Augusta of Prussia was stiffening the resolve of her husband against the sinister Junker. In a memorandum of July 1862 she wrote:

As envoy to the diet H.v.B. always sowed mistrust among the governments friendly to Prussia and made an impression on the princes hostile
to Prussia only by means of political views which do not accord with
Prussia's position in Germany, but with her position as a threatening
great power.[15]

The king had always lacked the power of decision and Bismarck, knowing
of the influences that surrounded him in his family, thought it unwise to
press him, much as he disliked the hand-to-mouth existence he had to live
in Paris. In a letter to Roon on 15 July he said that the king must have time
to decide of his own volition, otherwise he would hold those pushing him
responsible for what happened. In any case he, Bismarck, might be more
useful when liberals in the chamber had talked themselves to a stand-
still and had reduced the general public to boredom. Many among them
drawing salaries as judges would get alarmed by the cost of having to pay
for a replacement, he added with characteristic cynicism. Let them stew in
their own juice for a while and then the moment might arrive when his own
appointment would show that the fight was not over, 'especially if ahead
of it there is a bit of sabre-rattling with talk of an imposed constitution and
coup d'état'. Then his old reputation of frivolously resorting to violence
would come in useful and make them think 'hey, the balloon is going up.'[16]
But the balloon was not likely to go up in the torpid summer holiday
season and so Bismarck, with the permission of his chief Bernstorff, went
on leave on 20 July. Contrary to the impression given in his reminiscences
thirty years later, there was therefore nothing sudden or unforeseen in his
return to Berlin in mid-September. During his leave he kept a weather-
eye open on what was going on in Berlin and he could be contacted with
only small delay by Johanna as well as on public business by Roon and, if
necessary, others.

*

After travelling alone for a while in the Loire valley he turned south and
had a glimpse of Spain at San Sebastián. He felt lonely at times, surrounded
by French families. His letters to Johanna have their usual poetic quality.
From Bayonne he wrote:

The splendour of the violet-purple heather here is amazing, in between
there is yellow broom, the whole a coloured carpet. The river Adur, on

which Bayonne is situated, ends this *b minor* of the heath, which with its
softer reincarnation of a northern landscape increased my homesickness.
From St Vincent one sees for the first time, above heather and fir, the blue
outline of the Pyrenees, like a giant version of the Taunus, but bolder and
more jagged.[17]

He went to Biarritz in early August, found the bathing rejuvenating, but
was about to move on, when he fell in with more congenial company, Prince
Orlov, the Russian ambassador in Brussels, and above all his wife Katharina,
soon to become Kathy or even Katsch. She, née Trubetskoy, was twenty-
two, her husband forty-two and Bismarck forty-seven, and she and Otto
fell in love. It was probably an unconsummated *amitié amoureuse* common
in those days, but for Bismarck, as Johanna soon guessed, as engrossing as
years ago his love for Marie von Thadden had been. When the idyll was just
beginning he wrote jocularly to Johanna: 'You remember your partiality
for him, and now I am taking my revenge on you a little bit, by finding her
rather attractive and very amiable.' He and the Orlovs became inseparable.
A few days later he wrote to Pomerania: 'We are in a narrow gorge in the
rocky coast, grassy, with bushes, out of sight of everybody, between two
rocks with heather in blossom I can see the sea, green and white in foam
and sun; next to me the most charming of all women, whom you will love
dearly when you get to know her better. . . .' Later they went climbing in
the Pyrenees. Bismarck felt rejuvenated and Johanna, without any jealousy,
was glad of it. To his sister Malle he wrote on 20 August: 'Since the Orlows
have arrived, I live with them as if we were alone in the country, and I have
somewhat fallen in love with the dear little *principesse*. You know how that
occasionally happens to me, without doing any damage to Johanna.'[18]

A year later, when he was prime minister, in the midst of ferocious
political battles, he wrote to Kathy in French:

> I must suppress all *Sehnsucht* [longing] of seeing the sea again and
> everywhere else I fear I would find the Princess O and not Catty. I console
> myself by opening my cigar-case, where I always find by one of your big
> hairpins a small yellow flower plucked at Superbagnères, moss from Port
> de Venasque and a twig of olive tree from the terraces of Avignon;
> German sentimentality, you will say; no matter, one day I will have the
> satisfaction of showing you these souvenirs of happy times to which
> I think back as a paradise lost [in English].[19]

It was another side of Bismarck, so very different from the man of power that he was about to become after leaving Biarritz in September 1862. They met again in October 1864 in Biarritz and perhaps recaptured something of the lost paradise. Bismarck knew all along that Kathy could be no more than an interlude, but his nostalgia for an existence away from politics and power was genuine enough.

*

When he arrived back in what for him was the real world, he found, on reaching Toulouse late on 10 September, a letter from Roon, written on 31 August. It described the situation in Berlin as unresolved and asked if he could propose Bismarck as prime minister, but without a portfolio, something he had never been keen on. Bismarck replied to Roon from Toulouse on 12 September showing a certain amount of irritation, though not with his friend personally. Bismarck said that he had never refused to be prime minister without a ministry and would take the job if the king ordered him, but did not think it useful. He was never one to make difficulties, he claimed, but was quite content to be his majesty's ambassador in Paris if he could remain so for some years and bring his family there.[20] This correspondence had already been overtaken by events. On 9 September the Prussian cabinet had given the king their collective opinion that the constitution did not allow the government to govern without a budget voted by the chamber. The so-called 'gap theory', which Bismarck used for some years after coming to office, was thus declared untenable. It was the theory that when the chamber refused to vote money, the king resumed his right to carry on the government without parliamentary sanction. It was a theory which made a mockery of the fundamental tenets of parliamentary government. Roon was among those who had signed this collective opinion. Simultaneously with the letter to Roon Bismarck had also written to his chief Bernstorff from Toulouse, again requesting certainty about his position, but significantly asking permission to come to Berlin ad *audiendum verbum regis*, to hear the command of the king. Clearly Bismarck must have guessed that a moment of decision was approaching and did not want to miss his chance again. He says nothing about his own request to return to Berlin in his reminiscences, making it appear that Roon's famous telegramme, 'Periculum in mora. Dépêchez-vous. L'oncle de Maurice Henning' – [Henning was the second Christian name of Moritz von Blanckenburg, Roon's nephew and once the husband of Marie Thadden] – was the message that brought him back to Berlin.[21]

Matters were indeed reaching breaking point between the king and the chamber. A compromise proposal emerged, with the support of Twesten, Sybel, the historian, and other liberal leaders. It would have allowed the budget for the new regiments of the line to go through, in return for the general period of service to be limited to two years. The ministry, including Roon, were prepared to accept this compromise, but again the king was adamant. To his mind giving way to parliament on such an issue was to tarnish the crown he was sworn to preserve. He now threatened to abdicate and started to draft his abdication proclamation. Roon was, to the fury of the chamber, forced to revoke the government's acceptance of the compromise on the length of service. This was the point at which Roon despatched his coded telegram to Bismarck, in a panic lest the king should really abdicate in favour of his son and thus pave the way for a liberal ministry. The crown prince had been called to Berlin, but tried to persuade his father not to abdicate. There was an element of filial piety in it, but more importantly the perception that to take on the succession in these circumstances might put him in an invidious position. The opportunity, it was reasonable to suppose, would recur under more favourable auspices, within weeks or months. It was not likely to be too long delayed in any case, for the king was sixty-five. Nobody could foresee that he would live another twenty-six years and that Crown Prince Frederick William had given away for good his chance to make history on a grand scale. Bismarck arrived in Berlin on the evening of Saturday, 20 September, and was immediately called to see the crown prince. Frederick William was, like his wife and mother, among those who regarded a Bismarck ministry as a disaster, but he no doubt wanted to find out if Bismarck was really prepared to take office under these inauspicious circumstances. Bismarck gave away nothing, fearing that the king might interpret any real communication with his son as an attempt to curry favour with those with whom the future appeared to lie. The crown prince knew that up to this point the king had always reassured his family that he would on no account turn to Bismarck.

The next day, after church at Potsdam, Roon persuaded the king to grant Bismarck an audience. At some point the king was reported to have said: 'but he has already seen my son.' William clearly had little hope of Bismarck, and probably even now little inclination to turn to him. The decisive interview between the king and Bismarck took place at Babelsberg, the king's summer palace near Potsdam, on Monday, 22 September. The only record of it we have is Bismarck's own in his reminiscences.[22] This account of those crucial days is in many ways misleading, designed to show him as the knight in shining armour riding to the rescue of the house of Hohenzollern, which, in the shape of the king's grandson, had now treated him with such rank ingratitude. Bismarck says nothing about the plans he had already made in the summer to return to Berlin when the constitutional conflict was likely to reach crunch point, nor about Roon's willingness to compromise, which would have scuppered his chances. Nevertheless Bismarck's account of the interview at Babelsberg on 22 September is likely to be true in essence, but incorrect in some important detail. It cannot have been the case that Bismarck was surprised when the king showed him his yet unsigned declaration of abdication, for he must have heard about it from Roon. The line he took at this interview must have been planned with this knowledge in mind. Bismarck presented himself as the feudal vassal who would stick to his lord through thick and thin, regardless of the threats which had driven him to the extremity of contemplating abdication. To the king's question whether he was willing to implement the army reorganization to the full, in spite of the chamber's votes against it, he replied with a strong affirmative. 'Then it is my duty to attempt with you the continuation of the fight, and I will not abdicate.' The king tore up the programme he had drafted for the new ministry.

By this time the two men were walking in the park of the palace and the king was about to throw the shreds of his programme into the stream flowing through the park. Bismarck warned him that bits and pieces with his well-known handwriting might fall into the wrong hands and the king later consigned the discarded programme to the flames. Bismarck could take office, as prime minister and foreign minister, with his hands untied. The king was tied to him to a greater extent than he perhaps realized. For Bismarck it was the situation he had long hoped for, but even he did not anticipate how difficult it was to prove. The personal risks were high. Ministers who flouted the constitution might be impeached and stripped of their property. The king was forced to turn to Bismarck, because he was unlikely to find men of repute and ability to incur high risks in an unpromising situation. Next day William tried to justify himself to his wife by saying that it had been his duty to present a firm front to attempts to ruin the army and the country. The crown prince wrote in his diary: 'Poor mama, how bitterly she will feel this appointment of her mortal enemy!'[23]

Bismarck's appointment, so nearly aborted, turned out to be an event of historic importance, though few contemporaries realized it. Most of them gave him weeks rather than months in office. So far the liberal movement in the various German states, but above all in Prussia, had been the main force in pressing for the reform of the German Confederation of 1815. Now it was going to be Bismarck who, through the Prussian monarchy and its armies, would take the lead in the unification of Germany. The course he had advocated during the 1850s could now put into operation. It meant an alliance of the Prussian monarchy with the German national-liberal movement, but on terms that left the Prussian government in the driving seat. Bismarck had long divined the weakness of the liberals and their fear of the masses. He thought that the masses were loyal to kings and princes and could be mobilized on their behalf, but he did not fully realize the extent to which rapid industrialization was changing both the bourgeoisie and the classes below them. In the event, although getting the better of the liberal middle classes in narrow political terms, the society that emerged was much further removed from that in which Bismarck had his roots than he could have anticipated. His own handiwork, unification, gave even greater impetus to social transformation. During his long years in power the disjunction between the political status quo and the social advance grew. It could not be cured by the sort of manipulation of which Bismarck became a master. The notion of self-government as good and desirable in itself had no place in Bismarck's outlook.

5

PRIME MINISTER

Johanna, who had not seen her husband for months, learnt of the appointment only through the newspapers. Otto, in his first letter to her two days after the meeting at Babelsberg, took the fatalistic line he often affected: 'It's not a cheerful prospect and I feel frightened every morning when I wake up. But it must be . . . Accept what God has sent us, it is not an easy matter for me.'[1] It certainly was not easy and Bismarck's way of coping with it was to confuse all and sundry about where he was heading. He suggested that Johanna and the children should move into his official residence in the Wilhelmstrasse as soon as the prorogation of the Landtag would give him time to settle them in. It was a way of signalling to the public that he at any rate did not regard his tenure of office as shortlived. To the general public he was still the reactionary Junker and his appointment was seen as a last-ditch attempt to avoid the inevitable triumph of the parliamentary principle. For the same reason his appointment was welcomed on the right, in the *Kreuzzeitung*, where it was seen as the prelude to sweeping away the whole constitutional bag of tricks. It was recognized that Bismarck was a great deal more intelligent and resourceful than the average Junker and that he might have taken a leaf out of Louis Napoleon's book, with whom, it was known, he got on well. This might mean that he would try to use success abroad to keep the Prussian public quiet at home. His hostility to Austrian aspirations in Germany was also well known.

Bismarck's own political horizon was for the moment very restricted. He had to stay in power long enough for something to emerge to give him some room for manoeuvre. Within two or three weeks the chamber would go into recess and this would give a breathing space. This was the reason for the withdrawal of the government's budget proposals for military expenditure, which the chamber had rejected by a large majority on 23 September. The withdrawal was announced in the first declaration of the Bismarck government in the Chamber, on the ground that an immediate decision would not 'be useful for a future resolution of the matter in dispute'. In other words, the government was still hoping for a compromise and this was also the intention behind Bismarck's speech on the following day, 30 September, in the budget commission. No full report of this speech exists, but the direction of Bismarck's argument was clear enough:

> Germany does not look to Prussia's liberalism but to her power; Bavaria, Württemberg, Baden may indulge their liberalism, but no one will expect them to take Prussia's role; Prussia must gather and keep its forces for the favourable moment, which has already been missed several times; Prussia's frontiers since the treaties of Vienna are not suitable for a healthy state; the great questions of the day are not decided by speeches and majorities – that was the big mistake of 1848 and 1849 – but by iron and blood. The previous year's allocation [of military funds] was agreed; for what reasons does not matter; he was sincerely seeking the path of accommodation.

But there was also a threat: 'If no budget can be agreed, then it is *tabula rasa* [a clean sheet]; there is no way out under the Constitution, it would be one interpretation against another . . .'.[2] To emphasize his accommodating mood Bismarck sometimes took the olive branch out of his cigar case that Kathy Orlov had given him at Avignon. But what made the headlines and has stuck to him ever since was the phrase 'iron and blood', later usually reversed into the even more threatening 'blood and iron'. Even Roon, with whom Bismarck walked home after the meeting, does not seem to have been too pleased with his colleague's performance. He muttered that he found such 'clever discourses' not useful to the cause, as Bismarck remembered thirty years later. For the general public it reinforced Bismarck's image of a man prepared to resort irresponsibly to violence. When he tried to explain it away, that he was only thinking of the amount of equipment and number of men in the army, it convinced no one. Heinrich von Treitschke, already a leading liberal-national publicist and later a fervent admirer of Bismarck, wrote: 'When I hear a shallow Junker like this Bismarck boast of the iron and blood with which he will bring Germany under his yoke it sounds to me even more ridiculous than it is vile.'

Bismarck had to back-pedal hard. When a day later he met Twesten he at first stuck to his view that the crown and the upper Chamber could reject the amendments made to the budget in the lower chamber. The expenditure not agreed by the elected deputies could then still be spent, for the business of the state could not stand still. When Twesten remonstrated, he said that he was not for the moment anxious to make a stand on this principle. On the substance of the two-year period of service he was prepared to give way, as Roon had done. But, he confided, the king remained an obstacle: 'He was like a horse shying from a new object, that would get even more recalcitrant if force was used, but might gradually get accustomed. For the moment it was impossible . . . but by the winter he hoped to change the king's mind, by persuasion, and through the influence of people in whom he trusted, also through the advice given by generals and conferences with them. . . .'[3] A few days later at a chance meeting with Unruh on a railway journey Bismarck said that on entering office he had hoped for compromise, but that he had been disappointed. In spite of such conciliatory talk it is doubtful if his offer of ministerial posts to right-wing liberals like Vincke was serious. In fact Bismarck had difficulty in finding any ministers of even modest competence from within the bureaucracy and in his reminiscences he still described them in his most caustic vein. When his old ultra-conservative friend Kleist-Retzow criticized them, he replied: 'We are glad to find eight men and to keep them.'

The new prime minister was feeling his way, also putting up smoke screens. What really mattered to him was to retain the confidence of the king. He was again in Baden with his son-in-law and exposed to the influences that Bismarck feared. He wrote him a long justificatory letter on 3 October, in which he tried to explain away the public-relations disaster of the iron and blood speech by blaming it on false reporting. The following day he intercepted the king on his journey back to Berlin, at a station 50 miles south of Berlin, which was still being built. He sat on an upturned wheelbarrow left by workmen, waiting for the king's train to arrive. He had difficulty in finding his royal master, who was travelling alone in a dark first-class compartment. When he found him he was in low spirits, saying that 'I can foresee exactly how it will all end. Here on the opera square below my windows, they will cut off your head, and a little later mine.'[4] Whether the king was really in so pessimistic a mood as Bismarck described is doubtful. In Baden he appears to have rebuffed all attempts to argue with him and to have shouted so loud that it could be heard in the street. He was, according to Bismarck, certainly in a more resolute mood by the time they arrived together in Berlin. He had little alternative but to persevere with the minister he had just appointed. When on 13 October the Landtag was prorogued till the following session the door was left ajar for a future compromise.

Besides the constitutional conflict there was another element in Bismarck's political inheritance when he took office. It was Prussia's strong position in the affairs of the Zollverein. Renewed Austrian attempts in 1859 and 1860 to gain access to the Zollverein had been rebuffed by the New Era government. More important was the adhesion of Prussia, in March 1862, to the Anglo-French free trade treaty, also known as the Cobden treaty. The Austrian government tried hard to prevent the conclusion of agreement between Berlin and Paris and lobbied the other German governments against it, on the grounds that it ran counter to the treaty between Austria and the Zollverein, renewed for twelve years in 1853. Some of the major South German states like Bavaria and Württemberg supported Vienna, while Saxony, Baden and others voted through their parliaments for the Franco-Prussian treaty. The fact was that Austria was not economically in a position to join such an enlarged free trade area, while, as it turned out, the other member states of the Zollverein could not afford to cut the free trade link with Prussia. Saxony was under Beust's leadership always pro-Austrian, but economically it could not afford to leave the Zollverein. In August 1862, while Bernstorff was still foreign minister, the Prussian government went ahead in forcing the issue by giving the previously initialled treaty with France its definite signature. Ratification was made dependent on the adherence of the other Zollverein members, but it was made clear that if they refused to sign the treaty with France, Prussia would break the Zollverein.

Bismarck therefore inherited strong cards as far as the fundamental facts of economic life in Central Europe were concerned. So much was this the case that the unification of Kleindeutschland under Prussia can be seen as the almost inevitable outcome, rather than the consequence of the policies Bismarck was about to embark upon. But the economic pressures highlighted by the Franco-Prussian trade treaty also produced some crossed party-lines. All over Germany and in Prussia itself many leading liberals, who were appalled by the appointment of the reactionary Bismarck as Prussia's chief minister, were among the strongest supporters of Franco-Prussian free trade. These were the men of substance, the commercial and entrepreneurial middle class, who made up much of the membership of the Nationalverein. In May 1862, when the Franco-Prussian trade treaty and the opposition to it by Austria and her supporters had come into the open, the journal of the Nationalverein declared: 'On the day the Zollverein is torn apart, Prussia, for good or ill, will head not the movement for reform, but the German revolution.' In October 1862, by which time the battle lines on the trade treaty were fully drawn, the *Deutscher Handelstag*, an organization of chambers of commerce and commercial corporations throughout Germany, voted in favour of the Franco-Prussian treaty, a serious blow for Austria. What remained of Prussian conservatism, now mainly in the upper chamber, of which Bismarck was a member, was also in favour of the treaty. The Junkers were mostly still confirmed free traders. They opposed the constitutional demands of the liberal majority in the lower chamber, but they agreed with them on free trade.

Bismarck inherited much weaker political cards on the German question. The Habsburg monarchy had through two constitutional reforms, of October 1860 and February 1861, given itself a slightly more liberal-looking façade than its previous neo-absolutist regime; it might now appear rather more attractive than a Prussia riven by constitutional conflict and presided over by the reactionary Bismarck. Plans to reform the German Confederation abounded after the Italian war had produced a strong revival of the German national movement. Beust, the Saxon minister, put forward a plan tailored to the requirements of the intermediate German states, now generally called the Würzburg group from a meeting held there in November 1859, but this group was so disunited among themselves that it came to nothing. In December 1861 Bernstorff produced a new union plan, not unlike that of Radowitz which came to grief at Olmütz, but this then led to a joint counterproposal by Austria and the intermediate German states, tabled in February 1862. This was predictably seen as an affront in Prussia, even by the liberals in the Landtag, almost as a preparatory move towards another Olmütz. When Prussia recognized the new Italian kingdom on 21 July 1862, against the wishes of King William, it was part of the counter-offensive. Ten days later the Franco-Prussian trade treaty was signed. The liberals in the chamber had long been in the van of demanding Prussian leadership in Germany to the exclusion of Austria. The king naturally wanted to enhance Prussian prestige in Germany and avenge Olmütz, but could not possibly allow himself to become the catspaw of German liberalism. His reluctance to have Bismarck as his minister was due to the feeling that this was precisely what he would be reduced to by this Junker, who was too clever by half.

*

Meanwhile the constitutional conflict itself and finally Bismarck's appointment had progressively dashed the expectations of the German national movement and Prussia's loss was Austria's gain. In Frankfurt the Austrians had, with the support of some of the intermediate states, tabled yet another reform plan in August 1862. Its principal provision was the establishment of an assembly of delegates drawn from the representative bodies of the member states. Prussia had immediately declared that the adoption of such a plan required a unanimous vote, but it now fell to Bismarck to put paid to this Austrian plan. It was also for the new Prussian minister to make the next move in another long-running saga, the conflict between the fiercely reactionary elector of Hesse and the liberal opposition in his country. Here Bismarck chose to do exactly the opposite of what he was doing at home: he supported the liberal opposition in Hesse and forced the elector to give way. He did so in a deliberately brusque manner. A mere *Feldjäger* (field messenger) was sent to the elector with the note threatening force. It was a clear signal to the Prussian liberals that abroad the new minister might be on their side and it prepared the ground for the absorption of Electoral Hesse into Prussia in 1866. It is possible that Bismarck may have hoped that the elector would refuse to comply with a request transmitted in so humiliating a manner and that this would furnish an excuse for Prussian troops to intervene in this strategically important territory.

The situation that Bismarck found on taking office was thus highly complex and the usual battle lines were on many issues reversed. The fiasco of the 'iron and blood' speech showed that he had much to learn about public relations, but his diplomatic finesse and ability to play his cards close to his chest came increasingly into play. Not least among the devices he used to hide his true intentions was the 'utmost frankness' with which he sometimes spoke and that occasionally made others cast doubt upon his sanity. It was a way of talking he chose with the Austrian ambassador in Berlin, Count Karolyi, in December 1862. He protested strongly against the Austrian reform plan proposing an assembly of delegates at Frankfurt. In the past, he declared, such a plan would never have been introduced without a prior understanding between Vienna and Berlin. For the present government, involved as it was in a severe constitutional conflict, it was vital to maintain Prussian prestige abroad. He complained that the other German governments were making it difficult to maintain a conservative policy in Prussia. He went into a long, rather tendentious account of relations between Austria and Prussia within the German Confederation and stressed how vital it was for Prussia to 'move freely and unhindered in her natural region', North Germany. He then made the suggestion, that Austria, instead of seeking her centre of gravity in Germany, should transfer it to Hungary, killing two birds with one stone by reconciling the Hungarians without risking the alienation of the German provinces. It was unusual, to say the least, for the head of one government to tell the ambassador of another how to order its internal affairs. But there was not only advice from a candid friend, there were also threats. In his first talk with Karolyi in December 1862 he said:

> If Austria persists in her present direction and restricts our action and the air we breathe, then you will conjure up catastrophes, which in the last analysis must end in a fight, in which we each will have our allies, in which we might come out badly, but which we cannot prevent.[5]

A month later he talked to his old Frankfurt colleague Count Thun, now Austrian ambassador in St Petersburg, who was stopping off in Berlin on his way home. Thun was evidently charmed by the friendliness of the reception he got from a man with whom he had crossed swords in the past. They went over the course of Austrian-Prussian relations and Bismarck said if it came to hostilities between them Prussia would be bound to free her back by occupying Hanover, Electoral Hesse and other minor states. Thun then brought up the subject of France and what Prussia would do in case of her intervention in a 'fratricidal war'. Bismarck said one should spare him the spectre of France intervening against Prussia and remained undeterred by phrases about 'war between brothers'. 'I am impervious to this kind of sentimental policy-making; I have no feeling for German nationality, for me a war against the king of Bavaria or of Hanover [he must have meant the emperor of Austria, Thun added in his report to Vienna] is exactly the same as against France.'[6]

Already Bismarck was playing his cards, weak as they were in many respects in these early months of power, with growing virtuosity. He dispensed charm, candour, threats, offers of concessions in carefully graded doses, according to the circumstances of his interlocutor. At home he fought the liberals with a catalogue of brutal repression and chicanery and in many private utterances affected contempt for the 'caterwauling of 250 deputies and about the same number of their lackeys in the press'. He writes about them to Motley: 'these phrasemakers can't rule Prussia, I must resist them, they have not enough wit and too much complacency, dumm und dreist [stupid and brazen]'.[7] Yet he could not have done without them, for they made him indispensable to the king. Eventually he would shoot their fox, a united Germany. It would not have done to make this too obvious to the king. The gags on the press and other flagrant attacks on civil liberties also had the purpose of making his royal master think that plans for a *coup d'état*, as advocated by Manteuffel and others, were unnecessary.

Abroad he treated the Austrians to a constantly changing menu of threats and offers. Since the Italian war Austrian foreign policy was in the hands of another old Frankfurt colleague, Rechberg, for whom Bismarck had frequently expressed contempt and who in his turn regarded Bismarck with the utmost suspicion. But Rechberg was conservative and legitimist and had to hope that his Prussian counterpart, appointed to confront the liberals, would live up to his reputation as an arch-conservative. Luckily for Bismarck, Austrian policy was not consistent. Since 1860 Schmerling, once a *grossdeutsch* minister in 1848, had become influential. The internal Austrian reforms were largely his, but they were based on the assumption that the German element in the Habsburg empire continued to enjoy the moral reinforcement of an Austrian lead in the German Confederation. The last thing Austria therefore could do was to surrender its position in Germany, no matter what was offered as compensation in Italy or the Balkans.

Bismarck could thus build up alternative strategies and fall-back positions, something that became a hallmark of his policies. His skill should not blind one to the precariousness of his position nor his ultimate success to his frequent mistakes. Already his reputation as a subtle manipulator was adding to the miasma of mistrust that surrounded him. The fact that he always kept at least several ways forward open for himself does not mean that he thought them all equally likely. He cannot really have thought a division of Germany between Austria and Prussia roughly along the River Main was likely. The way the affairs of the Zollverein were developing after the Franco-Prussian trade treaty showed that leading intermediate states like Saxony or Bavaria had no option but to stay with Prussia, however much they wanted politically to go the other way. The Austrians were therefore confronted with an either–or situation and no one could expect them to retreat from Germany without a fight. But if it came to a fight Bismarck would have to mobilize all the support he could get, including German nationalism, even if it conflicted with conservative legitimism.

*

In the early months of 1863 Bismarck was fighting for survival and the vehemence with which, even in despatches to his own ambassadors, he rebuts rumours in the press and among foreign governments that he is about to resign shows how threatened he feels. He won a minor success when on 22 January the Frankfurt diet voted down the Austrian proposal of a delegate conference. In his declaration to the diet the Prussian delegate stated that his country could only consent to a representative body if it was composed of directly elected delegates drawn from each member state in proportion to its population. Since Austria could as a multi-national empire not participate in such a body, the reform of the Confederation would have to be decided within a narrower circle. Bismarck was thus playing the national-liberal card of a Germany led by Prussia without Austria, something he was to do at intervals during the next few years. For the moment it was academic and, coming from such a source, provoked only ridicule. A few days later he appeared before the reconvened chamber in Berlin. His policy still was to let them talk and stew in their own juice, but his interventions, on this occasion and subsequently, hardly helped his cause. His confrontational style, his glib tongue, his insuperable arrogance led him into remarks which showed that he had learnt little from the 'iron and blood' fiasco.

The famous surgeon Rudolf Virchow, now and for years to come a fearless fighter for liberal principles, moved an uncompromising reply to the address from the throne, declaring the government's conduct unconstitutional. In answering him Bismarck made no attempt to avoid provocation and seemed to take pleasure in deploying arguments which could justify a return to monarchical absolutism. 'With this address the royal house of Hohenzollern is being asked to surrender its constitutional rights in order to transfer them to the majority of this house,' he declared and then elaborated on this theme, pulling no punches. He said that the constitution provided for a balance between the three legislative powers, the king, the upper and the lower chamber. If one of these prevented a compromise with 'doctrinaire absolutism', then compromise fails and is replaced by conflict. Conflicts become questions of power. 'He who has the power, will then use it at his discretion, for the life of the state cannot stand still even for one moment.'[8] Not unreasonably a very moderate liberal, Count Schwerin, once minister of the interior, then accused Bismarck of proclaiming that 'might was right', something that went against the motto of the Prussian kings 'justice is the foundation of kingdoms'. But Bismarck did not, for the time being, dissolve the house and stuck to his policy of letting the members stew in their own juice. It was a weakness of the various liberal groups that so many of them were officials, judges and professors, so few belonged to the new entrepreneurial class. Bismarck made sure that those drawing official salaries were pressured if they did not toe the line, by denied promotions, unwelcome transfers and similar devices. He would make the appointment of every Landrat a cabinet question, he asserted. It was a policy that made few friends and many enemies.

Bismarck was about to make himself even more unpopular by his attitude to the Polish rebellion, which started in January 1863. Hostility to Polish nationalism was one of his most consistent convictions. The resurrection of a Polish state was diametrically opposed to the Prussian national interest, in his view, and everything had to be done to make sure that Russia and Austria kept their own Polish minorities under control. This was the official reason for the conclusion of the Alvensleben convention in February 1863, which, however he and events justified it later, was one of the rasher acts of his early diplomacy. The adjutant of the king, General Alvensleben, was sent on special mission to St Petersburg to conclude an agreement between the Russian and Prussian governments to assist each other in the suppression of the Polish insurgency, particularly in pursuit of fugitives crossing the border between the two countries. The agreement had little practical consequence, but as a red rag to provoke liberal feeling at home and abroad it could hardly be bettered. It was, however, the kind of sentiment that always aroused Bismarck himself to cynical contempt. It emerges in all its calculated arrogance from a report he himself made of a conversation on the Polish rebellion with the British ambassador in Berlin, Sir Andrew Buchanan. Bismarck did not hold Sir Andrew in high regard, perhaps because he was a liberal. 'His intellect lags behind the first impression made by his appearance,' he told his own ambassador in London, Bernstorff.[9] Buchanan asked the Prussian prime minister if the Alvensleben convention allowed Russian and Prussian troops to cross each other's borders, to which the answer was 'yes'; he went on to ask what would happen if the Poles managed to throw the Russians out of their country, to which Bismarck replied that in such an eventuality they would have to occupy the kingdom of Poland themselves in order to prevent the rise of a hostile power.[10] When Buchanan said that Europe would never tolerate this, Bismarck, according to his own note of the conversation, replied 'Who is Europa [sic]?', a remark quoted in innumerable histories and biographies.

In similar caustic vein Bismarck defended the convention in the Prussian chamber, going out of his way to inflame sentiment. When Waldeck, a leading left liberal and 1848 democrat, said that Prussia's policy on the Polish insurrection made his face go red with shame, Bismarck retorted that his sense of Prussian honour was at least equal to that of the deputy. In defence of his policy, both at the time and later, he made much of the fact that he had to strengthen those among Russian policy-makers who wanted to confront rather than appease Polish nationalism. Gorchakov, so Bismarck felt, had some sympathy with the appeasers, the anti-German pan-Slavs. This was the line he still took in his reminiscences thirty years later, when it was plainly part of his purpose to blame his successors for allowing the Prussian-Russian relationship to cool, thereby facilitating a Russian rapprochement with France. In 1863 the Prussian attitude to the Polish rebellion led to a cooling of relations with France, to which Bismarck had always attached so much importance. Napoleon III not only sympathized with Polish nationalism himself, it enjoyed so much support among French public opinion that he could hardly have done other than favour the Polish cause.

The Alvensleben convention was the kind of *Realpolitik* that Bismarck favoured and his fear of Polish nationalism was no doubt genuine. But on this occasion he paid a high price for his disregard of sentiment and the convention was not as important as he later made out in ensuring Russian benevolence or at least neutrality in the years that followed. When he found how much ill-feeling the convention caused in other European capitals he made an unsuccessful attempt to get Gorchakov to discard it. Even without the convention, the Polish rebellion would have disturbed relations between France and Russia, which was useful to Bismarck's schemes in the longer run. On the other hand it gave some substance to the possibility of an alliance between Paris and Vienna, which would have had the opposite effect and made his German plans impossible. Never was his position weaker than in the weeks and months following the Alvensleben convention. He could only hope that the king and the supporters of a coup d'état around him would be convinced by his forthright performances in the chamber that he was one of them. He was trying to satisfy the ultras with a kind of cold coup d'état, allowing the deputies to let off steam, while never giving way to them one jot and harassing them in every possible way.

*

It was a sign of his weak political position, but also of his boldness in exploring unorthodox avenues, that during the spring and summer of 1863 he found time for a series of conversations with the German socialist leader Ferdinand Lassalle. He was, as much as Marx, the forefather of the eventually powerful German socialist movement. He was ten years younger than Bismarck and came from a Jewish merchant family in Breslau. Organizations within the numerically still small German industrial working class were at this time still generally linked to liberalism. The organization which Lassalle founded, the *Allgemeiner Deutscher Arbeiterverein* (ADAV, General German Workers' Association), cut the link with liberalism and it was Lassalle's hostility to the Progressives that made him attractive to Bismarck. Lassalle was influenced by Marx, but sought to realize socialism within a national context through means such as universal suffrage. In the immediate short term he was looking to a unification of Germany under Prussia. There is no authentic record of the talks and they would probably not have continued as long as they did if the two men had not found each other fascinating. Bismarck said many years later: 'Our conversations went on for hours and I was always sorry when they had to end.' But to those around him he called Lassalle a fantasist and utopian.[11]

The talks seem to have gone over ground like the possibility of a socially responsive monarchy, indirect taxation, on which they disagreed, and above all universal suffrage, which was essential to Lassalle's vision and with which Bismarck was flirting. The talks led nowhere, for Lassalle was a leader with a minute following and Bismarck, for all the precariousness of his future at this time, was the quasi-dictator of Prussia. The meetings were widely noticed at the time. Bonapartism was in the air, but there were many reasons why the French example could not be exactly transferred to Prussia and why Bismarck could not be Louis Napoleon. Eventually Bismarck introduced universal male suffrage for the Reichstag and thereby unwittingly laid the foundations for the great socialist party that Lassalle envisaged. But at this moment universal suffrage was outside practical politics for Bismarck and a great socialist party looked utopian. When Bismarck was thinking of mobilizing a wide suffrage to strengthen the monarchical order and undermine the liberal parties, he was looking to the rural masses, the peasants, not the industrial workers, as yet a small group of whom he knew little.

*

In May 1863 the constitutional conflict between the Prussian chamber and the Bismarck government reached yet another climax and so did the repressions practised by the regime. During the ever more acrimonious debates on the military service law, Roon, backed by all his colleagues collectively, refused to acknowledge that the president of the chamber had any disciplinary powers over ministers when they appeared and spoke in the chamber. It was a deliberate affront, for it would mean that the deputies would have to listen to ministers in silence, however offensive their attacks on individual members of the house. The debate of the military service law was discontinued and it was therefore effectively rejected. On 22 May the chamber passed by 239 to 61 votes a motion declaring that no understanding with the present ministry was possible and that the gulf between the chamber and the crown could only be bridged if the persons and the system were changed. In a very sharply worded message the king then closed the session, dissolving the chamber three months later. On 1 June 1863 a press ordinance was issued which allowed the authorities to ban publication of newspapers and journals 'because of a continuous attitude endangering the public welfare'. Indignation in Prussia and Germany reached unprecedented heights and the blindly reactionary policy of Charles X in France before the revolution of 1830 was widely recalled.

The most striking protest, however, came from the crown prince. After first writing to his father and Bismarck he expressed his regret, at an official reception at Danzig (now Gdansk, in Poland) on 5 June, that matters had reached such a pass and denied his personal involvement. He was sharply called to heel by his father, but was forgiven on the understanding that he would remain silent in future. The crown prince's public dissent from the Bismarck government raised high hopes among liberals, but they were to be disappointed. There was no follow-up and Frederick William never spoke up again so bravely in public. In his memoirs Bismarck treats the whole affair with ironical contempt. He again pours scorn on the school of political writers who saw in the English constitution an example to be followed in Prussia. From this, he says, followed other misapprehensions 'by the crown princess and her mother', such as 'that there would be a repetition in nineteenth-century Prussia of the struggles and catastrophes of seventeenth-century England.'[12] Clearly Bismarck did not anticipate the fate of Strafford and Charles I for himself and his king, and in this he proved only too right. Nevertheless when elections to the chamber took place at the end of October all the pressure, manipulation and chicanery that the Bismarck government had applied achieved hardly any result. It is true that rather more conservatives were elected, 35 instead of 11, but the Progressives, the real hard core of opposition to Bismarck, also increased their numbers from 133 to 140. Altogether the various liberal factions made up about 70 per cent of the chamber. Some notable moderate Old Liberals lost their seats, while the Progressives were reinforced by some outstanding personalities like Theodor Mommsen, the famous historian of the Roman empire, and at a by-election in 1865 by Eduard Lasker. Voting participation declined in all three classes, overall from 34.3 to 30.9 per cent, which gave some substance to Bismarck's argument that the electorate would eventually tire of the conflict. But for the moment his government found itself in a cul-de-sac, with even less of a future than the Manteuffel regime had enjoyed in the 1850s.

*

The repressive, deeply reactionary Bismarck regime spread despair among all those throughout Germany who had put their hopes in a liberal Prussia taking the lead in solving the German question. It made Austria, for all its faults and difficulties, look more attractive again. It was still the highest priority for the policy-makers in Vienna to find a way of reasserting Austrian supremacy in Germany and forcing Prussia to take its place within it. All the world was now expecting a fresh Austrian initiative for the reform of the German Confederation and when it came it posed a challenge to Bismarck greater than any he had faced at home or abroad since taking office. On 3 August the Emperor Francis Joseph suddenly sprang a verbal invitation on king William of Prussia to attend a meeting of all German princes at Frankfurt on 16 August to consider a new Austrian reform plan. King William was taking the waters at Gastein, within the Habsburg dominion, when he and the emperor met. Bismarck describes in his reminiscences how he sat watching a tit feed its young while the king sat on a bench on the opposite side of a river gorge. By paying so much attention to the tit Bismarck missed the moment when king and emperor met.[13] When he reached the royal quarters he found a note from the king telling him of the invitation to Frankfurt. There now ensued the famous battle between the king and his minister, during which Bismarck had to pull out all the stops, including the threat of resignation, to prevent his royal master from going to Frankfurt. The Austrians had played their cards very cleverly and had taken Bismarck by surprise. That he was determined to frustrate their initiative goes without saying. To even start on the slippery slope towards an agreement with the Austrian proposals was, in his view, fatal. The king, on the other hand, had great difficulty in bringing himself to oppose an initiative which was to emerge from a collective decision of the German princes.

When the invitation reached the king in writing, Bismarck managed to get his royal master to write a reply which neither accepted nor rejected it, but took refuge in the argument that he could reach no decision without consulting his advisers. He proposed a preliminary conference of the ministers of the principal German states, to prepare the ground for the rulers. It was a curious line to take, when the king had just insisted in the Prussian chamber of deputies on his untrammelled prerogative. The crunch came when the Congress of Princes actually met and despatched the king of Saxony, accompanied by his minister Beust, to persuade his Prussian fellow monarch to come to Frankfurt after all. By this time the Prussian king had moved to Baden, where he was exposed to the liberal influences Bismarck always feared. The king found the invitation to go to Frankfurt now extremely hard to resist. 'Thirty ruling gentlemen and a king as courier!' he kept on repeating. After hours of debate lasting till midnight, both king and prime minister were emotionally exhausted. The king burst into tears and Bismarck smashed a washbasin on leaving the royal closet. He dropped any pretence of diplomatic delicacy in forcing the king of Saxony and Beust to leave Baden before they could further importune his master. Close to hysteria it had driven him, but Bismarck had got his way. William did not go to Frankfurt and the Austrian plan was thereby fatally damaged. Had he gone, Bismarck would have had to resign and the Austrian triumph would have looked like a second Olmütz. The Austrian reform plan attempted to give the Confederation an executive organ, which it hitherto lacked. There was to be a federal directory, chaired by Austria, in which Austria, Prussia and Bavaria were to have permanent seats. In this forum Prussia could have been outvoted. There was to be a chamber of deputies, not directly elected, but to be chosen by the parliaments of the member states. This was similar to the proposal of a delegate conference which Austria had tabled a year earlier and for the rejection of which Bismarck had laboured hard. In refusing to accept this further and more far-reaching Austrian reform plan the Bismarck government once more put forward the idea of a federal parliament based on direct elections, with its composition determined by the population size of the member states. Coming from such a source the proposal again met only with ridicule.

6

FIRST TRIUMPH

The crisis over Schleswig-Holstein, which came to a head in the late autumn of 1863, became the turning point in Bismarck's fortunes. Even after he had successfully emerged from it in the following summer he was sometimes, as he put it later in life, still closer to the gallows than to the throne. But after the Danish war neither friend nor foe could delude themselves that Bismarck was only a footnote in history. The case of Schleswig-Holstein was notoriously complicated and a full exploration of its antecedents is not necessary for the appreciation of Bismarck's place in it. It was one of the many instances in nineteenth-century Europe where the rise of rival nationalisms, German and Danish, created conflict. The king of Denmark was also duke of Schleswig and of Holstein and of the small territory of Lauenburg. The latter two duchies were part of the German Confederation and by virtue of his sovereignty over them the Danish king was represented in Frankfurt, just as the king of Holland was through Luxemburg and the king of England, until 1837, through Hanover. The population of Holstein was entirely German-speaking, but particularly in North Schleswig there were many Danish speakers and the language problem had begun to cause tension by the 1840s. It had to be the aim of the Danish kings to keep the whole of their kingdom, the Helstat, together. Danish liberal nationalists wished to maintain the Danish language and culture in Schleswig. They were Eiderdanes, the river Eider being the dividing line between Schleswig and Holstein. German nationalists wanted the incorporation of both duchies in Germany and frequently invoked the long tradition, going back to the seventeenth century, that the tie between the two duchies was indissoluble, 'for ever undivided' (*up ewig Ungedeelten*, in the north German patois).

When in 1848 the Prussians finally gave up the war to wrest the duchies from Denmark it was a scarring experience for the German national movement. It seemed to show that the great powers of Europe would never allow German national aspirations to be realized when they conflicted with their own national interest. When the upheavals of the years of revolution were finally laid to rest in the London protocol of 1852 the status quo was restored. Schleswig and Holstein were to have an equal but separate existence under the Danish crown. The protocol also secured the Danish succession following the then reigning King Frederick VII, who had no heirs. It would go to Prince Christian of Sonderburg-Glücksburg, from a cadet branch of the Danish royal house, thereby guaranteeing the integrity of the Danish monarchy. In Germany he was contemptuously known as the protocol prince, for the recognition by the great powers of his right to succeed in Denmark and in the duchies was in the Danish and not in the German national interest. Prince Christian's right of succession was never recognized by the estates of Holstein and Schleswig.

During his time in Frankfurt Bismarck had to deal with the Schleswig-Holstein question when the Danish government, through various constitutional measures, tried to emphasize the integrity of the Danish kingdom or at least bring Schleswig into greater union with Denmark, the aim of the Eiderdanes. The German Confederation had to intervene on behalf of the Holsteiners and, eventually in 1858, to threaten a federal execution against the king of Denmark in his capacity as duke of Holstein, but the implementation of it was repeatedly postponed. Moves by the Confederation on behalf of Holstein encouraged Danish moves for the full integration of Schleswig into Denmark. Against this, German nationalists continued to emphasize the inseparability of Schleswig from Holstein. Bismarck's advice to his own government was usually along the lines that Prussia should hold back and not expose herself for the sake of nebulous German national sentiment. The Confederation should not be encouraged to make demands it could not enforce, especially as the Austrians were making it clear, as he told Gerlach in April 1857, that they were against any armed intervention. If the Confederation came out of the affair badly, Prussia would, because of her geographical and historical connection with the situation, get the blame.[1] 'We have greater concerns and dangers to face than the misdemeanours of Danish overlords in Schleswig and the Holsteiners are, it seems to me, not favourable to the idea of being saved by German troops', he wrote to Schleinitz in April 1861.[2] Soon after coming to power, he put forward the view, in confidential communications, that the Schleswig-Holstein question could only be resolved by war, but that Prussia should contemplate such a war only in her own interest, and not for the establishment of a further separate German state. Nor should Prussia fight to enhance the importance of the German Confederation and least of all should she be yoked to the revolutionary German national movement.

The Schleswig-Holstein question assumed a high profile in March 1863. A Danish royal patent seemed to aim at the full incorporation of Schleswig into the Danish state, at the price of keeping Holstein separate and largely autonomous, but still under the Danish crown. The waves of German national sentiment over Schleswig-Holstein began to run higher than ever before, spurred by the fear of losing the duchies to Denmark. In July 1863 the Confederation reactivated the suspended threat of a federal execution. The great powers, Britain, France and Russia, had to get more heavily involved, for there was now the risk of war in a strategically sensitive area. In November the Danish parliament adopted the constitution foreshadowed in the March patent. King Frederick VII was reluctant to sign it, knowing that it might involve his country in a war, in which it might not get the support of the great powers. On 15 November he died and the protocol prince ascended the throne as Christian IX of Denmark and duke of Schleswig, Holstein and Lauenburg. He signed the constitution immediately after his accession. In the protocol of 1852 another claimant to the Danish throne and to the duchies, Duke Christian August of Sonderburg-Augustenburg, had waived his claims and been compensated for it. His son Frederick of Augustenburg refused to recognize the waiver and had himself proclaimed Frederick VIII of Schleswig-Holstein, immediately upon Christian IX claiming his succession.

The Augustenburg duke now became the candidate of almost all sections of the German national movement. More than was the case at the time of the Italian war in 1859, a movement of clubs, associations and armed volunteers willing to fight the Danes sprang up to support the establishment of an independent German Schleswig-Holstein under the Augustenburg duke. There was every indication that German nationalist emotions now reached beyond the articulate classes down to the grass roots. Even the governments of the medium and smaller German states, normally so fearful of popular movements and their revolutionary implications, came out in support of the Augustenburger. Their motives were obviously different from those of the German national movement. They hoped that the creation of another medium-sized state would reinforce their ranks and strengthen their influence at the expense of both the two German great powers. Once more the idea of a third Germany as a powerful magnet and focus for German nationalism came into view.

*

Bismarck was faced with a difficult choice. He could swim with the tide of German nationalism and thereby at a stroke end the conflict with the liberals in Prussia and beyond, something he had in one way or another attempted to do since coming to power and was to do again later on. But by doing this now over Schleswig-Holstein he ran the risk of putting himself at the mercy of the national-liberal movement. They would do the pushing, he would have to follow. He put this very sharply in a despatch of 20 December 1863 to Robert von der Goltz, his ambassador in Paris:

> Seeing the impulses, which motivate the latter [public opinion in Germany], the possibility of aligning Prussian policy with them appears to me remote and improbable. Within the movement, which pervades Germany, the more reflective and moderate elements form a tiny minority. I regard it as impossible to act with the real leaders of this movement, for it would be incompatible with the maintenance of ordered conditions in Prussia. I therefore believe that we must attach more weight to our relations with the other major powers than to any agreement with the present trend of public opinion and I further believe that we must prepare for an open fight against rather an alliance with the incipient national and revolutionary movement.[3]

Goltz was not only a subordinate, he was also a rival, all the more dangerous at this moment as the king, and many of those around him, were inclined to support the Augustenburg claimant. It was something like the resurrection of the Wochenblattpartei, to which the king had once been sympathetic and to which Goltz had belonged.

A few days after his official despatch to Goltz, Bismarck wrote him, on Christmas Eve 1863, a sharply worded letter warning him against giving the king advice that differed from that of the responsible minister. An ambassadorial report is one thing, he tells Goltz, but to offer the king an alternative ministerial programme is quite another and would not be tolerated. He repeats again the substance of his argument on the Schleswig-Holstein problem:

> The question is, are we a great power or simply a German federal state, and whether, in the first case, we are to be governed monarchically, or, as would be permissible in the second case, by professors, circuit judges and small town gossips. The chase after the phantom 'popularity in Germany', which we have carried on since the 1840s, has cost us our position in Germany and in Europe.

Later in the letter he says:

> If we now turn our backs on the great powers, in order to throw ourselves into the arms of the policy of the small states caught in the net of democratic clubbery, it would be the most wretched state into which one could deliver the monarchy at home and abroad.[4]

Goltz was not to be deterred and told Bismarck 'you are strengthening the revolution by leaving it to the revolutionaries to fight a just cause.' And in reply to Bismarck's warning not to persuade the king to adopt a different policy he said: 'You are not a parliamentary government, but neither are you a monarchical one, yours is the dictatorship of the minister for foreign affairs.'[5]

Bismarck did not know at the outset of the crisis whether he could achieve the absorption of the duchies into Prussia, but he had a very clear idea what he needed to avoid. Nothing must be done to enhance the standing of the German Confederation, which he had done his level best to destroy; an even more negative result would be the creation of yet another medium-sized German state in a region of the utmost strategic sensitivity for Prussia. The Augustenburg prince belonged to the liberal grouping of German princes, in which Duke Ernst of Saxe-Coburg-Gotha, brother of the recently deceased Prince Albert, played a leading role. The Coburg connection figured high in the list of Bismarck's bugbears. He had to take into account the interests of the other European great powers. Napoleon III was pursuing his own agenda on the Schleswig-Holstein problem, possibly a deal with Austria, trading concessions to the Habsburg empire in Italy in return for a strengthened French position further north, possibly on the Rhine. Napoleon could hardly disavow his commitment to the nationality principle over Schleswig-Holstein. He was prepared to leave Schleswig-Holstein to Prussia, provided North Schleswig with its Danish majority would be left to Denmark. Britain had a strategic interest in the integrity of Denmark and had recently strengthened her dynastic ties with the Danish royal family through the marriage of the prince of Wales with Princess Alexandra. The Danish government had high hopes of British assistance in case of war and the Palmerston government had done nothing to disillusion them, but in practice Britain could do little on the Continent without France, and the Franco-British alliance of the Crimean War was in bad repair. This was of great help to Bismarck on the Schleswig-Holstein question. It was even more important to him that Russia had, like Britain, a strategic interest in the integrity of Denmark, but that this was secondary to the tsar's fear of revolution and of Napoleon and his dislike of the democratic Danish regime. Russia also had her own dynastic candidate for the succession in the duchies, the grand duke of Oldenburg. All these international complications and dangers notwithstanding, the strength of feeling over Schleswig-Holstein in Germany was such that the king and others in the Prussian establishment, the crown prince especially, found it difficult to resist the temptation to go along with it. It was another paradox that for the first time the Confederation, which for years had aroused the contempt of the German national movement by acting only as an instrument of repression, was shaping up to be the champion of German nationalism against Denmark. Bismarck was determined not to allow it to do so and equally sure that the Augustenburg cause would have to be ditched.

Perhaps the most surprising consequence of Bismarck's determination not to follow the Augustenburg movement was the restoration of collaboration between Vienna and Berlin, which had only recently broken down in acrimony over the Austrian proposals for the reform of the Confederation. It has often been portrayed as one of the outstanding diplomatic masterstrokes of Bismarck that he now managed to drag Austria in the wake of Prussia over the Schleswig-Holstein question. This is, however, a judgment made with hindsight, from the point of view of the eventual successful incorporation of both duchies into Prussia. In late 1863 there were compelling reasons why it should suit both Berlin and Vienna to come together. Austria was even less than Prussia in a position to set aside international agreements, such as the protocol of 1852, and put herself at odds with the other great powers of Europe. Nor could the multi-national Habsburg state align itself with the German national movement, with all its revolutionary nationalist connotations. The Austrian policy-makers, from the emperor down, were still smarting under their defeat at the hands of the French and remained intensely suspicious of Napoleon. Rechberg, the Austrian foreign minister, had been sceptical of the initiatives which had led to the abortive Congress of Princes in Frankfurt in August. They were the work of Schmerling, the man chiefly responsible for the attempts to reorganize the Habsburg empire along more liberal lines, and of Biegeleben, the head of the department of German affairs in the Austrian foreign office. Rechberg still feared Bismarck as a violent and unpredictable operator, but did not shed tears over the failure of the Frankfurt congress. He thought the way forward lay in some kind of Austrian-Prussian collaboration on a conservative basis. He therefore welcomed the fact that over Schleswig-Holstein Bismarck was acting as a conservative cabinet politician and refusing to pander to German nationalist emotion. The recent clashes over the German question were swiftly forgotten and informal agreement on a common front over Schleswig-Holstein was reached when the death of the Danish king in November made the problem acute.

In consequence there developed a strong divergence between the two major German powers on the one hand, and the Confederation, backed by the majority of German opinion, on the other. Leaving aside the legal complexities, the Confederation wanted to secure both duchies for the Augustenburg claimant. It was fully entitled to act in Holstein and it could be argued that, given the historical and to some extent legal connection, could by extension also act in Schleswig. In contrast, Austria and Prussia were proceeding on the basis of the 1852 protocol. Their occupation of Schleswig, which began on 1 February 1864 and started the war against Denmark, was initially justified as a move to enforce the withdrawal of the Danish constitution incorporating Schleswig into Denmark. Once the Danes withdrew the constitution, it could be inferred that the rule of King Christian of Denmark over the duchies would be restored. German opinion was outraged by the attitude of the two German great powers andtheir flagrant disregard for the wishes of the people in the duchies. The Nationalverein and its *grossdeutsch* counterpart, the *Reformverein*, organized a meeting of deputies from the various German parliaments in Frankfurt. This meeting of 491 deputies demanded the recognition of the Augustenburg duke as the ruler of Schleswig-Holstein and set up a committee of 36 to promote the cause. The governments in Vienna and Berlin tried to suppress the activities of this committee. In setting aside decisions of the Confederation and threatening to bring it to an end altogether, the Austrians had far more to lose than the Prussians. They lost the moral high ground they had recently gained in Germany and were going against their usual allies among the lesser German governments. Yet Vienna had no guarantee that the Prussians would not eventually take over the duchies and that in a region so remote from Austria and close to Prussia they would not get their way. In their actions against Denmark, Austria and Prussia based themselves on the 1852 protocol, but the outbreak of actual war was likely to render this agreement meaningless. Everything would then be up for grabs and Prussia would be in a strong position to do the grabbing.

Robert von Keudell, an old family friend and then his secretary, describes Bismarck at the New Year celebrations of 1864. He was sitting in front of his dining room fireplace, into which he had tossed branches from the Christmas tree and watched them burn. He was talking politics, something he rarely did in the bosom of his family.

> The 'old inseparables' [the Schleswig-Holsteiners] must eventually become Prussians. That is my aim; whether I can get there is in God's hands. But I could not be responsible for shedding Prussian blood to create a new small state, which in the confederation would always vote against us.

He then said that the Augustenburgs had no real right of succession and that fortunately Rechberg did not believe so either. His Austrian colleague was annoyed by the hasty recognition and support for Augustenburg by the Nationalverein, by the democrats, by princes like Coburg and Baden and by the machinations on behalf of Augustenburg of von der Pfordten, the Bavarian envoy at Frankfurt. Rechberg had no time for the lesser German states since the failure of the Frankfurt Congress of Princes and, in short, he, Bismarck, and the Austrian minister were heart and soul together. 'How long it will later hang together I don't know, but the beginning is good; and the obstinacy of the Danes will probably give us what we need, a reason for war.'[6] Bismarck, for all his imperiousness, was mercurial and had moments of discouragement. He was talking like this in his intimate circle to reassure himself, when the tide was flowing so strongly for Augustenburg and when in public he had to fight on so many fronts. Keudell had written to him, four weeks earlier, what a marvellous opportunity they now had to put themselves at the head of a tremendous German national movement and free the duchies from the Danish yoke. Bismarck found such advice from his own secretary hard to take and Keudell had to apologize.

The most dangerous and nerve-racking battle he had to fight was again in his own backyard. He may have intended the annexation of the duchies all along and foreseen that it would require a war to achieve it and had said as much in official documents. But for all his calculated indiscretions and frankness, this was an aim he could not fully reveal even to his own king. William believed that he had no rightful claim to Schleswig-Holstein, quite apart from the advantages that support for the Augustenburger might earn Prussia with German public opinion. In order to show how indispensable he still was as the minister who would protect the monarchy from the liberals, Bismarck took again a deliberately confrontational line in the Prussian chamber of deputies in January 1864. He accused the deputies of wishing to usurp the conduct of foreign policy, which was none of their business and which would turn the strong Prussian monarchy into a parliamentary lapdog. He virtually accused them of betraying Prussia by their support of the Augustenburger. He poured sarcastic contempt on their refusal to vote further credits, at a moment when Prussia might have to take up arms.[7] In reply to Virchow, who accused him of having disappointed all expectations and of having given himself to evil and to the extreme right, he used a favourite Latin tag, 'flectere si nequeo superos, acheronta movebo' (If I cannot move the Gods, I will turn to the Devil).[8] He meant that he had offered a pact with the Devil, namely with the national-liberal German movement, on his terms, but that his overtures had so far been rejected. The king had once more to show his full support for his prime minister by closing the session of the House on 25 January. But Bismarck was at times in serious doubt about the king, for only a few days before he had written to Roon: 'I have the premonition that the cause of the crown against the revolution is lost, for the heart of the King is in the other camp and his confidence rests more with his opponents than with his servants.'[9] When he wrote this letter to Roon, he had one of his moments of discouragement. For all the contempt he showed for the liberals in the Landtag, he felt, as he would only let on to his intimate friend and comrade in arms, that having to swim against this tide was debilitating.

> I have not slept a wink this night and feel miserable, and don't really know what to tell these people, who will for sure refuse to vote credits, when it

> is as good as clear, that HM, in spite of the danger of breaking with Europe and to suffer a worse Olmütz, will give way to democracy and the Würzburger [the medium states], in order to establish Augustenburg and create a new medium state.

In writing thus Bismarck no doubt had the ulterior motive of enlisting Roon, who was close to the king, in his sisyphean task of persuading their royal master to steer clear of associating with revolution and risking a European war.

Bismarck in the end always succeeded in keeping William on side. At a crown council on 3 February, immediately after the troops of Prussia and Austria had crossed into Schleswig, he spoke of the possibility that the annexation of the duchies by Prussia might well be the final outcome. He told the king that this was his chance to add to the territory of Prussia, as all his predecessors had done. At this remark the crown prince, according to Bismarck's memoirs, raised his hands to heaven, as if doubting the sanity of his father's chief minister. Most of the time Bismarck was not discouraged, but gloried in the skill with which he was playing off all sides against each other. Not infrequently he boasted about the way he had taken Vienna in tow. In his Christmas Eve letter to Goltz he wrote: 'There has never been a time when the policy of Vienna has to this extent *en gros* and *en détail* been conducted from Berlin.' Later, at a ball, he met the Italian ambassador de Launay and pointing at his sword joked 'the sword of Italy!'. De Launay quipped back 'it seems you do not want to use it, for you have chosen another comrade in arms.' The Austro-Prussian alliance was naturally unpopular in Turin. Bismarck flashed back 'Oh. We have only hired him.' 'For nothing?' 'It is *travailler pour le roi de Prusse*,' the old proverbial saying signifying hard work for little gain.[10]

These weeks and months when the Schleswig-Holstein crisis was moving from one climax to another enabled Bismarck to use his formidable personality and intellect with growing confidence and virtuosity. He choked off the king's Augustenburg leanings by frightening him with the spectre of revolution and a general European war. He brazened it out with the liberals in the chamber of deputies and made them look absurd. They had failed to vote the military budget just when the Prussian army was needed in defence of German interests. He quelled the doubts of Rechberg and other Austrian players by invoking conservative solidarity and played on their fears of great power intervention and of French designs in Italy. To the French he held out the possibility of vindicating the triumph of the nationality principle in Schleswig. He opened beguiling vistas to Napoleon and his advisers by telling them that Prussia's Polish frontier was more important to him than the Rhine frontier, but he made sure that there was no understanding between Paris and Vienna at the expense of Berlin. He reassured the great powers, especially the British, by stressing the moderation of his aims, when the other courses, like those being advocated by German nationalists, would be so much more disturbing to the status quo. He frightened them with the spectre of a more liberal Prussian government, should he be forced to resign. He could be charming and brutal in carefully graduated doses. The reports of foreign envoys from Berlin give vivid evidence how seductive they found his brilliant and witty analysis and how convincing his apparent frankness.

The long-delayed federal execution against Holstein had at last been carried out by Saxon and Hanoverian troops on 23 December 1863. It had only been agreed by the narrow margin of eight against seven votes. The medium-sized states led by Bavaria were among the seven, because they did not only want action against King Christian as duke of Holstein; they, along with most of German public opinion, wanted to replace him with the Augustenburg duke. The federal execution, on the other hand, implied the recognition of the Danish king as the rightful duke of Holstein. In the wake of the Saxon and Hanoverian troops Frederick of Augustenburg was in fact allowed to enter Holstein, to the general acclaim of the population. An Austrian-Prussian proposal that the duke of Augustenburg should be expelled from Holstein was rejected at Frankfurt. The decisive parting of the ways between the two German great powers and the smaller German states came on 14 January, when the Frankfurt diet voted by eleven votes to five against the Austrian-Prussian proposal that the Confederation should threaten the occupation of Schleswig for the limited purpose of forcing Denmark to withdraw the November constitution. What the majority wanted was an occupation of Schleswig to enforce the succession of the Augustenburg duke. Two days after the vote of 14 January, which put the Confederation finally at odds with its two most powerful members, the first agreement between their two countries was signed by Bismarck and Karolyi, the Austrian ambassador in Berlin. The two countries agreed to present an ultimatum to Denmark to withdraw the November constitution and, in case of rejection, to occupy Schleswig. If the Confederation did not go along with this narrow purpose of the occupation the two powers would act independently of it. They would not tolerate any demonstrations in the Schleswig territory occupied by them in favour of Augustenburg. Bismarck skilfully avoided any firm commitment in case the war put an end to the agreements of 1852, which it was obviously going to do. All the *Punctation* said was that the two powers would take decisions on the succession question only by mutual agreement. In his conversations with Karolyi Bismarck emphasized how difficult it was for him to carry the king along with him. The Austrian seemed entirely convinced by Bismarck's professions of friendship for his country and by his anti-revolutionary zeal.

*

Bismarck had thought it unlikely that the Danes would withdraw their constitution, though the pressure on them was such that they came close to doing so. In the end Austria and Prussia retained their excuse for occupying Schleswig. The Confederation's Saxon and Hanoverian troops had to allow the Austrians and Prussians to march through Holstein, although Bavaria and Saxony had refused to allow Austrian troops to be transported north through their territories. The Austrian and Prussian troops, under the command of the Prussian Field Marshal Wrangel, moved into Schleswig on 1 February and met little Danish resistance. The Danes abandoned the fortifications guarding most of Southern Schleswig, the Danneverke, and withdrew to the Dybbøl (Düppel) fortifications and the island of Als in Northern Schleswig. In this stage of the hostilities Prussian troops did not distinguish themselves and the eighty-year old Wrangel failed to make proper use of the plans prepared by Helmuth von Moltke, the chief of the general staff.

In the meantime the British efforts to deal with the situation by way of a European conference moved into high gear. Palmerston and Russell, prime minister and foreign secretary, had encouraged the Danes to expect British assistance, when both military resources and will were lacking to give such assistance. British public opinion was pro-Danish, but the queen was pro-German and Britain could not fight a continental war without allies. The international conference was to be a means of securing the integrity of Denmark without the need for armed intervention. In the interval before the conference met in London, on 25 April, Bismarck moved adroitly to leave his hands untied while creating *faits accomplis* on the ground. It was a decisive moment when in early March Bismarck and Karolyi signed a second Austro-Prussian Punctation to extend military operations into

Jutland if necessary and, to secure their flanks, to seize the Danish positions at Dybbøl (Düppel) and Als. There was an uncomfortable moment when a Prussian detachment prematurely occupied the town of Kolding in Jutland and Bismarck had to do some careful footwork in London and Paris. To keep the two western powers apart was an essential part of his strategy. In the impending European conference the two German powers would no longer consider themselves bound by the treaties of 1851–2. This implied that Austria and Prussia no longer considered Denmark as having any rights in either Schleswig or Holstein and that the most that might be conceded was a purely personal union of the duchies under the Danish king. Again Bismarck managed to avoid making any commitment to his Austrian partners about the future of the duchies. On 18 April, a week before the meeting of the London conference, Prussian troops stormed the fortifications of Düppel. It was the first military victory arising from Bismarck's policies and it gave public opinion throughout Germany its first heady taste of victory. It was a sensation that now began to drown out the hostility and the disgust that had hitherto gathered round the name of the Prussian prime minister. The sweet smell of success was to prove intoxicating and disorientating.

Bismarck therefore entered the London conference in a strong position. Although in many ways the central figure, he did not personally attend it and thereby gave himself even more room for manoeuvre. A hostile coalition of powers that might have saved the Danish position was never very likely and Bismarck's preliminary moves had made doubly sure that it would not happen. He made the most of the fact that for the first and only time the German Confederation, just before its final demise, was given separate representation at an international conference. The representative of the Frankfurt diet was Beust, whose personal vanity Bismarck was only too ready to exploit. He made sure that the Prussian representative at the conference, Bernstorff, kept in step not only with the Austrian representative but also with Beust. He used public and parliamentary opinion in a way that later became natural, but was still relatively novel at this time. In Prussia he encouraged the raising of a petition demanding the incorporation of the duchies into Prussia and it received 30,000 signatures; he instructed Bernstorff to make contact with those members of the British parliament who were opposing the Palmerston government's ineffective pro-Danish policy. The 'personal union' solution was so heavily hedged about with conditions that the Danes not unexpectedly rejected it. At this point the

Augustenburg solution seemed to come to the fore again, and in an important dispatch to Vienna on 21 May Bismarck mentioned this as the first of three alternatives, the other two being the Oldenburg candidature and the third annexation by Prussia. The Oldenburg succession was an option that was now being given some discreet Bismarckian encouragement, both in London and in Frankfurt. Rechberg, however, now came out in favour of Augustenburg, something that the Prussian prime minister had perhaps not expected when he raised it as a possibility. Bismarck had always done his utmost to feed Rechberg's fears of the duke of Augustenburg's liberalism and the dangers of having his semi-revolutionary regime ensconced in the heart of Germany. There was nothing for it but to go along with Austria, for at this moment a breach with Vienna was the last thing Bismarck wanted. The two German powers therefore proposed, on 28 May, the total separation of Schleswig-Holstein from Denmark under the duke of Augustenburg.

News of this proposal was greeted with enthusiasm throughout Germany. It was naively supposed that Augustenburg was now home and dry. On the face of it Bismarck had lost a round and was being diverted from his ultimate goal, but he was far too resourceful to be pinned down. On 1 June he had a three-hour meeting with the Augustenburger in Berlin. The duke had received support from the king and even more from the crown prince and entered his talks with Bismarck entirely willing to satisfy reasonable Prussian demands, such as granting naval and military facilities. But Bismarck contrived to humiliate the duke with demands that would have reduced him to a Prussian provincial governor. Any liberalism that the estates and populations of the two duchies might have expected from the duke was to be strictly disallowed. Bismarck made it clear to the unfortunate young man that he would not tolerate any interference from Vienna and that he could easily switch his support to the grand duke of Oldenburg. To his own king Bismarck made it appear that the Augustenburger had been entirely unreasonable in rejecting moderate Prussian demands, such as a canal linking the North Sea with the Baltic. It was a heavy blow to the Augustenburg cause, especially as in Prussia the movement for annexation was gaining ground and providing grist for Bismarck's mill.

In London in the meantime another hare was running: that a plebiscite should be held to decide which part of Schleswig was to remain Danish and which was to become German. Such a solution along the lines of the nationality principle was supported by Napoleon, but also by the

Palmerston government, which had to do something to satisfy the pro-Danish mood it had allowed to arise in British public opinion. In his talks with the Austrians Bismarck always made full use of the argument that Prussia and Austria together had to defend German aspirations and honour against British arrogance. On 15 May the Austrian chargé d'affaires in Berlin reported to Bismarck in a high state of excitement about 'a European dictatorship reminiscent of Louis XIV or Napoleon, which England was now assuming *vis-à-vis* Germany', which he could no longer tolerate.[11] If Austria was not prepared to continue the war against Denmark energetically, then Prussia would have to give up the alliance with Austria and go it alone, though it was the last thing he wanted. Thus Bismarck was always playing on the numerous anxieties in the Austrian government, fear of Napoleon, of being drawn into hostilities with Britain, above all of Prussia abandoning the alliance founded on conservative solidarity. When on 10 June Alexander II and Gorchakov arrived in Berlin, Bismarck played up the ideological implications of the war with Denmark. It was a fight against revolution and any weakness on the part of Prussia would give encouragement to the revolutionaries.

The London conference ended on 25 June 1864 without result. No agreement could be achieved on what part of Schleswig should the subject of a plebiscite. Hostilities were resumed and the conquest by the Prussians and Austrians of the island of Als and the occupation of most of Jutland followed swiftly. The king, always a soldier at heart, was pleased and his feelings towards his formidable prime minister grew noticeably warmer. During these events they were both at Carlsbad, and Bismarck wrote to Johanna: 'The king is very well and the sip of Als from the cup of victory agrees with him even more than the Carlsbad waters.' In telling her how moved the king had been in thanking him for his great service to Prussia, with God's grace, he wrote:

> Don't let's invoke Him gratuitously and let us hope that He will continue his grace and not leave us to our blindness. One learns in this trade that one can be as clever as the best in this world and yet the next minute go like a child into the unknown.[12]

Usually only the second sentence is quoted, with its apparent humility, while the first gives it the typically wry Bismarckian note. And indeed all was far from over. Against Austrian reservations, Bismarck made sure that the threat of further military action forced the Danes into agreeing to a total cession of the duchies. In a preliminary peace on 1 August Denmark ceded the duchies of Holstein, Lauenburg and Schleswig to Austria and Prussia. Neither the German Confederation nor the Augustenburger were parties to these proceedings. During the peace negotiations Bismarck was in Vienna and drew crowds wherever he went: 'people look at me like a new rhino for the zoo,' he wrote to Johanna. He still found time, amid pressing public business, to dine with his old American friend Motley and his family. 'We drank a lot, were very gay, which does not often happen with him, what with worry about the war.'[13] (Motley must have had the American civil war on his mind.)

*

Another point of decision was approaching. The Prussian-Austrian alliance had been victorious in war and had gained a certain amount of kudos for having vindicated the German national cause. In Germany as a whole support for Augustenburg, the clear choice of the people of the duchies, was still strong, but in Prussia there were now voices even among the liberal opposition advocating Prussian annexation of the duchies. Heinrich von Treitschke was moving from his previous liberalism towards worship of Bismarckian *Realpolitik*. More steadfast liberals like Theodor Mommsen and Karl Twesten were, with reservations, reaching the conclusion that the annexation of Schleswig-Holstein was a necessary step towards German unity. If it temporarily favoured the hated Bismarck cabinet, it was a price worth paying. These signs of divided counsel among the opposition caused some to advocate the recall of the Landtag, closed down since January, or even dissolution and fresh elections, but Bismarck resisted this. The big question now looming was the future of the Prussian-Austrian alliance. It had been Bismarck's great achievement to have kept it going this far, but the pressures against its continuance were formidable. It was a juncture where his underlying strategy of always keeping a number of options open was coming into operation on the largest possible scale. Continuing alliance with Austria on the basis of conservative solidarity had in his eyes much to commend it. It was the course which from an ideological point of view would have offered him the greatest comfort. From a power-political view it would have meant an Austrian-Prussian duopoly in Germany, along the lines he had sketched to Karolyi in December 1862, with Prussia predominant to the north of the Main. But it might also mean a war with

France, because Austria would want to recoup herself for the loss of position in Germany by the recovery of Lombardy and the retention of Venetia. It was doubtful if an alliance of the conservative powers, Austria, Prussia and Russia, against the liberal western powers was any longer realistic and Bismarck must have been well aware of it. Austria and Russia were no longer allies and some in St Petersburg, including Gorchakov, had visions of a French alliance.

There were powerful forces pulling Austria and Prussia apart and they arose from the future of the Zollverein. The renewal of the Zollverein treaty was due in 1865 and the Franco-Prussian free trade treaty made Austrian adherence virtually impossible. The other member states were confronted by Prussia with the choice of remaining in the customs union and accepting the French treaty, or leaving it altogether. For most of them this second option was no longer viable. There was thus a direct conflict between the political alliance of Berlin and Vienna and the incompatibility of their interests in the economic sphere. The same economic trends were lending weight to what Bismarck, in the shorthand he used in so much of what he wrote, called the Nationalverein view of the future. He did not like the Nationalverein, he called it democratic and revolutionary, particularly when he was trying to frighten his interlocutors. At other times he was contemptuous and explored all avenues, including Lassalle, to lift the whole phenomenon off its hinges. But he knew it would not really go away and since the 1850s he had advocated a strategy of using and manipulating the national-liberal movement. When he applied it on coming to office it had shown no results, but success in the Danish war was beginning to make the liberals more amenable. Bismarck's long-standing hostility to Austria was based on the rivalry of the two countries in German affairs, but it was just in this battle that he could tell himself that he had now won some notable victories. Austria had lost out in the German popularity stakes and had deeply disappointed the governments of the lesser states. In the final settlement of the future of Schleswig-Holstein Prussia would always have much greater leverage than Austria. A continued alliance with Vienna must therefore have been attractive for Bismarck, a balance of power in Germany on a secure ideological foundation that would have greatly enhanced the standing of Prussia and yet made the competitive wooing of German national liberalism unnecessary. The indications are that Bismarck wanted to keep this option open as long as possible, without conceding anything of substance.

By 20 August Bismarck and his king were back in Vienna for a state visit. Bismarck had rooms in the Schönbrunn Palace looking out into the private garden into which he had penetrated with Johanna seventeen years earlier on their honeymoon. 'When I look over my right shoulder, I see through a glass door the dark beech hedge along which we walked, secretly enjoying forbidden fruit by looking through the windows, behind which I am now living.'[14] He had come a long way since then and he was now on business that was to decide the future of Europe and the world for the next century. In his talks with Rechberg he dangled the prospect of a continued alliance, the attractions of which were even greater to his Austrian colleague than they were to him. Rechberg had staked his reputation on the Prussian alliance and there were many in Vienna who accused him of having been taken for a ride by Bismarck. He decided to take the Prussian at his word and presented the meeting of monarchs and ministers with a draft, worked out by Biegeleben, but based on suggestions thrown out by Bismarck, tying Prussia to the recovery of Lombardy in return for Austrian agreement to the Prussian annexation of Schleswig-Holstein. This Schönbrunn convention was never signed and Bismarck left it to his king to keep it in suspension. When asked by Francis Joseph whether he really wanted to annex the duchies, William replied with some hesitation that he had no real right to them. Bismarck clearly had no intention of being tied to a war with France for the recovery of Austrian territory, but nor was he simply engaged on a deception of the Austrians.

In the subsequent weeks he made considerable efforts to keep the idea of an alliance alive and to prevent Rechberg's fall. In long letters to Rechberg he played down the significance of the differences between their two countries over the renewal of the Zollverein treaty. He sought to put the onus on ministers and officials which he could only with difficulty control, particularly as an illness of Johanna had kept him away from Berlin. Complex legal disputes and tensions on the ground had arisen between the troops and commissioners of the German Confederation and Prussian troops in Holstein. Bismarck tried to justify the Prussian position and persuade Rechberg that Austria should not allow herself to be seen as the protector of the smaller states against Prussia, otherwise

> we would revert to the old track, on which Austria and Prussia had
> got stuck to their mutual detriment for more than a decade. You will
> recognize with me the difficulty of the task we have set ourselves, to

relegate years of differences and conflicts to the past; we will only succeed if we maintain for our alliance the fresh life of an active common policy . . . which would without doubt bring us to our desired goal, to the unity of Germany against internal and external enemies, to the restoration of the basis for a monarchical regime, to the emasculation of revolution.[15]

Such fine words buttered no parsnips and Rechberg in the end lost faith in his own policy of working with Prussia under Bismarck. Just before his resignation on 27 October he wrote to his emperor:

One is dealing with a man, who admits his political cynicism so openly, that he replies to the passage in my lettter that we need to make the maintenance of the Confederation and of the well-established rights of the German princes the basis of our policy . . . with the hair-raising phrase, that we should together stand on the practical basis of cabinet policy, and not allow ourselves to be disorientated by the fog rising from the dogmas of German nationalist sentimentalism. It is language worthy of a Cavour.[16]

The absence of Prussian concessions on the Zollverein was a factor in Rechberg's fall. Bismarck had no desire to see him go prematurely and argued for leaving in the Zollverein treaty a clause, which would have provided for another renegotiation with Austria when next it expired, after another twelve years at the end of 1877. He pleaded that such a clause would have little practical significance, but might just throw Rechberg a life line. The ministers of trade and finance, Itzenplitz and Bodelschwingh, were adamant that such a clause, raising false expectations, should not be included and Delbrück threatened resignation. It seems to have been this threat that finally determined the king to come down against the inclusion of the clause. As usual it is difficult to decide how seriously Bismarck took all this.

He had by this time gone on leave and was in Biarritz with the Orlovs, a kind of Indian summer in the company of Kathy. To Roon he wrote:

It is clear that Delbrück, his technical usefulness notwithstanding, belongs, along with other high officials, to a political colour, which likes to see the present ministry in difficulties, and where there are none seeks to create them. If Bodelschwingh and Itzenplitz are now carrying out Delbrück's policy against my judgment, let them make Delbrück their

> colleague for external affairs and not expect me to carry the can for
> mistakes in treating Austria now, before the peace treaty, in such a
> way, that Rechberg and the emperor will conclude that we are already
> otherwise engaged and that the break is only a question of time.[17]

He hinted that if there was any deviation from the course he wanted, by
other ministers or officials, he would not return from his holiday. The
recovery of something of the 'paradise lost' of the summer of 1862 made
him conscious of the price he was paying for the now all-absorbing exercise
of power and there were moments when he felt like giving it all up. It is
unlikely that he meant it, but it was neither the first nor last time that
Bismarck argued in this way – 'Do it my way or without me' – and it
became second nature to him. He was more than ever confident of the
superiority of his judgment and that he was indispensable. He clearly had
little expectation that his *pas de deux* with Austria would go on for very
much longer, whatever happened to Rechberg, but it was his strength that
he had no wish to force the pace of events.

On his way back from Biarritz Bismarck had another interview with
the French emperor. If it came to renewed tensions between Vienna and
Berlin, the attitude of Paris would be crucial. Even during the festivities
surrounding the Schönbrunn meeting in August Bismarck had had a long
tête-à-tête with Gramont, then French ambassador in Vienna, holding out
all sorts of enticing propects for Napoleon, should Prussia's current alliance
with Austria fall apart. To keep such possibilities open and to make them
sound convincing was an established part of his technique. It was a game
that two could play and Napoleon did not commit himself either. The
course history now took, ending in the exclusion of Austria from Germany,
had catastrophic consequences in the twentieth century and makes the
alternatives that seemed to beckon at Schönbrunn look attractive. Bismarck
had more of a hand in making it go the other way than anybody, but he
would have been the last to claim that it was simply his handiwork.

Rechberg's successor as Austrian foreign minister was Count Mensdorff-
Pouilly. He was less committed to the Prussian alliance than his predecessor,
but he was no more anxious than Bismarck to end it unnecessarily or
prematurely. But tensions in the relationship were becoming more evident
by the day. They chiefly revolved round the part the German Confederation
and the medium states would play in the future disposition of the duchies.
Bismarck had no wish to see them play any part and the Prussians began to

harass the federal commissioners and the federal troops in Holstein. At one point Bismarck directly threatened Saxony, where Beust was in charge, with intervention if Saxon troops were not withdrawn from Holstein. Any such open conflict would have torn the Confederation apart there and then and made no sense for the Austrians. They had to keep the Confederation alive and restore their relations with the lesser German governments and this would sooner or later drive them back to the Augustenburg cause. Mensdorff, and even more Schmerling and Biegeleben, whose influence in Vienna was stronger again, wanted to keep the joint ownership of the duchies by Prussia and Austria strictly provisional. For the moment there was compromise. The Frankfurt diet voted the end of the federal execution in Holstein and for the time being refrained from endorsing the Augustenburg duke as rightful ruler of Schleswig-Holstein. The Austrian commissioner did his best to protect the Augustenburg cause in the duchies, while Zedlitz, the Prussian commissioner, under Bismarck's instructions promoted all elements and organizations in favour of outright Prussian annexation or at least close association with Prussia. It was obvious to all and sundry that this situation carried the seeds of a future Austrian-Prussian conflict.

7

FRATRICIDAL WAR

For Bismarck the great question of the Austrian-Prussian relationship in Germany was inextricably interwoven with the domestic conflict he had fought since coming to power. The progress he had achieved towards a more united Germany by the victorious war against Denmark was splitting the liberal movement in Prussia and in Germany. Nationalists could not but applaud the fact that the whole of Schleswig-Holstein had finally been wrested from the Danes; liberals could not but abhor the way the two German great powers had ridden roughshod over the wishes of most of the inhabitants of the duchies. For the sake of German defence and security the predominance of Prussia in such a strategically sensitive area was inescapable, but no liberal would happily hand over the Schleswig-Holsteiners to the repressive, reactionary Bismarck regime. These dilemmas were particularly painful for the liberal movement in Prussia itself, but the point had not yet been reached where liberals would relent sufficiently in their opposition to Bismarck to make a deal on his terms possible. However, the domestic situation now offered the prime minister better opportunity than ever of provoking, dividing and generally tormenting his opponents. A further element in the growing divisions among the liberal opposition was the successful renegotiation of the Zollverein by the Bismarck government. There were not a few liberals for whom material considerations were now more important than ideological ones. After a year of being closed down, the Prussian chamber of deputies reconvened in January 1865. The Bismarck government was still 'collecting money where it could find it' without parliamentary sanction and was doing so successfully, in the absence of a tax boycott, which the liberal opposition did not have the strength to mount. It was also continuing its brisk campaign of suppression, harassment and chicanery against officials, many of them deputies, judges and mayors, and against the press. The immunities of the deputies were constantly under threat. Even government contracts were awarded on political grounds.

An incident that caused particular bitterness occurred after the renewed closure of the Landtag in June 1865. The city of Cologne refused to commemorate the fiftieth anniversary of the Rhineland's adhesion to Prussia and instead decided on a meeting to honour the returning opposition deputies. This was repeatedly blocked by the police. Whenever Bismarck was personally involved he took the view that all means were justifiable to make those holding official positions toe the line. It was he who proposed in the crown council of 19 June 1865 that Twesten and another liberal deputy, Frentzel, be prosecuted for having accused the justice minister Count Lippe, one of the most reactionary of Bismarck's colleagues, of having misused the justice system for political purposes. The facts completely justified this accusation. The prosecution of Twesten and Frentzel, like the case of the prohibited Cologne festivities, continued to reverberate and cause great bitterness in the 1866 session of the Landtag. Whenever Bismarck himself spoke in the lower chamber his tone was calculated to exacerbate the conflict. It was a measure of the prevailing personal bitterness that the prime minister saw fit to issue a challenge to a duel to Virchow arising out of a debate on 2 June 1865. Bismarck had homed in, with all his ironical acidity, on the refusal of the chamber to vote the funds for the establishment of a naval base at Kiel and the building of two frigates. He recalled how, amidst the ruin of German hopes after the collapse of the revolution in 1849, the German fleet had been auctioned off: 'This German fleet came to grief, because in the regions of Germany, in the higher governing circles, as well as lower down, party passion was more potent than a sense of solidarity.'[1] Virchow then accused him of untruthfulness for ignoring the tribute which the chamber had paid to the Prussian fleet in the recent war. It did not come to a duel, but the incident illustrated how hopelessly entrenched both sides in the constitutional conflict had become.

Bismarck had by no means given up the strategic concept that he had advocated before coming to power and had tried to put into operation since. He still wanted to solve the problem of ensuring Prussia's survival as a great power by enlisting the dynamic of German nationalism and to do so by concentrating on the goals that were common to the German national movement and to Prussian great-power ambitions. But for him it was the German national movement that was to be instrumentalized not the Prussian state. Strengthened by its success in the Danish war, the Bismarck government was prepared to make some conciliatory gestures and even in the bitter debate that had produced the challenge to Virchow the prime minister had said: 'If we could explain to you the likely course of our policy in the duchies with the same clarity as I can to HM the King, then, I believe, the vehemence of your opposition to what we are doing would be considerably reduced.' At the beginning of the session the interior minister Eulenburg, trying to be conciliatory, had urged the chamber to assert its budgetary rights in an area other than the military, for in anything touching his power of command the king remained adamant.

Bismarck still could not risk trying to soften the stance of his master. After the peace with Denmark William had conferred the Order of the Black Eagle on his prime minister and, what was more, embraced him warmly, as he told Johanna, but Bismarck knew that the favour of princes was fickle. There were still those around the king who tried to persuade him that the only way out of the debilitating struggle with parliament was to abolish it. Edwin von Manteuffel was the most able of them and closest to the king; he remained for Bismarck a dangerous rival. The prime minister's indispensability rested precisely in the fact that there was a parliament and only he knew how to confront it. The confrontational manner of his parliamentary performances was intended to make its mark on to those behind him as much as on those in front of him. Bismarck and even Roon would have liked more flexibility on the length of military service and the size of the army, but the law which the latter introduced in April merely served to harden the conflict with the liberal opposition. Roon was often more exposed to the raw hostility of the liberal deputies than Bismarck himself and had moments of discouragement. Another factor making for caution was the financial situation. In spite of lacking parliamentary sanction the government had built up a war chest, but it still needed more funds and more time to raise them. In July 1865 an agreement was negotiated through Bismarck's banker Bleichröder for the sale of the government's rights in the Cologne–Minden railway. This sale made considerable further sums available in the next few months.

Bismarck was also pursuing tactics similar to those that had induced him to talk to Lassalle. He was trying to outflank the liberal entrepreneurs, who were increasingly important in the liberal movement, by showing the government's sympathy for their employees and for the poor and vulnerable in general. He encouraged the king to receive a deputation of unemployed Silesian weavers. When attacked for this by a liberal textile employer in the chamber, he hit back in his usual aggressive style. Why should he prevent poor weavers from having access to the king? The kings of Prussia had never just been the kings of the rich: as Frederick the Great had said when crown prince, 'je serai un vrai roi des gueux' (I will be a true king of the beggars). Bismarck was collecting around him a number of men who were helping him with domestic affairs and manipulating the press on his behalf. Hermann Wagener was advising him on social policy and the ex-1848 revolutionary Lothar Bucher had just joined his staff and was to remain one of his most intimate confidants. In his English exile Bucher had become disillusioned with parliamentarism and the fact that he had been in communication with Lassalle until the latter's death in November 1864 did not deter Bismarck from employing him. On Bucher's advice an offer of employment to Karl Marx was considered. If conservative solidarity came to an end and there was war with Austria, Bismarck would have to seek allies where he could find them. One can sense his growing confidence and feeling of exhilaration that he, and only he, could find the narrow path forward.

*

The situation on the ground in Schleswig-Holstein was still critical and Bismarck had no compunction in exacerbating it. Sometimes he was on the offensive, sometimes he played the injured party. The propaganda techniques that became familiar in the twentieth century, portraying yourself as the victim of those you are about to attack, were used by Bismarck with a subtlety that Hitler and Goebbels could not match. Bismarck was a master of cabinet diplomacy, but he knew that it was being played out in front of an increasingly large and influential public audience. His efforts to strengthen the pro-Prussian forces in the duchies had only limited success, for it was mainly the nobility that was in favour of close association with Prussia. The Austrian chargé Chotek reported him as saying, with the levity characteristic of him, 'as for the recalcitrance of the inhabitants, our two governments have always been used to oppositional war cries . . . it doesn't amount to more than that.'[2] Bismarck took the line that the dislike of Schleswig-Holsteiners for Prussia was selfish, due to the refusal to pay higher taxes or do military service, but that wider German opinion was aware that a Prussian take-over was in the German national interest. He fended off the French pressure for a plebiscite in the Danish-speaking areas of Schleswig by emphasizing how difficult it would be to ascertain the true wishes of the inhabitants. But Bismarck knew that sooner or later he would have to show more of his hand to the Austrians and he did so in the so-called February conditions. By not demanding full annexation, Bismarck presented them to the Austrians as a concession, but they amounted to a virtual control of the duchies by Prussia. The military and naval forces of Schleswig-Holstein would be fully integrated with those of Prussia, come under Prussian command and take an oath to the king of Prussia. The duchies would be economically integrated with Prussia and become part of the Zollverein. A canal to be built between North Sea and Baltic, as well as certain fortified areas, would become Prussian territory.

Austria could not agree to these conditions without incurring a virtually fatal humiliation of her position as a German power, but the Vienna cabinet, beset as it was with difficulties all round, still could not bring itself to break with Prussia. It did, however, encourage the medium states to put forward a proposal at Frankfurt asking the two powers exercising the condominium over the duchies to hand over the administration of Holstein to the Augustenburg duke. This proposal was passed by the Frankfurt diet by nine votes to six on 6 April. Austria, along with Bavaria, Saxony, Württemberg, Baden, Hesse-Darmstadt and other lesser states, was among the majority; Prussia, Hanover, Electoral Hesse and Mecklenburg, as well as a few minor states, among the minority. Austria accepted the decision provided Prussia did so as well, but Berlin refused point blank. On the day before, Roon had announced in the Landtag the building of a Prussian naval base at Kiel and the Austrians had protested. Bismarck told Karolyi sharply that 'Prussia would not withdraw; only a lost campaign, a victorious Austrian army of 200,000 entering Berlin would deter us from this decision . . .'[3] An open breach had again come closer.

On 29 May the king called a crown council to discuss the deteriorating relationship with Austria. Without consulting his prime minister he invited the advocates of rival policies, Manteuffel and Goltz. The crown prince was also present. The king himself was no longer reluctant about annexation, for the crown lawyers had given their opinion that the Augustenburg duke had no rightful claim to the duchies and that their legitimate owner had in fact been King Christian, who had now been forced to cede them to Prussia and Austria. Even though this opinion undermined, *ex post facto*, the juridical basis of the war against Denmark, it put the king's conscience at rest. Along with the king, most of those present at the crown council were in favour of annexation, even it meant war with Austria. Bismarck had to tread warily if he was not be outflanked with the king by hardliners like Manteuffel. He made it clear that a war with Austria might eventually be unavoidable, but he was not prepared to advise it immediately, even though he gave a favourable account of the international situation. Anything short of annexation, or involving heavy compensation, including monetary indemnities, to Austria, Augustenburg and others, might be seen by public opinion as a Prussian retreat, but annexation now might mean war and it might be better to allow the situation to develop. Bismarck repudiated the crown prince's argument that a war with Austria was a civil war. Since Frederick William wanted a close association of the medium and smaller German states with Prussia, such an outcome could only be secured by the incorporation of Schleswig-Holstein into Prussia and not by the creation of another medium-sized state under its own ruler. Bismarck was therefore already looking forward to the next stage, the big solution of the German problem, without wishing to force the immediate issue. Moltke expressed confidence about the military outcome of a war with Austria, but thought it would help if the Habsburg empire was simultaneously forced to fight in Italy. Bismarck pointed out that the benevolent neutrality of France was essential and that Austria would have no compunction about seeking a French alliance.[4]

For the moment the crown council adopted the wait-and-see policy that Bismarck had recommended. The campaign of harassment against the Austrian commissioner in the duchies, Halbhuber, and against the Augustenburger and his supporters continued, as did the confrontation between the Bismarck government and the liberals in the Prussian chamber. Even when the resignation of Schmerling at the end of June 1865 indicated that the anti-Prussian party was losing ground in Vienna Bismarck pressed on relentlessly, risking war without wishing to bring it about. This manouevring on the edge of hostilities went on even when the leading Prussian actors, the king, his prime minister and their entourage, had moved to Austrian territory. William stuck to his routine of taking the waters at Carlsbad and Gastein. The Austrians showed some flexibility regarding the Prussian military requirements in the duchies, but Bismarck continued to demand rigorous action against the Augustenburger and his supporters. Privately he expressed a good deal of pessimism if what was compatible with Prussian honour could be secured without war. He caused soundings to be made with the Italian government about their attitude in case of war, hinting that the Italians, if they did not move swiftly, might find that such a war was over before they could realize their aims. Thus the situation which actually came about a year later was foreshadowed, but Bismarck probably thought that the Austrian political and economic situation was sufficiently precarious to make his hard line profitable and that it was unlikely that his bluff would be called.

And so it turned out by the time the Prussian party had moved first to Salzburg and then to Gastein in late July 1865. A war with Prussia, which might detonate another revolution and expose the Habsburg empire simultaneously on the many fronts, where it was challenged, was too dangerous for the Austrians. To pay the price for an accommodation with the fundamentally conservative Bismarck regime seemed preferable. Its replacement by a more liberal New Era type of regime would be much worse and this might be the consequence if the Augustenburg cause prevailed in the duchies. Francis Joseph was at this time much influenced by Count Moritz Esterhazy, an ultramontane Catholic, who still believed in the feudal-aristocratic order. The negotiations with Bismarck were largely conducted by Count Blome, the Austrian envoy in Munich, who came from the Holstein aristocracy and whose family had often been in the service of the Danish crown. His outlook was similar to Esterhazy's and he had little time for the liberal Augustenburg duke. All these circumstances were well known to Bismarck and he played upon them with his usual skill, using charm, cajolery and threats as only he knew how. Even as he was negotiating with the Austrians he was still sounding out the French and Italian attitudes. With the Austrians he reverted to a proposal that he had floated before, namely a division of the duchies, Holstein becoming an Austrian, Schleswig a Prussian responsibility, but he left it to Blome to make the running on this. Once this had been accepted as a basis for an agreement, the Austrians were concerned that this would undermine their previous support for the principle of the indivisibility of the duchies. Coming on top of dropping their support for Augustenburg it would virtually destroy what was left of their standing with German public opinion, as well as with the lesser German governments. In this respect the Austrians had far more to lose from an agreement to divide the duchies than Prussia under the Bismarck regime. Vienna therefore suggested that there should not be a definitive division of sovereignty, but only a provisional division of administration. Bismarck was not reluctant to go along with this, because he knew that it would give him unlimited ammunition to exacerbate the relationship with Austria again to any extent it suited him.

This then became the basis of the Gastein convention, signed by Francis Joseph and King William at Salzburg on 20 August 1865. Beyond the division of the duchies the convention still gave Prussia considerable rights even in Holstein. Kiel was to become the base for a German fleet, but immediately it was to come under Prussian administration. Prussia was given secure lines of communication through Holstein to Schleswig and the right to build a canal through Holstein from the North Sea to the Baltic. The duchy of Lauenburg was sold to the Prussian king for 2.5 million thaler. There was a certain amount of face-saving for Austria, but it was apparent that Vienna only maintained a toehold in North Germany, while the Prussian gains were much more solid. That it was another triumph for Bismarck was made evident by the fact less than a month later his king raised him to the dignity of a count. Otto and Johanna affected to think little of this elevation, but Otto knew only too well how vital the king's favour was to him. In retrospect it looked as if the Prussian prime minister was on a continuous upward curve of success, brought about by his own almost superhuman foresight and dexterity and this was certainly the picture Bismarck himself drew for posterity. It was a useful by-product for him that the Gastein settlement facilitated the removal from Berlin of his rival Manteuffel, who became governor of Schleswig. But the Gastein convention caused furious resentment throughout Germany, more damaging for the moment for Austria than for Prussia, but any setback would quickly have produced Bismarck's fall. He did not for a moment delude himself that a permanent settlement with Austria had been achieved. On all the many fronts on which he had to fight he continued to move with the utmost circumspection while not giving an inch on the positions he considered vital, namely at least the *de facto*, if possible the *de jure*, incorporation of the duchies into Prussia.

Not the least among the many risks was the continued uncertainty about the French attitude. The Gastein convention was not well received in Paris, nor for that matter in London. It rode roughshod over German aspirations to self-determination, with which there was much sympathy in both capitals. In France there was also the fear that a Prussian-Austrian understanding was detrimental to the French semi-hegemonial position in Europe. A circular from the French foreign minister Drouyn de l'Huys to his diplomats was overtly critical of the Gastein convention as an affront to national self-determination and therefore took exactly the same line as the German national movement. In a despatch to Goltz on 1 September Bismarck pointed out that Napoleon was overestimating the importance of the 'so-called national movement', which had its location in the parliamentary and media circles of Prussia and the lesser states. Even if as a result the representatives of these states at Frankfurt voted against Prussia, this signified little. The governments of the lesser states would not allow themselves to be driven into actual opposition to Prussia and even if they did, they were so disunited and their military capability so low as to constitute neither a substantial support nor a serious danger for Prussia. 'The real essence of successful and really practical national aspirations in Germany was a strong Prussia and the pursuance and development of an independent Prussian policy,' he declared to Goltz, no doubt for transmission to the government to which he was accredited.[5] It was also meant for the ambassador himself, of whom Bismarck remained intensely suspicious and whose despatches home he still regarded as arguments directed towards the king for an alternative policy, rather than as objective reports.

Directives to the press, in so far as it was amenable to the influence of his government, had now become an important aspect of Bismarck's political methods. Following Gastein he laid it down that there should no triumphalism with regard to Austria. German public opinion should be reminded that Britain and France could hardly be regarded as guardians of the German national interest and that their attacks on Gastein as an offence to German self-determination were thoroughly false. The party that attracted this foreign patronage, namely the German national-liberals, thereby revealed themselves as anti-German. After dictating this directive to Keudell at high speed, he said to his secretary:

As long as the Augustenburger remains in Kiel we have no certainty of being able to get along with the Austrian administration; Edwin [Manteuffel] thinks in three months we will see where Vienna stands. If Mensdorff reverts to a Würzburg [the alliance of the lesser German states] policy we will rub some black-red-gold [colours of the 1848 revolution] under his nose. The Schleswig-Holstein and the great German question are so closely linked that, if there is a break, we will have to solve both together. A German parliament would confine the particularist interests of the medium and small states to their proper limit.

After a short pause he added: 'and if there was a great leader among the medium states, the giant German national movement would squash him and his master.'[6] It was a revealing insight into the way Bismarck's mind was moving.

It remained vital to stay on friendly terms with the French emperor. At the beginning of October Bismarck went once more to Biarritz, where the French court was on holiday. This time the Prussian prime minister was accompanied by his family, but it had also been arranged that he would again meet up with the Orlovs. On arrival Bismarck was unpleasantly surprised by the news that Kathy had cancelled her visit a week earlier, allegedly because rumours of an outbreak of typhoid had caused her to go on holiday in England rather than Biarritz. Perhaps she had no taste for encountering Bismarck *en famille*. Before leaving Biarritz her uncle, as Bismarck always called himself, wrote to her saying how desolate the place was without her, how wet and stormy it was and that he would never go there again. He never saw her again before her early death ten years later, though there was some further correspondence. He saw Napoleon twice at Biarritz and once more at St Cloud on his way home. Neither side gave away anything, but Bismarck may well have guessed that Napoleon now lacked the power of swift decision that might have enabled him to turn the smouldering rivalry between the two German powers to his advantage. But of all the risks which a war between Austria and Prussia would entail, the possibility of French intervention remained one of the greatest. However, there were plenty of others. The uncertain outcome of any war would force Bismarck to use all available means to strengthen his position. He would be driven to alliances which could turn a war between the two German powers into a revolution, the course of which he might not be able to control. The prospect of such a war was encouraging all the forces that saw their future in revolution and far-reaching change. Italy was a vital factor in weakening the Habsburg empire if it came to war, as the remarks of Moltke at the crown council of 29 May had indicated.

A despatch which Bismarck sent on 13 January 1866 to the Prussian ambassador in Italy, his old rival Usedom, again gives a good insight in how he assessed the situation at this point.[7] He stressed that he had always regarded the Gastein convention as provisional, rather than as a definitive solution. Austria had shown no sign of wishing to make it definitive by some compensatory deal over the duchies. It had on the contrary allowed the Augustenburg supporters to agitate in Holstein. The old anti-Prussian attitude in German affairs had once more prevailed in Vienna and the Austrians had not given up exploiting their links with the lesser German states against Prussia. He again stressed that Prussia had nothing to fear from a hostile intervention by other powers, not from Russia and above all not from France. If Austria encouraged the lesser German states to move against Prussia at Frankfurt and to interfere in the policy of the great powers then the present form of the German constitution might be called in question. 'We might have to revert to the principles which we invoked in opposing the Frankfurt meeting of princes in 1863 [the calling of an elected German parliament].' It proved difficult for Usedom to bring La Marmora, the Italian prime minister, on side, for the Gastein convention had naturally made the Italians feel that they were only being used as a pawn in the Austro-Prussian dialogue.

*

A point of decision was approaching that involved a greater gamble than anything Bismarck had faced hitherto. He did not flinch from it, but neither did he wish to hasten it. He knew that stormy weather and high seas had, as he often put, always favoured the expansion of Prussia and these were the conditions best suited to his own hold on power. In the early months of 1866 he was in a highly excitable state, his tendency towards psychosomatic pains and ills accentuated. His religious faith had always been a means of confirming him in his certainty that he knew best. When he was attacked for not acting as a Christian, it hit a sensitive nerve and he defended himself vigorously. To a fellow-Prussian landowner he wrote: 'As a statesman I am not sufficiently ruthless, I feel almost a coward, because it is not always easy, in the questions with which I have to deal, to gain the clarity which promotes trust in God.'[8] To Bismarck trust in God was a by-product of political clarity, not the other way round.

His guerrilla war with Austria, over their administration of Holstein and failure to curb the Augustenburg movement, came to a head when on 23 January a big demonstration took place at Altona, near Hamburg, calling for a summoning of the Schleswig-Holstein estates. Bismarck could now assume with greater conviction than ever the posture of the injured party. He told Werther, the Prussian ambassador in Vienna, to imagine what a painful impression it must make on the king when his ally in war, the emperor, was now in peace allowing 'revolutionary tendencies, inimical to every throne, to spread themselves under the sign of the Austrian double eagle.'[9] The ambassador was to ask the Austrian government for an unequivocal assurance that all agitation in Holstein hostile to Prussia would be suppressed, otherwise the common policy of both governments agreed at Gastein would be at an end. 'If Austria continues to provide a haven for the activities of the republican democracy . . . then the king will prefer an open breach to this kind of struggle.' Once more the Austrians were confronted with the choice of virtually surrendering their position in Germany or facing the all-out hostility of Prussia. It is obvious with hindsight that Vienna was fighting on too many fronts at once, in Germany against Prussia, in Italy against the new Italian kingdom backed by France, in the Balkans against Russia. But to give up any of these positions voluntarily was difficult and none was more deeply woven into the historic fabric of Habsburg rule than their German role.

Almost simultaneously with this exacerbation of the conflict with Austria another of the many fronts on which Bismarck had to fight was also reopened, with the reassembly of the Prussian Landtag. When it suited him Bismarck always expressed contempt for the liberal movement and their 'caterwauling' in the press and on platforms, but he knew full well that in a conflict with Austria German nationalism would play a vital role. The German national movement was not synonymous with the liberal opposition in the Prussian Landtag, which was itself increasingly divided, but nor were they entirely distinct. When the Nationalverein had met in Frankfurt in October 1865 to pass a strong resolution against the Gastein convention, not many Prussian deputies had attended. Even so principled an opponent of Bismarck as Theodor Mommsen had publicly distanced himself from the Frankfurt proceedings. In words reminiscent of Bismarck himself he wrote of the 'sovereignty swindle' of the German princes and declared that there was now a stark choice between subordination to a German great power, namely Prussia, and the disappearance of the German nation.[10] Bismarck had pressured the Austrian government to agree to strong measures against the city of Frankfurt, always a liberal stronghold, for allowing the meeting of the Nationalverein. When the Austrians hung back, it was one of the many small steps in the deterioration of relations between Vienna and Berlin in the aftermath of Gastein. In these pinpricks Bismarck always took the initiative. The campaign against Frankfurt sheds a particularly lurid light on the methods he was prepared to use.

All the while, the conflict between the Bismarck government and its domestic liberal opposition was raging as fiercely as ever. Feelings were inflamed by the case of the suppressed Cologne demonstration in the previous year and the continuing attack on the immunities of the deputies. The sale of the government's stake in the Cologne–Minden railway without parliamentary sanction was branded as illegal by a parliamentary commission headed by Lasker. The purchase of Lauenburg by Prussia and the establishment of a personal union between that duchy and Prussia, part of the Gastein convention, came under attack. Virchow moved that the union of Lauenburg with Prussia was invalid in law, because the duchy was a foreign realm. Bismarck called this a linguistic quibble and in his best polemical form quoted Schlegel's famous German Shakespeare translation, in this case *Henry VI, part III*, and its use of the words realm and dukedom as antithetical terms. Later he said in reply to Twesten that he was not using foreign policy only to further his fight against his domestic opponents: 'Foreign affairs are to me an end in themselves and stand higher than the rest. You, gentlemen, should think the same, and if you should give some ground domestically, you could regain it quickly under a liberal ministry, which might come about [laughter].'[11] It was a kind of hidden olive branch, more carefully phrased than that in his 'iron and blood' speech at the outset of his ministry, but also a clue to how Bismarck saw the way ahead. For the moment the differences between the government and the majority in the lower house remained so irreconcilable that there was nothing for it but to close and adjourn the Landtag once more. It was the last time in the history of Prussia, and even of Germany, that an array of distinguished speakers, men like the famous constitutional lawyer Rudolf von Gneist, could proclaim liberal principles with equal boldness and confidence.

On the day following the closure, on 28 February 1866, there was another crucial meeting of the crown council. Bismarck had been in daily contact with the king and this was the front on which his fight was always most difficult, uncertain and yet crucial. The crown prince reported in his diary that Bismarck had faced his father with three alternatives: either a change to a liberal ministry; or a *coup d'état* and suspension of the constitution; or war. His father was against the first two alternatives, but had not yet reached a decision on the third. It would be entirely in character with Bismarck's methods that he should frighten the king in this way and keep him dependent on his advice. He had to convince the king that a war with Austria might become necessary and keep him convinced. He was, he said, like a clockmaker who had to rewind the clock every morning. A fratricidal war with Austria would be intensely repugnant to the king and to his legitimist, anti-revolutionary convictions, but any repeat of the humiliation of Olmütz would be equally unbearable. At home it was out of the question for William to give ground to the liberal opposition, if only they could be brought to heel without a *coup d'état*.

Bismarck by now knew his royal master intimately and usually succeeded in making him feel that he was retaining the power of ultimate decision, when in fact he was doing what Bismarck wanted him to do. The guerrilla warfare with the Austrian administration in Holstein, in which Bismarck had so effectively played the injured party, was not only designed to make a breach with Vienna possible at any moment, it also had the purpose of convincing the king that he really was the injured party. William's opening remarks at the crown council showed that Bismarck had succeeded well in rousing the king against Austria. The prime minister then launched into a long historical review of relations with Austria. He said that 'Prussia was the only viable political creation that had emerged from the ruins of the old German empire, and this was the basis of her destiny to be at the head of Germany.' Austria had always fought against this well-founded Prussian aspiration out of jealousy, while herself incapable of providing the lead in Germany. He gave a rather selective review of relations with Austria since the Napoleonic period. He claimed, rather surprisingly, that 1848 would have given Prussia the chance to lead Germany if she had resorted to the sword. Austria was not willing to concede to Prussia the position in the duchies that was her due and that was demanded by public opinion. Retreat would mean humiliation. Austria would, if it came to war, not be deterred from concluding alliances especially with France. This was said to impress upon his audience, especially the king, the importance of Prussia's good relations with Napoleon, into which Bismarck had put so much effort. He therefore regarded the current constellation as favourable for Prussia.[12]

An immediate consequence of the crown council meeting was to develop the now more hopeful possibility of an alliance with Italy. Moltke again pointed out that an Italian campaign for the conquest of Venetia would be an important pre-condition for Prussian success in a possible war with Austria. Shortly after the council it was in fact decided to send Moltke on a special mission to Florence, though this proved in the end unnecessary, because the Italians sent a negotiator, General Govone, to Berlin. When Eulenburg, the interior minister, said at the crown council that a war with Austria might solve the Prussian domestic conflict, Bismarck declared that this could not be a motive for war, though it might be a by-product.

All those present were thus prepared to contemplate a war with Austria in the near future, though no decision was taken to bring it about. The only person who spoke against war was the crown prince. Manteuffel was more bellicose than Bismarck, perhaps to impress the king. The prime minister's other rival, Goltz, now saw little chance of his policy of a closer association with the German national movement, possibly by allowing the Augustenburger to prevail, being adopted by the king. At least this was the report of Benedetti, the Corsican who was French ambassador in Berlin and whom Bismarck frequently made the repository of confidences, particularly when he wanted to see these spread around other European capitals. The Prussian king was sensitive about dealing with what he regarded as revolutionary governments like the Italian, squeamish about undermining his fellow German princes, who were legitimate even if their sovereignty looked anachronistic, but he had gone a long way with Bismarck. He could no longer retreat easily from the policies, however revolutionary their implications, into which his prime minister had led him. But it continued to strain Bismarck's nerves to breaking point that so many in the inner circle of the Prussian establishment opposed his policies and were plotting his downfall. Not only Goltz, but his two predecessors in the foreign ministry, Schleinitz, now minister of the royal house and close to the queen, and Bernstorff, the ambassador in London, were opponents.

The crown prince was again to the fore among those who attempted to turn the course of events in a different direction from what he had called 'Otto Annexandrovitch's piratical policy'. Frederick William lent a hand to efforts at mediation by the British foreign secretary, Lord Clarendon, by his mother-in-law, Queen Victoria and by the liberal duke of Saxe-Coburg-Gotha. This 'Coburg intrigue', encouraged by Mensdorff, was the kind of dynastic interference that infuriated Bismarck and he stifled it before it could get off the ground. He inspired articles in the *Kreuzzeitung* attacking the duke of Coburg, which evidently displeased the king. Relations between sovereign and his nominal subject became distinctly strained. With scarcely disguised allusion to the queen and the crown prince Bismarck wrote to his master that he could not expect him to be superhuman and remain silent when his difficult, all-consuming duties were made even more difficult by those 'for whom the success of Prussian policy, the repute of your majesty and the royal house ought to rank above all else'.[13] He had no intention of allowing backstairs royal influences to interfere with what was now his major preoccupation, namely to give Prussia the best possible starting point if it should come to war with Austria. He had the advantage that Austrian mobilization procedures were much slower than those of Prussia. Cautious moves by the Austrians to protect their Bohemian frontier could be made to seem offensive and gave Bismarck more than ever the chance to make Prussia look the injured party.

In this *mise-en-scène*, as he described it to Manteuffel,[14] he now moved the German question centre-stage. It was no longer just a matter of the future of the duchies, he argued, but of the future of Germany's federal constitution, a problem the solution of which had been interrupted by the Danish question. Barely a week after the crown council he instructed his envoy in Munich to take this line with von der Pfordten, now the Bavarian prime minister, who was seriously aggrieved by the Austrian treatment of the medium states.[15] The envoy was to discuss with the Bavarian minister the suggestion, made before at the time of the Congress of Princes in 1863, that there should be a German parliament 'composed on a conservative basis'. The proposal of an elected German parliament was now used again by Bismarck as a principal weapon in his fight to gain an advantage over Austria in the eyes of the German national movement. Soon he was suggesting to the Bavarians that they should join him in proposing at Frankfurt the summoning of a parliament based on universal suffrage, which he argued was 'a better guarantee of conservative attitudes than an artificial electoral law designed to achieve ready-made majorities'. Von der Pfordten was not in principle opposed to universal suffrage, but he was not prepared to takes sides in the growing conflict between Vienna and Berlin by associating himself publicly with Bismarck's ideas. Bismarck was also trying to appeal to the Bavarians with the suggestion that when Prussia became the undisputed master in North Germany, they might become the leading power in South Germany.

The proposal for a parliament elected on universal suffrage was made public on 9 April. Nothing was initially said about the functions of the parliament and further details were only reluctantly given by the Prussian government. Coming from Bismarck these proposals almost everywhere provoked derision. A Berlin comic journal, the *Kladderadatsch*, said it might have to cease publication, because it could think of no better joke. In Dresden Beust told the Austrian envoy that such a proposal from the hand of Count Bismarck had only provoked laughter, but he added 'One can't guarantee that given the Germanizing disposition of many of the Saxon people this mood of ridicule might not soon turn more serious.'[16] It was due to von der Pfordten's mediation that the Frankfurt diet did not turn down the detailed Prussian proposals outright, but referred them to a committee. Bismarck cannot have been surprised by the negative reception, but his real purpose was to have as many irons in the fire as possible in his struggle with Austria and to prepare alternative as well as fall-back strategies. A war against Austria, as he had kept pointing out within the Prussian decision-making circle, had to be presented to the wider public not merely as a fight by Prussia for Schleswig-Holstein, but as something much bigger, the solution of the German question.

The jockeying for position went on for three months, from March to June 1866. It tested Bismarck's nervous strength to its limits and he was tortured by rheumatic pains in his injured leg. On occasion Karolyi found him lying on a sofa like a wounded boar. Nothing took it out of him as much as the battle for the king's heart and mind, which he could never regard as finally won. In the exchanges between Berlin and Vienna, in which accusations and counter-accusations about troop movements were flung to and fro, Bismarck was pressing ahead, but more than once the king held him back. War was increasingly the most likely and for him the best outcome; hesitation and divided counsel could easily bring his carefully constructed edifice tumbling down. Even in these weeks of almost unbearable tension Bismarck rarely spoke of politics when in the evening he left his study and joined his family. Keudell thinks that this release from political discussion in his domestic circle helped him to recover his equanimity.

He could not keep the dangers that beset him from his wife after an assassination attempt on him on 7 May. He was walking back from the royal palace in Unter den Linden to his office in the Wilhelmstrasse when a student fired three shots at him. He was Ferdinand Cohen-Blind, stepson of the 1848 revolutionary Karl Blind, who was living in exile in London. Bismarck, strong and physically courageous as he was, seized the assassin's right arm, but he managed to fire two more shots with his left hand, before the prime minister overpowered and arrested him with the help of a passer-by. The bullets had caused only slight bruising to Bismarck's ribs and Cohen-Blind killed himself in prison the following day. When the news of the attempt spread a crowd gathered outside Bismarck's official residence to cheer him and he addressed them briefly. In general Bismarck was still so unpopular throughout Germany that there was if anything more sympathy for the assassin's motives than for his intended victim. Bismarck himself felt an increasing sense of divine justification. In his devotional book he underlined 'ye must be reviled for my name's sake' and kept Blind's pistol by his bedside. He noticed the absence of Goltz from the official congratulations on his escape and later said that Goltz had never been good at hypocrisy. He even made use of the attempt in his diplomacy. He had been worried by the alarm caused in Russian official circles by his suggestion of an elected German parliament. He now instructed his envoy in St Petersburg to tell Alexander II that the attempted murder by a Württemberg republican showed that he was seen by South German revolutionaries as their inveterate enemy and that they regarded his German reform proposals as an obstacle to their plans.

By coincidence, on the day of the assassination attempt, an article by Ludwig von Gerlach appeared in the *Kreuzzeitung*, attacking him on grounds of political morality. Ludwig was the surviving of the two brothers, who had once been so close to him and advanced his career. Gerlach argued once more the strictly legitimist conservative position, that the same principles laid down by divine authority must govern the conduct of public policy, diplomacy and war as governed the conduct of individuals and that there could be no *raison d'état* divorced from morality. Gerlach sent Bismarck the article with congratulations on his escape, but adjuring him solemnly to preserve Prussia from an unjust war. Benedetti, the French ambassador, suspected a court intrigue against the prime minister behind the article. Gerlach made a last attempt to restore friendly relations with his former protégé, but in vain. Gerlach described Bismarck as 'abrupt, pale, passionately excited, incapable of a friendly word . . . there was something restless and desperate about him. He spoke of God, of prayer, as if to say that he would make his case with God, with God alone, but not with friends or party colleagues'.[17] The gulf that was dividing Bismarckian *Realpolitik* from the liberals and their principles was now also estranging him from his former conservative friends.

The one concrete advantage that emerged from Bismarck's tireless manoeuvres during this period of latent hostilities with Austria was a treaty with Italy. It resulted from the negotiations with General Govone and was signed on 8 April, the day before the Prussian reform proposals were made public in Frankfurt. It was a secret defensive–offensive alliance. Italy was obliged to declare war on Austria if Prussia should be forced to resort to arms as a result of the failure of the reform proposals about to be tabled. Italy would obtain the cession of Venetia from such a war. Napoleon had encouraged the Italians to conclude the treaty in his efforts to set the two German powers at each other's throats. It was valid only for three months and therefore effectively established a time limit by which Prussia had to go to war if she was to secure the Italian alliance. The secret of the treaty, which Bismarck had made no great effort to keep, was soon breached and brought the situation appreciably nearer to war.

Linked with the Italian negotiation Bismarck took even more revolutionary steps to make life difficult for the Austrians. Usedom, who had good contacts in Hungarian emigré circles in Italy, suggested that these should be given encouragement and Bismarck, although advising caution, eventually agreed. He had already himself made contact with a man who had been a colonel in the Hungarian revolutionary army of 1848–9, Kiss de Nemeskér, who had links with French official circles. The Prussian government joined with the Italian government in giving financial support to the establishment of a Hungarian legion. These facts leaked out as early as July 1866, after the Austrian defeat, and caused Bismarck considerable embarrassment. He tried to attribute the whole affair to Usedom, but even at the time few believed this. The episode has always lent credibility to the argument that Bismarck was a man with few scruples, that he had an utterly Machiavellian approach to politics and that to call him a white revolutionary is entirely appropriate. He probably thought that this particular undertaking would in practice have limited consequences and would be effective mainly as a threat.

This turned out to be the case with Hungary, but his assessment of the consequences of universal suffrage was much less accurate. He envisaged it mainly as a device to take the liberals in the rear and, with his proposals of 9 April for a German parliament, to put the Austrians on the spot. He saw the masses as still mainly consisting of a loyal peasantry. When Bernstorff reported to him from London that Clarendon had been horrified by the universal suffrage proposal, he wrote the marginal comment:

> In England only the higher classes are loyal to the monarchy and the constitution, because these embody *their* privileges, *their* rule over the country. The masses are brutal, ignorant, and their attachment to the crown is not of the kind it is in Prussia.[18]

He could not envisage that in the not too distant future the masses would be largely synonymous with the industrial proletariat. He regarded

industrial workers as a small group, who should be given some encouragement to assert themselves against oppressive and greedy entrepreneurs.
Occasionally he had given such encouragement or had allowed men like
Wagener, his advisers in this field, to do so. The rise of a large-scale trade
union movement had not yet entered his field of vision. The leaders of the
workers, such as Lassalle, he regarded as allies against the liberals, but of
limited utility and caught up in utopian fantasies.

Such an assessment was not wide of the mark when it came to Lassalle's
successor as president of the General German Workers' Association,
J.B. von Schweitzer. There seemed no harm in releasing him from prison,
into which the government's repressive policy had put him, and supporting
his newspaper with a small subvention, when it was in fact taking the
Bismarckian line in the summer of 1866 and commending his proposal of
an elected German parliament. Another faction in the infant German labour
movement, in which August Bebel and Wilhelm Liebknecht were coming
to the fore, was anti-Prussian, *grossdeutsch* and up to this point had links
with the liberals. Bismarck was simply seeking allies where he could find
them and it was a measure of his awareness of the dangers and risks of his
situation that he left no stone unturned, even it was only a small pebble.
But to liberals everywhere a parliament elected on universal suffrage was,
coming from Bismarck, not only a joke in bad taste, but a signal that he
was a Bonapartist.

Napoleon was still much the biggest problem. German nationalist
historiography was subsequently anxious to prove that Bismarck never
made any offer of German territory in order to purchase French neutrality
in a Prussian war with Austria. Even though he later denied it, he held out
such bait from time to time. The Italian negotiator Govone reports him as
saying that he was much less German than Prussian and willing to cede the
region between Rhine and Moselle. But then, as so often, he took refuge
behind the king: 'If I could have him always on my side, if I could sleep with
him, as the queen does, it would work [si je pouvais coucher avec lui, comme
fait la Reine, cela marcherait]', hardly the language of a loyal subject.[19]
At times it looked as if Napoleon would demand the frontiers of 1814,
before the return of his uncle from Elba. On 30 April 1866 Bismarck
recommended to the Prussian cabinet that the state-owned mines in the
Saar should be sold to private investors, in case the region had to be ceded
to France. None of this proves that he was really willing to cede any German
territory to France, if he could help it. He guessed correctly that Napoleon

was unlikely to make binding demands prematurely. France was still seen as the prime potential disturber of the peace of Europe and Napoleon hesitated to lend colour to such views by aiming too obviously at territorial aggrandisement. When in May 1866 rumours surfaced that Austria was making offers to Paris, Bismarck pointed out that in a competition with Austria for French support, based on the bait of German territory, it would not be difficult for Prussia to unleash the full fury of German national feeling against Austria. However, what Austria was offering the French emperor at the expense of Prussia, he could secure more directly from Prussia without compromising his aims in Italy, which he would have to do with Austria. It was another of Bismarck's vague and veiled hints that he might offer Napoleon chunks of German territory on the Rhine if it became necessary.

But the uncertainties were so great that Bismarck left lines of compromise open, even as mobilization measures, with all their attendant expenses, made it progressively more risky for his own survival to pull back from the brink into an unsatisfactory compromise. An effort at mediation was made, with some encouragement from the Prussian prime minister, by the brothers Gablenz in late April and May 1866. Ludwig von der Gablenz was the Austrian commissioner in Holstein; his brother Anton, a Prussian officer and member of the Prussian Old Liberal party. They belonged to a family of imperial knights, whose members had seen service under a variety of German princes. Anton von der Gablenz went to and fro between Berlin and Vienna with plans that would have amounted to a division of Germany between north and south, as Bismarck himself had proposed from time to time. Schleswig-Holstein was to be ruled by a Hohenzollern prince, while retaining formal independence. For Bismarck the Gablenz mediation held open a fall-back position, at a time when the French attitude caused him much disquiet. It also helped to assuage the king's misgivings.

But it was becoming too late for compromise. Austria was mobilizing the German Confederation against Prussia and succeeding in pulling most of the lesser states along. Even in states as exposed to Prussian military power as Saxony and Hanover, Bismarck's threats and blandishments failed. In the case of Hanover he anticipated, and almost hoped, that the strongly reactionary blind King George would take his stand on his sovereignty and on his binding compact with the German Confederation. The refusal of the Hanoverian government to remain neutral made an excuse, even in the eyes of King William, for the outright annexation of the country after a Prussian victory, something of great strategic importance for Prussia. The inter-mediate position of Bavaria, which Bismarck had encouraged and which might have made it impossible for other South German states to abandon their neutrality, in the end crumbled and the country took up arms on the side of Austria.

War had become for Bismarck the most convenient solution, for all its high risks. But there was also a war party at Vienna. Since the summer of 1865 three counts had dominated the Austrian cabinet, Belcredi, the prime minister, Mensdorff, the foreign minister and Esterhazy, without portfolio. Mensdorff, the most influential, worked hardest for peace, but he was surrounded by others who felt that this was politically and militarily the best opportunity for the Habsburg empire to reassert itself. There was much anti-Prussian feeling, exacerbated by hatred of the Bismarck regime, to be exploited in the Habsburg dominions and in Germany. A Catholic, ultra-montane tide was running strongly, against Protestant Prussia and the new Italian kingdom that was threatening the papacy. Belcredi, Esterhazy, Blome, the man who had negotiated the Gastein convention with Bismarck, the emperor himself, were men of that persuasion. Even the constantly threatening bankruptcy suggested that a swift solution on the battlefield was necessary. There was still a widespread belief, shared on the Berlin stock exchange, that Austria was militarily stronger than Prussia.

For these reasons the Austrians did not make the most of the French initiative to call a European conference to settle the outstanding issues in Germany and Italy, which could have been very inconvenient for Bismarck. When the invitations went out on 24 May Prussia had little alternative but to accept, even though a successful conference could not but have resulted in limiting Prussian gains. Bismarck was spared this eventuality by the Austrians, who, while accepting the invitation, imposed conditions which amounted in fact to a refusal. The Austrians asked that all the participants should in advance declare that no territorial aggrandisement or increase of power would be sought by them at the conference. This would have reduced the room for negotiation to virtually nothing. But Vienna was already negotiating directly with Paris and Napoleon, anticipating an eventual Austrian military victory, was now ready to come at least partially off the fence. In a secret treaty signed on 12 June, just before the outbreak of hostilities, Austria agreed to cede Venetia to France. Napoleon envisaged that he would subsequently, under conditions, cede the province to Italy. In return France agreed to an increase of Austrian territory in Germany, provided this did not amount to a complete Austrian hegemony in Germany. The members of the Austrian ruling house that had been dispossessed in Italy would be compensated in Germany. There was a verbal understanding that this compensation might come from the Prussian Rhine provinces, which might be formed into a new independent state. If Austria had at an earlier stage made this choice of giving up her Italian possessions for the sake of maintaining her German position she would have been spared a two-front war.

Nevertheless it looked as if the Austrian politicians, divided and indecisive as they were, had been more successful in their preparations for the impending conflict than Bismarck. German public opinion was flowing more strongly for Austria than for the Prussian government. The domestic situation in Prussia remained so intractable that the Landtag was once more dissolved on 9 May. About this time Bernstorff wrote to Goltz of 'the mad Bismarck policy' and 'how can we get through such a life-and-death struggle without peace in our own country, against the overwhelming majority of our own people with an unwilling and mainly recalcitrant Landwehr and reserve?'[20] Bismarck had done a good deal to court the German national movement, but when the courtship was palpably unsuccessful he could still be contemptuous. When told of the negative response of Hanoverian liberals, in particular of the later important leader Bennigsen, to overtures made on his behalf, his characteristic reaction was 'one does not shoot with public opinion, but with powder and lead.'[21]

The Austrians now initiated moves, beginning on 1 June, at the Frankfurt diet which made war inevitable. They asked for the law of the Confederation to be restored with regard to Schleswig-Holstein, against the illegal pretensions of Prussia. They thus renounced the Gastein convention, in agreeing to which they had themselves gone against the consensus of the Confederation. On 9 June Prussian troops invaded Holstein to prevent the Austrians from summoning the Holstein estates, though as a *casus belli* this failed, for the Austrians withdrew. For once Manteuffel, as governor of Schleswig commander of the Prussian troops, had acted in a conciliatory manner, much to Bismarck's consternation. On 10 June Prussia put forward another reform proposal, which excluded Austria from the Confederation and also repeated the proposal of a parliament elected by universal suffrage. Austria then asked the diet to mobilize its forces in response to the Prussian incursion into Holstein. The diet agreed to this on 14 June and Prussia then declared the Confederation at an end. All the larger states, Bavaria,

Saxony, Württemberg, Hanover, Electoral Hesse, Hesse-Darmstadt and finally even Baden went with Austria. Only states virtually surrounded by Prussian territory, such as the two Mecklenburgs, Brunswick and Anhalt, went with Prussia.

*

Everything now depended on the outcome of the fighting. After the triumphant completion of German unity the man in the street attributed the national glory to a trinity of heroes, Moltke, Roon and Bismarck, and the two former seemed no less important than the latter. Bismarck had relied on the Prussian army's ability to mobilize quickly in comparison with the cumbersome and cash-starved Austrian forces and this had played an important part in his diplomatic manoeuvres. He was confident that this military machine would deliver the victory he needed, but paradoxically the near-perfection with which it performed its task, essential to his political purpose, made it that much more difficult to keep it under political control. Moltke was very different from Bismarck, unemotional, cerebral, self-sufficient, an intellectual in his approach to the art of warfare. Moltke's genius consisted in his appreciation of the impact of modern technology, railways and telegraph, on the conduct of operations. The planning and staff work that was his most original contribution to the development of warfare was designed to deliver on to the battlefield forces that could win an annihilating victory. Even in the nineteenth century wars could easily get out of control and the kind of fighting that Moltke envisaged might well have done so. Bismarck's gamble came off because the Austrian military defeat was so swift. At the decisive battle of Königgrätz, or Sadowa, in northern Bohemia (now Hradec Karlové in the Czech Republic), on 3 July 1866, Moltke's plan, to bring the three Prussian armies together on the battlefield, worked.

During the campaign in Bohemia Bismarck made the most of the military rank he then had, only that of a major, but he did so mainly to ensure his standing at a time when the major figures of the state, from the king downwards, were physically present on the battlefield. Anecdotes about Bismarck on the battlefield entered German folklore. There was the occasion at a crucial point in the battle when he offered Moltke a cigar to test his mood; or when his excellent pair of field glasses enabled him to spot the arrival of the crown prince's army, decisive to the outcome of the battle; or when he found no quarters prepared for him after the battle and, crossing a farmyard, fell into a dungpit. He found some sleep on a discarded carriage seat, until the duke of Mecklenburg took him into his room. Unlike his king, Bismarck did not love war for the sake of it and his shock at its horrors was genuine. When with the royal party he rode past some hideously disfigured corpses he said to Keudell: 'When I think that some time in the future Herbert [his eldest son] might fall like this, I feel ill.' Bismarck's presence on the battlefield in the company of the king had its uses. William's soldierly blood was up and he frequently rode into danger. The only person whose warnings he would listen to was his prime minister. 'No one would have dared to speak to him so harshly', he wrote to Johanna, 'he cannot forgive me that I deprived him of the pleasure of being hit. Only yesterday he said, pointing his finger at me "at the place where I had to ride away on all-highest orders".'[22] Bismarck truly was a servant who had become a master.

It was a mastery that had to be constantly reasserted, never more so than after Königgrätz, one of the decisive battles of modern history. Within two days of the battle Napoleon's offer of mediation reached the Prussian headquarters in Bohemia. So did the news that Austria had ceded Venetia to France, even though she had, ten days earlier, beaten the Italians at the battle of Custozza. It was ominous that France was helping Austria to disengage from her southern front to enable her to meet the Prussian threat. There was the hidden threat that France might demand compensations or attack from the west. Bismarck said to Keudell and his faithful amanuensis Abeken: 'In a few years Louis will regret taking sides against us; it may cost him dear.' Austria had to be brought to a permanent armistice and an agreement on peace conditions as rapidly as possible. In the days immediately following Königgrätz Bismarck was keeping up the pressure on Vienna by encouraging more resolute Italian action and by maintaining the measures to encourage revolution in Hungary.

His most difficult task was to restrain his king and the generals from ramming home their victory by marching on Vienna. To his wife he wrote five days after Königgrätz:

> We are in good shape in spite of Napoleon; if we are not too exorbitant in our demands and do not believe we have conquered the world, we will get a worthwhile peace. . . . But we are as quickly intoxicated as discouraged, and I have the thankless task of pouring water into the effervescent wine and to point out, that we do not live alone in Europe, but with three other powers that hate and envy us.[23]

The king would have liked to march into Vienna in revenge for Olmütz and the trial of wills Bismarck had over this with his master were among the most serious of their long relationship. In later life he said: 'My greatest difficulty was first to get the king into Bohemia and then to get him out again.'[24] When in response to this mood there was a military presentation on a march to Vienna, Bismarck became ironical:

> If the hostile army surrenders Vienna and withdraws into Hungary, we must follow them. Once we have crossed the Danube it will be advisable to concentrate on the right bank, because the Danube is such a mighty ditch that one can't march along it on horseback. Once we are across we lose our communications to the rear; then it will be best to march on Constantinople, found a new Byzantine empire, and leave Prussia to her fate.[25]

In his memoirs Bismarck gives a highly coloured account of his struggle against the hubris that victory had induced in the king and the generals. He describes himself being driven almost to the point of suicide and rescued only by his old enemy, the crown prince, who talked reason to his father. In the end Bismarck put his advice into a formal document and William added to his acceptance the comment 'the victor at the gates of Vienna has to swallow this sour apple.'[26] As far as the generals were concerned, Bismarck may have exaggerated their bellicosity. They were well aware that to continue the war against Austria, with a possible new front against France, was highly risky, especially as the Prussian army was weakened by cholera and shortages caused by long lines of communication. When Bismarck was writing his memoirs twenty-five years later, it rankled with him that the generals of that period, particularly Waldersee, the chief of staff in the 1880s, had been part of the Fronde that helped to bring about his fall. He wanted to show that his wisdom was always superior to everybody else's, to the military, who owed their high status to him, and to the Hohenzollerns, whom he had lifted into supreme glory.

When it came to the annexation of Hanover, Hesse and Nassau, Bismarck argued that if the rulers of these states were, because of legitimist scruples, left in control of truncated territories, they would prove a focus for discontent in areas of strategic importance to Prussia. William was much troubled by arguments from his nephew, the tsar, that irreparable harm would be done to the monarchical principle by these dispossessions. In the end the king's territorial greed overcame his legitimist fears all too easily, but it stuck in his craw that Saxony was to be spared. The Austrians stood loyally by their Saxon ally, as the Saxon king had stood by them, but since Saxony was to become a member of the North German Confederation, Bismarck the realist saw no reason to exact any further revenge.

In dealing with Napoleon Bismarck showed his usual dexterity and psychological insight. He played him along, making him feel that he was a genuine mediator. He affected moderation, by limiting the Prussian sphere to North Germany, something that he had already aired in previous exchanges with Paris. Bismarck was sorely tried by the fact that within days of Königgrätz Benedetti managed to make his way to Prussian headquarters in Bohemia. Bismarck was also worried by the Russians and had to fend off their call for a European congress, for the tsar was shocked by what was happening in Germany, saw the spectre of revolution and was directly involved through his German relations. Manteuffel was sent to St Petersburg to reassure the Russians. When by 5 August Napoleon came out with far-reaching demands, the Bavarian Palatinate and the left bank of the Rhine including Mainz, Bismarck flatly refused. He could not now, he said, give way to demands that might be the consequence of a lost war, when earlier he had found it difficult to agree to what was called the frontiers of 1814. He professed bewilderment that Napoleon, who knew the strength of national feeling and was its champion, could ask for something that risked outraging German national feeling, if it became public. It was a veiled threat. To give it substance Bismarck had already, within days of Königgrätz, ordered the ground to be laid for the calling of a *Vorparlament* to prepare a German Reichstag, steps reminiscent of the prelude to the 1848 revolutions. He told Manteuffel that this 'national swindle' would come in useful against French demands. Manteuffel was also instructed to use it against Russian demands for a European congress and against the tsar's complaints about the proposed dispossession of the king of Hanover and other princes. In Manteuffel's instructions of 11 August there occurs the often quoted passage: 'Pressure from abroad will drive us to the constitution of 1849 and to really revolutionary measures. If there has to be revolution, it is better to make it than to suffer it.'[27]

Goltz was instructed to divert the French emperor's attention to Luxemburg and Belgium. He had no wish to include the former in the North German Confederation and with the demise of the 1815 Confederation its fortress was no longer of military value to Prussia. Bismarck stored up for future use against France documents from the diplomatic by-play with Benedetti over Luxemburg and Belgium, which for the moment led nowhere. Once the preliminaries of peace were signed on 26 July at Nikolsburg, the Bohemian castle of the wife of the Austrian foreign minister Mensdorff, the French threat lost credibility. Napoleon had missed a historic opportunity. He knew better than his wife Eugénie and the foreign minister Drouyn de l'Huys, who were pressing for more resolute action, that France was not ready for war. He personally was certainly not ready for it, being incapacitated by an agonizing bladder complaint. His downfall, and even more importantly, the end of any French aspirations to hegemony in Europe, were already in sight.

8

HIGH NOON

When riding home from the battlefield of Königgrätz, an aide-de-camp said to Bismarck: 'Your Excellency, now you are a great man. If the crown prince had arrived too late, you would be the greatest villain.'[1] It was the turning point when Bismarck ceased to be a gambler living precariously and became the towering, overwhelming figure that dominated Germany and Europe for the next twenty-five years. Talking to the Hungarian exile Count Seherr-Thoss a few days after the battle he said: '. . . they took me for a Junker, a reactionary . . . with the king they denounced me as a secret democrat . . . this fight has cost me my nervous strength, my vitality! But I have beaten them all! all!' and with splendid scorn he, 'the mighty one', thumped the table.[2] Seherr-Thoss was shortly afterwards imprisoned by the Austrians and the Prussians threatened the shooting of hostages to have him released. Bismarck had recast Europe and he now turned to recasting Prussia and Germany.

On the day of Königgrätz and before the victory became known, the Prussian voters went to the polls. A few days earlier a minor victory against the Hanoverians, at Langensalza, had aroused some enthusiasm in Berlin, brought out the flags and Bismarck, about to leave for Bohemia, came to the window of his office to address a cheering crowd. The poll confirmed the weakening of the liberal opposition, who for the first time since the constitutional conflict suffered serious losses. The Progressives (Fortschrittspartei) dropped from 141 in 1863 to 95; the conservative groups rose from 35 to 136; and the centrist liberal groups dropped from 106 to 77. Bismarck could now put into operation, from a position of strength, his long-standing strategy of making a deal with the liberals on his own terms. Suggestions had for some time been around that an act of indemnity might be passed, drawing a line under the long-running constitutional conflict. When at the height of the pre-war crisis the finance minister Bodelschwingh, whose competence Bismarck had never rated highly, resigned, the former finance minister von der Heydt was recalled. He wanted a bill of indemnity, but he turned out to be the only one of Bismarck's colleagues to do so. The others went to the length of trying to persuade the king, behind the prime minister's back, to refuse and there was a weight of conservative feeling behind them. Bismarck's old and intimate friend, Hans von Kleist-Retzow, had stirred up feeling among ultra-conservatives and had written to Otto that 'it was throwing the prize of victory into the lap of the astonished defeated enemy. It would be ignominy in the face of all Europe.' Otto wrote to Johanna:

> Lippe [the reactionary justice minister] talks big against me in the conservative sense, and Hans Kleist has written me an excited letter. These little people do not have enough to do, can't see anything except their own nose and exercise their swimming ability on the stormy waves of phrase-making. One can deal with one's enemies, but these friends![3]

Bismarck, in the daily company of the king in Bohemia while the rest of the cabinet were in Berlin, managed to keep the monarch on side. William probably failed to see the full implications of the indemnity. In the speech from the throne on 5 August the government asked for an indemnity to bring the constitutional conflict to an end. The bill was passed on 3 September by 230 to 75 votes.

It was a great watershed in Prussian and German politics and must occupy a central place in any analysis of Bismarck's career and in any interpretation of the history of imperial Germany. Many commentators have regarded this outcome, whether they approve of or deplore it, as the almost single-handed work of the mighty Junker, genius or demon. In his saner moments Bismarck himself always stuck to his Latin tag 'unda fert nec regitur' (you can ride a wave, but not make it), but he now had boundless confidence that he could ride the wave with greater virtuosity than anybody else. The men who had fought the repressive Bismarck regime, some of whom did not give up the fight in his hour of triumph and did not accept the indemnity bill, were formidable figures to whom history was not kind. They did not get their just deserts from the national-liberal school of historians that became dominant in Germany. Behind the leaders of Prussian liberalism stood equally formidable figures in other parts of Germany. The question whether they could have solved the German problem avoiding Bismarck's 'iron and blood' can never be answered. It is doubtful whether a more whiggish solution was really available in Germany and such doubts are still voiced by historians today, when the national-liberal certainties are long gone. Whatever might have been, the fact was that in Bismarck the Prussian *ancien régime* found a man able to take the German question in hand on its own behalf and in its own interest. In doing so he had to make more concessions to liberalism and all its works than they wanted and even he bargained for. But if they denounced him to the king as a secret democrat, they were certainly wrong. He was far too intelligent to be a reactionary Junker, but neither was he a liberal. Through his exceptional political gifts, and through an ample measure of luck, he rebundled all the prevailing tendencies and forces into a new package. This new equilibrium could not have been reached if it had not suited the times. But its creator's preternatural success, the heroic status he derived from it as well as his political longevity maintained many features of the settlement long after they had outlived their usefulness. His solutions proved to be unstable and his rebundled package unravelled within a time span scarcely longer than his period in power.

It was widely suspected that Bismarck's prime purpose in proposing the indemnity bill was to split the liberals and this he certainly achieved. His tone in the chamber was now sweet reasonableness, but the king nearly spoilt the effect by telling Forckenbeck, the president of the chamber and a moderate pro-indemnity liberal: 'I had to act in this way and I will always act in the same manner should similar circumstances arise.'[4] The exact meaning of the indemnity was difficult to pin down and whatever it was, it was certainly not an act of repentance by the government and more a matter of legal exoneration. The legal arguments that divided the liberal opposition were complex and the divisions that occurred on questions of law and principle left individuals not necessarily on the same side as their disagreements on the political judgment that they now had to make. In the long run it was the latter that really counted. The realists felt that more could be achieved by cooperating with the Bismarck government, now firmly in the saddle and enjoying hitherto unknown popularity, than by a purely negative, if principled opposition. That was the view of a man like Twesten, at the centre of the conflict about parliamentary immunity, a man hardly lacking in principle. Ludwig Bamberger, a South German liberal in exile in Paris after 1848, who later became an opponent of Bismarck again, wrote: 'This act was not the best the government could have offered the chamber, but in fact it was the best it was willing and did offer. Could hostility have secured anything better than what the government conde-scended to concede?'[5]

Bismarck had created a powerful German state that had the potentiality for further enlargement. For many liberals this seemed to be a prerequisite for achieving their aims, which were meaningless within the existing dwarf states. Unity was, in other words, a necessary pre-condition for freedom. Bismarck would not last for ever and in a new reign, under the liberal crown prince, a quite different wind would blow. The acceptance of the indemnity bill was therefore not just a capitulation, an act of worship to success, as with hindsight it has often seemed in the twentieth century. There was even at the time much talk of a revolution from above and Bismarck himself at times adopted such a perspective. Revolution from above was to the taste of many liberals and even the left of the liberal opposition, the Progressives and those near to them, were fairly evenly divided on the indemnity pro-posal. Among those who were for it were such strong former opponents of Bismarck as Lasker and Unruh as well as Twesten, against whom judicial proceedings had still not been dropped. The Conservatives voted for it, but, leaving aside such principled legitimists as Gerlach, who had already parted company with Bismarck earlier, there were among them many who felt uneasy. They were disconcerted by the sweeping way in which Bismarck was changing the political landscape at home and abroad. What he had saved did not any longer look like the old Prussia with which their loyalties lay.

As for the liberals, it cannot be denied that many of them experienced a kind of Pauline conversion as a result of Bismarck's success. An influ-ential article in the *Preussische Jahrbücher*, 'Liberalism: a self-criticism' by Hermann Baumgarten, a liberal historian, is often cited as the archetypal example of conversion. After paying tribute to the political and military virtues of Junkerdom, Baumgarten writes of the 'extraordinary ineptitude' of liberalism, which proved that the middle class 'is little suited for real political action' and is 'only in exceptional cases able to participate in great political endeavours with success'.[6] This kind of a self-abasement and loss of confidence shows the side-effects of Bismarck's *Realpolitik* at their worst and boded ill for Germany's future.

*

By September 1866 the management of the cataclysm he had done so much to unleash left Bismarck physically and psychologically exhausted. On 20 September he rode in triumph through Berlin, in front of the king's carriage and alongside Moltke and Roon. The rank of major-general had been conferred on him. A few days later he departed from the capital with his family on one of those prolonged leaves of absence that was to punctuate his tenure of office until his fall. He was away from Berlin for nine weeks until the beginning of December, most of the time staying with Prince Putbus on the island of Rügen, off Pomerania. That he could operate in this way shows the extent to which the climacteric of 1866 had turned him into a Bonapartist, Caesaristic figure, a law unto himself on the political scene. His health caused Johanna much anxiety and he was largely shielded from the daily transaction of affairs. When he saw newspapers, he complained that Brass, a former radical, but now the subservient editor of the *Norddeutsche Allgemeine Zeitung*, was giving too much publicity to anti-Prussian sentiment in Hanover. For Bismarck freedom of expression always came second to what was politically expedient.

His stay at Putbus became famous for two directives he dictated, on 30 October and 19 November, that decisively shaped the constitution of the North German Confederation and of the German empire.[7] Much preparatory work had already been done by his assistants, but when Lothar Bucher gave him an oral report on their work, Bismarck hardly listened and then dictated, out of his head, the essentials he wanted incorporated. He was entirely guided by pragmatic considerations. He wanted to make the new confederation look as much as possible like the old, while in fact bringing about a much more centralized structure in which Prussia was unequivocally in control. It had to look like the old, because this would respect the susceptibilties of the members other than Prussia and above all make it easier for the remaining South German states to adhere at some point in the future. The central feature was therefore not to be a ministry, but a diet, *Bundestag*, later renamed *Bundesrat* 'with which, I believe, we will do good business, if we for the moment adopt the curial system [voting system] of the old diet.' In the directive of 19 November he goes into detail on the voting system, which was to arise out of the allocation of votes at Frankfurt, with Prussia taking on the votes of the annexed states. Prussia would then have 17 out of 43 votes, which, with the five smaller enclave states, would her give her a majority. This Bundesrat, consisting like the Frankfurt diet of the representatives of the member governments, would share the legislative power with the elected chamber, the Reichstag, which Bismarck had proposed in the previous April and from which he could not now retreat. He does seem to have had cold feet about universal suffrage, at least in the directive of 30 October, but in the end went through with it.

But the powers of the Reichstag would be severely circumscribed, since it shared legislation with the Bundesrat and there would be no federal ministry which it could hold to account. The Bundesrat, based on the federal principle, would restrict the powers of the Reichstag, based on the citizenry as a whole and therefore incorporating the unitary principle. As regards federal ministries, some might arise *au fur et à mesure*, gradually and as required. Initially there would be only the Prussian war ministry. The king of Prussia would be the supreme military authority and retain the full power of command, which had been at the bottom of the constitutional conflict. The privileged position of the military was more complete under this constitution than it was under the Prussian constitution and it was carried over into the second Reich. The Prussian king would also hold the presidency of the Bundesrat. The Prussian government, in practice Bismarck himself, would thus remain firmly in control of the whole structure. It was a halfway house between absolutism and parliamentarism and it was precisely this equilibrium that had given him his position of exceptional power. It was now to be enshrined in a constitution, which, as Bismarck knew only too well, would need to leave room for future developments, but would also perpetuate, as far as possible, his personal power.

When Bismarck returned to Berlin in December 1866 a full constitutional draft was worked out, to be placed before a federal constituent parliament, a Reichstag, elected on the basis of universal manhood suffrage. In preparation for these elections the parties regrouped themselves under the impact of the indemnity vote in particular and the upheavals of 1866 in general. The liberal deputies in favour of the indemnity and of collaboration with the Bismarck government, particularly on the German question, had already constituted themselves into a separate parliamentary group in the Prussian chamber in November. In the North German Reichstag they became the National Liberal party, with 80 deputies the largest group. It included such prominent figures as Twesten, Forckenbeck, Gneist and Lasker from the old Prussian liberals; but many of the deputies were so-called 'New Prussians' from the annexed countries, principally Hanover. The Hanoverian Bennigsen became the leader. Bismarck had succeeded, with the indemnity and his unwonted conciliatory tone, as well as with some further concrete concessions, in accentuating the differences of opinion between liberals into this definite party split. Some stayed with the Progressive party; they included Benedict Waldeck, an 1848 democrat, who had in fact supported the annexation of the duchies, while maintaining his pronounced left-liberal orientation. Schulze-Delitzsch, the champion of the cooperative movement, also stayed with the Progressives, but they were reduced to nineteen seats.

There was also a less drastic split among conservatives. Those who went with Bismarck without reservations, *sans phrase* as it was later called, constituted themselves into the Free Conservative party, later called the Reichspartei, which had 39 seats. Many of them did not come from the Prussian core provinces, were Catholic or large-scale entrepreneurs. The old Prussian Conservatives were not yet as anti-Bismarckian as many of them later became and an old-fashioned legitimist like Gerlach was rather isolated. But a situation was beginning to be foreshadowed in which Prussian particularism, as represented by the Prussian Conservatives, became the most formidable of particularisms. There was, however, in this Reichstag, a clear majority for the line Bismarck was determined to steer between particularism, which included the establishment of a Prussian hegemony, and centralism, which would have brought the danger of a fully parliamentary regime.

During its passage through the constituent Reichstag between February and April 1867 a number of important changes were made in the draft submitted by the government. The most important of these concerned the position of the federal chancellor. Originally he was intended to be purely an executive officer conducting the business of the Bundesrat and appointed by the *Bundespräsidium*, which was permanently vested in the Prussian king. He would have taken his instructions from the Prussian foreign minister, who disposed of the 17 votes in the Bundesrat. It was thought the position might go to Savigny, son of the famous constitutional lawyer and recently Prussian envoy to the Frankfurt diet. In the constituent Reichstag strong efforts were made to insert in the constitution an independent executive responsible to the Reichstag. They came from the left but were also supported by the National Liberals. Bismarck was absolutely determined to prevent any control of the executive by the Reichstag and could not be shifted.

What finally emerged was a provision which made the chancellor accountable to the Reichstag, in the sense that he could be interrogated there and would have to defend the policies decided in the Bundesrat. It did not mean that the chancellor was responsible to and removable by the Reichstag in the western parliamentary sense. Even the limited accountability inserted in the draft meant that the chancellor now became the key political figure in the whole edifice. It also meant that potentially the Reichstag could become more significant, for it would be the forum in which the executive, consisting initially only of the chancellor, could be confronted by the representatives of the people. It was obvious that the position of federal chancellor, or *Reichskanzler* as he came to be called, could be held only by Bismarck and no one else and he had a hand in getting the amendment into the draft. Paradoxically it became known as the 'lex Bennigsen', because in its eventual form it was based on a proposal put forward by the leading National Liberal, Bennigsen. In fact it created a constitutional situation quite different from that always aspired to by liberals of all persuasions, namely an executive dependent on parliament. It created that peculiar mixture of authoritarianism and constitutionalism often called German constitutionalism, which remained in operation until 1918. The chancellor was appointed by and dependent on the monarch. Bismarck himself remained in power until a monarch less than half his age effectively dismissed him. The same monarch and not the parties in the Reichstag appointed the last chancellor of the empire in October 1918. Bismarck had got what he wanted, an executive independent of parliament. But he did not anticipate the weight the Reichstag would acquire as a result of its share in the legislative power, and also because it was popularly elected and could at least question the chancellor and subsequently other ministers heading federal departments, as these were gradually established.

In the tussle between Bismarck and the leading men of the constituent Reichstag he threatened from time to time that he would have to withdraw the draft and impose a constitution. He took refuge behind the governments of the North German Confederation, claiming that they would not accept some of the changes proposed in the Reichstag. This waving of the big stick, in fact the threat of a *coup d'état* by returning sovereignty to the constituent rulers and dissolving the constitution, became part of his style of government, particularly in his last decade of power. It was no more realistic now, at the beginning, than it was later on. Bismarck needed the Reichstag and its representation of the popular will as a counterpoise to what would otherwise have been the absolute power of the monarch. His own power was derived from the fact that he stood at the pivotal point between monarch and parliament. He also needed the Reichstag as the representation of the unitary principle, against the power of the federated rulers, whose position he had done so much to save by making his new edifice look as much as possible like the confederation that died in 1866.

A few other changes were made in the draft constitution. Bismarck was obsessed by the idea that state officials should not be allowed to sit in the Reichstag. In spite of all the harassment he inflicted on them, servants of the state had been the backbone of the opposition to the government in the Prussian Landtag, as they were in the parliaments of other German states. On this point he gave way and civil servants continued to make up a high proportion of Reichstag deputies, while representatives of lobbies and special interests were relatively slow in coming forward. Bismarck, however, insisted on retaining the bar on any payment, expenses as well as salaries, to the deputies. He wanted at all costs to avoid the rise of a professional political class. The absence of payment caused problems in the later history of the imperial Reichstag. It was often difficult to obtain a quorum and necessary legislative work was thereby held up. Expense payments were therefore introduced in 1906.

Another point on which Bismarck made a partial concession was the budgetary competence of the Reichstag, the cardinal point of conflict between him and the liberal opposition in the previous four years. He envisaged that the Reichstag would have no control over military and naval expenditure, 90 per cent of all expenditure, which would be fixed in perpetuity. In the end he accepted that it would be fixed for four years initially, on the basis of a peacetime strength of 1 per cent of the population and 225 thaler per man. If after 31 December 1871 there was no further legislation, the government would revert to the 'gap' theory on which it had raised revenue since the days of the constitutional conflict. The renewal of the conflict was thus for the time being deferred. The parties in the Reichstag were more successful in asserting their rights over ordinary revenue and expenditure, which was to be subject to annual vote. This became, in course of time and with the ever increasing scope of government, a very important prerogative of the Reichstag. Together with the amendments that widened the legislative powers of the Reichstag in many social and economic areas, it created the basis for making the North German Confederation and thereafter the Reich into a unified country. There was, however, no charter of basic rights, as many of the liberals would have wanted. Bismarck argued that this would be incompatible with the federal character of the constitution and would have to be left to the member states. In this respect the constitution lagged behind the Prussian constitution, which had a bill of rights.

In spite of the concessions he made, Bismarck had put his stamp upon this constitutional settlement to a great degree. He had been guided entirely by pragmatic considerations, not by theoretical or ideological preconceptions. As he put it in his first directive written in Putbus, 'the desire to allow a perfect Minerva to emerge from the head of the Präsidium would lead the matter into the quicksands of professorial quarrels'. It was an article of faith with him that professors were the last persons to be entrusted with political decisions. Now he had imposed what he required for his own survival in power upon a major country for the next half century. The constitution was accepted by the Reichstag on 16 April 1867 by a vote of 230 to 53. The crown prince, who in the past had so often been hostile to Bismarck, was active in bringing about some of the compromises that enabled the constitution to pass. He knew that it might fall to him to preside over the new system in the not too distant future and this thought was never absent from Bismarck's mind. As in the days between Königgrätz and Nikolsburg, circumstances were driving the two men together. Nevertheless he told a visitor in the summer of 1867 that the political principles of the crown prince were not his, for the prince would want to govern with the majority. 'In my opinion that is not always right for us, and presupposes a yielding character and conviction, of which I do not feel myself capable.'[8] He said that he would not remain in office beyond the lifetime of the king.

*

While the tussle between Bismarck and the parties over the constitution was going on, his attention was once more mainly concentrated on a foreign policy issue, the crisis over Luxemburg. He again applied what had always been a basic political tactic, the use of a foreign crisis to achieve domestic objectives and vice versa. Ever since the tense days stretching from Königgrätz through the preliminary peace of Nikolsburg to the final peace of Prague the future of Franco-Prussian relations had been at the centre of Bismarck's preoccupations. He had by no means completely given up his earlier guiding strategic concept that good relations with Napoleon were a *sine qua non* of Prussian advancement, but the price he was prepared to pay for a French alliance was clearly diminishing. To Goltz he sent a despatch in early September 1866:

> Provided Napoleon takes a similar attitude towards the Prussian task of German national development, HM is prepared to put no obstacles in the way of French expansion on the basis of French nationality . . . the initiative for such a policy must naturally come from the imperial Government.[9]

This was in line with the encouragement he had given to a possible French move in the direction of Luxemburg and Belgium, but also to his refusal to commit himself in any way. Luxemburg, of which the king of Holland was the ruler as grand duke, had been part of the German Confederation, but Bismarck had not made it part of the North German Confederation and had thereby left room for French aspirations. On the other hand the fortress of Luxemburg had been a federal fortress and was still occupied by Prussian troops, whose presence was now of doubtful justification under international law.

When after his return to Berlin in December Bismarck was asked to associate himself in some way with Napoleon's attempts to solve the awkward question of Rome and the papacy, on which he had impaled himself to the detriment of his domestic popularity, Bismarck refused any commitment. Benedetti hoped to get a more definite agreement on Luxemburg, but Bismarck made himself scarce and gave nothing away. In the meantime French opinion was moving more in the direction of 'revenge for Sadowa', even if this was not the view of the emperor himself nor of his minister Rouher and the foreign minister de Moustier. Drouyn de l'Huys, more inclined to take a hard line with Prussia, had resigned the previous autumn. Napoleon began negotiations with the Dutch king over the cession of Luxemburg. William III of the Netherlands was willing to sell the grand duchy, but was suddenly halted in his tracks by Bismarck's publication of the offensive–defensive alliances between Prussia and the three South German states Bavaria, Württemberg and Baden. These military alliances had been secretly concluded in the previous August as part of the peace settlement with these states. In deference to France Bismarck had then made no attempt to extend Prussian control beyond the line of the Main and the possibility of forming a South German federation analogous to the North German Confederation had been left open. But these secret military alliances were exacted from the southern governments, particularly Bavaria, in return for dropping territorial demands on them; but they were also a deterrent against French territorial demands, which were just then being made, or possible future Austrian attempts at revenge.

Bismarck's motives in making them public in March 1867, with the agreement of the three governments, were as usual manifold. It helped him in the debates in the constituent Reichstag, where among the deputies on whom he was relying to pass his constitutional draft there was much impatience about progress on the German question. It sent a signal to Paris that he was not prepared to expose himself in any way on their behalf over the Luxemburg question. Public opinion in Germany was increasingly stirred up about the possible acquisition of Luxemburg by France and Bismarck refused to make it appear that his government had in the slightest way encouraged such an acquisition. To the French emperor and his advisers it looked as if he had set a trap for them, encouraging them to negotiate with the Dutch king and then frightening the king off. Whether Bismarck really intended this is questionable, but he caused Bennigsen to direct an interpellation to the government about their intentions on Luxemburg, which enabled him publicly to deny any part in the negotiations between Paris and The Hague. In a speech on 1 April 1867, his fifty-second birthday, he replied in moderate tones to Bennigsen's passionately nationalist inter-pellation. In a private conversation with a leader of the Free Conservatives, Count Bethusy-Huc, he said that he thought a war with France sooner or later inevitable, but that he would do nothing to bring it on. With emotion he said he had seen the misery and suffering of war on the battlefield and in hospitals, that he had seen war cripples look up at his window in the Wilhelmstrasse , 'thinking if it was not for that man up there I would now be sitting well and sound with mother' and that he would not have a moment's peace if he brought on war lightly.[10]

Bismarck probably did think war with France inevitable, may even have underestimated the influence of the peace party at the French court at this time, but neither Napoleon nor he were for the moment ready to fight it. The constitution of the North German Confederation was not yet high and dry, the South German states were by no means itching for a fight on the side of Prussia, nor was Bismarck keen to bring large numbers of potentially disaffected Catholics into the North German fold prematurely. Austrian foreign policy was now under the control of Beust, who had been forced out of office in Saxony. It was to be expected that he might look for opportunities to recover Austria's German position, possibly in concert with France. When the Luxemburg crisis was submitted to a conference of the European powers in May 1867 Bismarck went out of his way to allow Napoleon an honourable way out by agreeing to the neutralization of Luxemburg and the withdrawal of Prussian troops from the fortress. For the time being peace was saved, but the idea of a Franco-Prussian alliance was dead. The prevention of further Prussian aggrandisement became a priority in Paris and therefore the completion of German unity was unlikely without war.

When the constituent Reichstag had accepted the constitutional draft Bismarck left Berlin to complete the acquisition of Varzin, an estate in eastern Pomerania, which he was purchasing with the money voted to him by the Prussian Landtag in recognition of his services. What especially attracted him to this estate were its extensive woods and the feeling of being far away from the daily press of affairs. Varzin was 'safe from dispatches' (*depeschensicher*) and it required several hours journey by rail, followed by a further journey over poor roads, to reach it. The house was old and draughty, but then made more comfortable by the building of an annex. Otto and Johanna cared little for either architecture or beautiful interiors and only wanted to be comfortable. He was becoming a landowner on an ever larger scale – after 1871 the Sachsenwald, near Hamburg, would become his, another gift from a grateful sovereign – just when he was becoming alienated from his old conservative friends.

Nothing got on his nerves more than attacks from that quarter. When talking to his old friend Below-Hohendorf and his wife in February 1868 he said,

> You talk of sacrifices that you, the conservatives, have made for me . . . . It's the other way round – I have made the heaviest sacrifices for you and continue to do so. Regard for you involves me again and again in difficulties with the more reasonable members of other parties, which otherwise I would be spared. In return I get only the blackest ingratitude.[11]

The more reasonable members of other parties were clearly in Bismarck's mind: those, the National Liberals, the Free Conservatives, and others like them, who in domestic and foreign policy envisaged the future in his own terms. To make Prussia prevail he had to hitch German nationalism, 'the national swindle', to her cause. Even his diplomacy had increasingly to use the language of German nationalism. At home he had had to coopt, rather than fight, the commercial and entrepreneurial middle classes. Prussian Junkerdom saw itself surrounded by alien tides, while Bismarck himself, in his personal life style and with his ever growing possessions and wealth, managed to insulate himself against developments which his own policies allowed to proceed at breakneck speed.

The insulation he achieved in his private life became also the most characteristic feature of the public position he had built for himself. He always rebutted the frequently made suggestions that he was aiming at a Bonapartist or Caesarist type of rule. He was no Caesar basing himself on a demagogic appeal to volatile masses. Nor was he aiming to build a movement to support his rule. What he wanted and largely got was an independent position above parties that left it open to him to cooperate with those willing to support his policies. It was nevertheless a form of charismatic rule, for it was dependent on the unique and heroic stature he acquired as the founder of the German nation state. In 1867 this task was not complete, and while he was not under immediate pressure to complete it, his exceptional position rested on the fact that he had taken it in hand and was the only man likely to complete it. Like all charismatic rulers Bismarck was now dependent on success. Neither liberals nor conservatives could regard him as one of theirs. Much of his legendary dexterity consisted in obscuring his true intentions and talking with forked tongues. Nobody could trust him, but his triumphs were so great that they had to admire him. Only further triumphs could justify him.

As the Bundeskanzler, federal chancellor, of the North German Confederation he was the sole executive minister of the federation and he needed an office to support him. The chancellery was established under the presidency of Rudolf Delbrück, with whom Bismarck had worked since his days in Frankfurt. Over the next few years Delbrück, in cooperation with the leaders of the National Liberals and the Free Conservatives, created the legislative framework for the economic and social unification of the North German Confederation and subsequently of the German Reich. A common currency was introduced and a central bank in due course established. A code of commercial law was promulgated and a court set up to administer it. The market economy, already to a large extent operating in Prussia, was extended to the North German Confederation and then to the whole Reich. The basis was laid for the rise of Germany into a great industrial powerhouse, which became the one enduring legacy of the whole Bismarckian enterprise. It also gave those liberals who had opted for cooperation with the regime their principal justification. They got unity and its economic consequences and for a while they consoled themselves that freedom would follow later. Bismarck himself took little direct part in this process, for it did not fit in with the style of governing he had now adopted. His prolonged absences, his olympian detachment, his concentration on foreign affairs, would not have made the day to day transaction of these affairs possible. He knew what was going on and occasionally he intervened administratively and in the Reichstag. He usually preferred to keep himself in reserve, as he explained to Delbrück in connection with the debates on the new penal code in 1870. Above all he was fully aware of the wider implications. He was giving economic liberalism its head, but he never believed that political liberalism, which he did not want, would follow. There were now many among the middle classes who were quite prepared to settle for economic liberalism and who were increasingly losing interest in liberal political principles. Others still deluded themselves that political liberalism would follow the free market, particularly once the overpowering personality of Bismarck had left the scene.

There were other implications that Bismarck was aware of. The legislative underpinning of the free market would further consolidate Prussian pre-eminence in Germany, as the Zollverein had already done. It would also encounter opposition in those corners of German society who felt themselves overwhelmed and pressured by this onrush of modernity. Such corners existed particularly in the more pre-industrial regions of South Germany and would therefore generate opposition to the adhesion of the southern states to the North German Confederation. The German *Bildungsbürgertum*, on which the liberal movement was predominantly based before its increasing domination by the economic middle classes, would also consider themselves threatened. Bismarck's former friends, the Prussian Junkers, were at this stage themselves still free traders, but they would find other aspects of the nationwide market economy difficult to swallow. It threatened the local autonomy and patrimonial power that the Prussian landowners, and Bismarck himself in his earlier days, had tried to preserve.

When one of his old friends, von der Marwitz, with whom he was on *Du* terms, told him that the deviation from the old Prussian order for which they held him responsible was not acceptable to him and his friends, he got very angry. Such conservative criticism, reminding him of his growing dependence on the National Liberals, made him even more irritable than usual. Keudell says about one such occasion, conservative opposition to his favourable treatment of Hanover in matters of local self-administration, that he was deeply shaken. 'Leg pains, gall bladder attacks and facial neuralgia were the immediate result.' Even an old comrade-in-arms like Roon told his nephew Moritz von Blanckenburg: 'He talks conservative with Conservatives and liberal with Liberals' and his old friend Blanckenburg himself grew increasingly disillusioned and bitter. But as the great landowner that he became, he himself clung to the old order and went on resenting state interference and taxes. He continued to have nothing but contempt and dislike for the bureaucracy over which he distantly presided. It was a strange paradox for one who more than most could say 'l'état, c'est moi'. The freedom he craved as a private individual he did not as a statesman extend to others.

The Luxemburg crisis ended inconclusively and that was largely Bismarck's own choice. He had gone as far as he could in saving French *amour propre* without giving up his alliance with the German national movement. But the crisis showed that the extension of the North German Confederation to South Germany was universally expected and that it was unlikely to be achieved without a French war. It had to be Bismarck's strategy, which always left alternatives open, to lower expectations. On many occasions he now said that one could not hurry the pace of history, that one might put the clocks on but time would not move any faster, that one could not harvest fruit that was not ripe for plucking, that it might not happen in his lifetime. Such remarks were not merely tactical, to lower expectations, but were entirely in accordance with Bismarck's view of politics. But it would not have been compatible with the maintenance of his own charisma if he had simply contented himself with postponing the completion of German unity to the Greek calends. On the other hand he was still enough of an old-fashioned, conservative cabinet politician not to give public opinion, charisma and similar considerations too high a place in his calculations.

His usual minute scanning of the European horizon was now clearly governed by the expectation that at some point he might have to move forward on the German question. But the fact that this was so generally expected made it all the more incumbent upon him to appear to be on the defensive and not to look like the disturber of the status quo. It was convenient for him that Napoleon, still suffering from his Mexican fiasco, could not free himself from the papal imbroglio. French troops, having been withdrawn in September 1866, drove Garibaldi out of the papal states in November 1867 and were back in occupation. Bismarck professed to be not unduly disturbed by high profile meetings between Napoleon and Francis Joseph, in Salzburg in August 1867, and in Paris on the occasion of the world exhibition in October 1867. Beust was now the imperial chancellor of what had become, through the so-called *Ausgleich* (settlement) with Hungary, the dual monarchy. He was enough of a realist to know that a war in alliance with France to recover Austria's position in Germany was not really on the cards. The Hungarians would not support it because it would threaten their newly established autonomy within the Habsburg empire. The Germans in the Habsburg dominions were now too nationally minded to want another fratricidal war in alliance with France. Bismarck could use the *furor teutonicus* to give himself diplomatic leverage, while Napoleon and Beust were afraid to arouse it.

Then there was the Russian drive to recover their European strength lost since the Crimean War. The Cretan revolt against the Turks moved the eastern question higher up the agenda again. Another factor was Romanian designs on Hungarian territory in Transylvania. Bismarck warned the Hohenzollern prince of Romania not to press these, for he did not want to reduce Hungarian reluctance to support a Habsburg alliance with France in pursuit of revenge against Prussia. No one was a greater master than Bismarck in the operation of such intricate diplomatic networks. For Vienna the position in the Balkans appeared as a greater threat than the German situation, where it was mainly a matter of maintaining the line of the Main. A Franco-Austrian alliance would provoke a Russo-Prussian one, in which the Russian objective would be gains in the Balkans and on the Black Sea. Nevertheless, an alliance between Vienna and Paris remained a possibility and negotiations went on in great secrecy right up to the outbreak of the Franco-Prussian War. Bismarck knew about them in general terms, though not in detail, but remained fairly confident that they would not be successful. A Franco-Russian alliance was also a possibility, but a more distant one. France had ultimately no real interest in exposing herself for Russian aspirations in the Near East, nor could Russia be expected to forward French designs on Belgium. Britain was in her post-Palmerstonian isolationist phase, interested in the maintenance of peace and the status quo in Central

Europe, but sensitive to any French designs in the Low Countries. Bismarck waited and watched and gave nothing away. He kept an eye on public opinion and the press. When he saw hostility, for example in the French press, he saw to it that there were appropriate counterattacks in those newspapers susceptible to his directives. 'À corsaire, corsaire et demi' (to give as good as you get), was his motto in this matter, as in so many others.

*

The Zollverein was an area where Prussia could take the initiative without touching too directly on pre-existing diplomatic arrangements and sensitivities. In the war of 1866 its members had fought on opposite sides, but after the war the Zollverein went back into operation. The economic vice in which Prussia had held the South German states before the war was now even stronger. There were many ideas in the air about the future relations of the South German states with the North German Confederation that would not constitute a breach of the Peace of Prague and the line of the Main. There were also long-standing plans to turn the Zollverein into something more like a federal state, or an economic counterpart to the German Confederation. At the beginning of 1867 the recently appointed Bavarian prime minister was Prince Hohenlohe-Schillingsfürst, a liberal Catholic, a supporter of greater German unity and eventually a successor of Bismarck as imperial chancellor. He proposed new arrangements to regulate the customs union between the southern states and the now enlarged and unified economic area of the North German Confederation. Hohenlohe's plan would have maintained a South German veto over Zollverein legislation. By the summer of 1867 Bismarck came up with a counterproposal: there was to be a *Zollbundesrat*, the North German Bundesrat expanded by South German representatives, and a *Zollparlament*, the North German Reichstag of 297 members expanded by 91 deputies, to be elected by universal male suffrage. In spite of reservations the South German states had to agree to these proposals, otherwise Prussia would have ended the Zollverein. Bismarck clearly hoped by this mean to bring movement into the German question, to strengthen centralism against federalism and to have a ready means of putting pressure on the South German governments. It would also lend weight to the use of the German national movement in his diplomacy.

The elections to the Zollparlament held in February and March 1868 ran almost entirely counter to Bismarck's expectations. Except in Baden and Hessen they became a demonstration of the surviving strength of particularism. In Baden the national party had always been strong and enjoyed the favour of the establishment. In Hesse-Darmstadt the grand duke and his minister Dalwigk remained strongly anti-Prussian, but their repressive regime had aroused strong resistance. There was no supporter of particularism elected among the six Hesse representatives. But in Bavaria and Württemberg, the two largest states, particularism triumphed. In the latter particularists won all the seats, in Bavaria 27 against only 12 nationalists. The roots of anti-Prussian feeling in the south were diverse. There was real fear of the autocratic, military side of Prussianism, in particular of the consequences of the military alliances with the north. They entailed a reorganization of southern forces, involving longer periods of military service and higher expenditure which were widely resented. To be taken over by Prussia meant 'pay taxes, become a soldier and keep your mouth shut.' Then there was the Catholic suspicion of the Protestant north and the survival of *grossdeutsch* as well as particularist sentiment. The economic liberalism of the North German Confederation was attractive to the commercial and entrepreneurial middle classes in the south and they were the main supporters of the pro-Prussian parties. The social groups disadvantaged by the spread of the market economy, mostly to be found in the Catholic regions, feared the spread of the market. The particularist deputies from the south combined in the Zollparlament with northern groups opposed to the National Liberals. These included a good many Prussian Conservatives, as well as northern Catholics and opponents of the take-over of Hanover and other states by Prussia, among them the later leader of the Centre party, Windthorst. The Zollparlament could not therefore become a focus for furthering the unity of north and south. There were subsequent setbacks. The most serious was when in November 1869 the Patriot party in Bavaria, opposed to further unification, won an absolute majority in the lower house of the Bavarian parliament. Three months later Hohenlohe decided to resign. Jörg, the leader of the Patriot party, spoke of the defensive alliances of 1866 as 'the source through which the evil of militarism was spreading into the formerly happy lands of South Germany'.

Bismarck had therefore to step with extreme caution and his frequent remarks that the completion of German unity was not on his immediate agenda could come as no surprise. It was the general view in the two years following the Zollparlament elections that the prospect of German unity had receded. In German affairs Bismarck went out of his way to discourage unification moves, which mainly came from Baden, where the national-liberal movement was strongest. When in February 1870 Eduard Lasker moved a motion to congratulate the Baden government on its national attitude and to welcome its earliest possible adherence to the North German Confederation, Bismarck voiced his opposition in the sharpest terms, not stopping at personal insults to Lasker. The adherence of Baden by itself could not possibly further the cause of unification. 'I may be wrong about this – perhaps I have lost the lucky touch, which I had for a time, perhaps it has been transferred to the previous speaker [Lasker],' he said with biting irony.[12] He was not prepared to allow the National Liberals any say in the conduct of his German policy and Lasker's move brought on stomach cramps.

At about this time he was toying with the idea of giving King William the title 'emperor' and had confidential talks with some National Liberal deputies, including Forckenbeck, the author of the compromise by which the military budget was fixed for four years. Bismarck hoped that the title might satisfy those in the national movement who were growing impatient about the pace of the unification process. He may even have thought that the title would have some attraction in the south. The Bavarian Patriot party found a Hohenzollern kaiser acceptable if paired with the Habsburg kaiser. In many quarters it aroused suspicion, particularly with the Bavarian king, who had tried to keep Hohenlohe in office, even when the Patriot party won a majority in the Bavarian parliament. If Bismarck thought it might be acceptable elsewhere in Europe, particularly in Paris, by creating the impression that there was a certain finality about the North German Confederation, he was soon disillusioned. The plan was quietly dropped before the king even learnt of it. He had dropped hints about it to the crown prince, but Frederick William hoped that the restoration of the German empire would mark the beginning of his own reign.

*

Another scheme was already afoot, not without Bismarck's encouragement, that was to bring German unity to completion. It was the plan that Prince Leopold of Hohenzollern-Sigmaringen should become king of Spain. Hohenzollern-Sigmaringen was the small territory north of Lake Constance, where the castle of Hohenzollern, the cradle of the dynasty, was located. The territory was now part of Prussia and the Sigmaringen family, who were Catholics, considered themselves part of the house of Hohenzollern. Prince

Leopold was a Prussian officer; but he was also quite closely related to the Bonaparte dynasty. The Romanian prince, later king, belonged to the Sigmaringen branch of the family. The head of the branch, Prince Karl Anton, had ceded his small principality to Prussia in 1849 and was for a time Prussian prime minister in the New Era; Prince Leopold was his heir. The vacancy on the Spanish throne occurred through the overthrow of the dissolute Queen Isabella in September 1868. Bismarck realized that from the start that this opened a kind of second front on France and would at the very least become a preoccupation for Napoleon. When the possibility of Prince Leopold's candidature surfaced he encouraged it discreetly. Some German historians argue that Napoleon could have vetoed the idea at the start, but did not do so, because he saw a chance of demonstrating that the interest of the Hohenzollerns and of Greater Prussia was not identical with that the German national movement, which he always felt reluctant to offend.

When Prince Karl Anton and then King William clearly opposed the candidature, which Prince Leopold himself did not want, Bismarck became more active in its support. A long letter, dated 9 March 1870, from prime minister to king, following on from previous discussions, argued strongly in favour of accepting the candidature, in the interests of Prussia, Germany and the Hohenzollern dynasty. 'It is in the political interest of Germany that the house of Hohenzollern should assume the prestige and elevated world position, to which only the Habsburg antecedents since the time of Charles V form an analogy.'[13] It was just the analogy with Charles V that now agitated French public opinion and that made it essential for Napoleon to prevent a Hohenzollern from ascending the Spanish throne. As always Bismarck was, in more actively promoting the candidature, pursuing a variety of objectives. Counteracting rumours of a Franco-Austrian alliance and hopes of importing some movement into the stagnating German situation were probably his most pressing motives. The king was not to be moved in favour of the candidature and in April the Sigmaringen prince and his father formally rejected the Spanish offer. Bismarck was much annoyed and retired sick to Varzin. 'The Spanish affair has taken such a miserable course, what was undoubtedly the national interest has been subordinated to princely idiosyncracies and ultramontane, female influences. Depression over this has tried my nerves sorely for weeks', he wrote to Delbrück.[14] His frequent absences in Varzin and his constant complaints about his health had given rise to the impression that he might really soon retire or at least do so, as he frequently asserted, when 'the old gentleman', now seventy-three, shuffled off his mortal coil.

Such appearances were deceptive and changes in the French political situation, about which he was exceedingly well informed, led him to renewed efforts to keep the Hohenzollern candidature going. The increasing domestic vulnerability of the Napoleonic regime, accentuated by the emperor's foreign policy failures, had led to a liberalization, bringing to power as prime minister Ollivier, a politician sympathetic to German national aspirations. But then the Bonapartist right staged something of a comeback in a referendum in May 1870. The duc de Gramont, long French ambassador in Vienna, became foreign minister and was expected to pursue a more prestige-conscious policy. When therefore Bismarck at this point made an effort to reactivate the Hohenzollern candidature and in great secrecy set Lothar Bucher and others to work on it, he knew that it might lead to a confrontation with France and probably to war. But then he had often expressed the view that without a French war the completion of German unity would not be possible and a war with France breaking out under the right circumstances might well be the catalyst for bringing the South Germans to the side of Prussia. War was still an instrument of policy, for Bismarck as for all the other cabinet politicians in control of the European great powers. In most diplomatic dispatches of this period, the possibility of war was part of the discourse. But Bismarck was not necessarily aiming for war and far from certain that it would happen. No one knew better than he that in high politics there was many a slip twixt cup and lip. He was assiduous in maintaining the fiction that Prince Leopold's candidature was purely a family affair and had nothing to do with official policy, thus leaving himself a line of retreat. It was just as well, because the slip occurred before too long.

It had been intended to create a *fait accompli* in Spain by making the official acceptance of the throne by Prince Leopold coincide with his election by the Spanish Cortes. This plan miscarried, because through a ciphering error the Cortes was adjourned before it could elect the new king, and the news of his acceptance leaked out. This made it virtually inevitable that the French government should demand the withdrawal of the candidature. Gramont did so in a very bellicose speech on 6 July, which left no room for retreat. At this point it looked as if things were going badly wrong for Bismarck, who was still at Varzin. Using the fiction that it was a dynastic affair, the French ambassador Benedetti was instructed to approach King

William himself, who was taking the waters at Ems. The king maintained the fiction that he had no direct influence over the decisions of
Prince Leopold and his father. But he did not want war, had never liked the
Spanish affair, and therefore recommended to the two Sigmaringen princes
to withdraw the candidature. This was promptly done and announced, on
12 July.

Bismarck had in the meantime set out from Varzin to see the king
at Ems and on his way arrived in the Wilhelmstrasse on the afternoon of
12 July. There he learnt of the withdrawal of the candidature, was naturally
displeased, though probably not surprised, by the way the king had handled
the matter, but immediately set out to save something from the wreckage.
The withdrawal could not be undone, but he was preparing the ground
for demanding some kind of satisfaction for the threats made by Gramont.
The Prussian ambassador in Paris was to be sent on leave and the North
German Reichstag might be recalled. At this point the air was full of
warlike noises both in France and Germany. Bismarck was stirring up
the press into a mood of outraged national honour. He was, however, saved
further embarrassment by Gramont's demand reported in the famous Ems
despatch. The original telegramme, sent by Abeken, Bismarck's aide, who
was accompanying the king, said that Benedetti had approached the king
to demand 'finally in a very obtrusive manner' that he should never again
give his consent if the Hohenzollerns reverted to the candidature. 'I rejected
this, in the end somewhat seriously, because one should not and could not
enter into such engagements *à tous jamais* [for ever].' Abeken went on to
say that the king had since received a letter from Prince Karl Anton and
had decided, on Abeken and Count Eulenburg's (the interior minister)
advice, not to receive Benedetti again, but to inform him through an
adjutant that he had now received the news (of the withdrawal) which
Benedetti had already had from Paris and that he had nothing further to
say. The king left it to Bismarck to decide 'whether the renewed demand
of Benedetti and its rejection should be made public'. The king was
therefore anxious to appear conciliatory and he kept quiet about the fact
that he had himself written to Karl Anton recommending withdrawal,
something entirely contrary to Bismarck's earlier advice. But Gramont's
and Benedetti's ham-fisted procedure had now put in the hands of Bismarck
the means of making the French look like the aggressors and to allow them
no retreat. It was just the conciliatory part of the king's action that in the
hands of Bismarck became the really inflammatory part: 'His Majesty

refused to receive the French ambassador again and caused him to be told, through the aide-de-camp on duty, that he had nothing further to say to him.'[15]

The account given of this whole episode by Bismarck in his reminiscences is seriously misleading. No doubt he was dining with Roon and Moltke that evening and the latter may well have said, when shown the edited version, 'it sounded like a retreat but now it sounds like an attack.'[16] What Bismarck did not reveal was that he had already taken steps to cover the king's retreat with a sufficiency of threatening noises. He had also, on returning to Berlin, seen Gorchakov, who happened to be there, and had assured himself that the apparent sympathy for the French predicament that existed in Britain and Russia would not lead to any Russian or British intervention. Moreover, he may well have anticipated the king's conciliatory reactions, otherwise he would have taken the trouble earlier to remove himself from Varzin and hasten to the king's side. All this does not add up to war guilt on Bismarck's part. Both sides were equally guilty and were, like everybody else, prepared to use war as an instrument of policy. Bismarck was, however, much more skilful in the *mise-en-scène* and in recovering from unpredictable setbacks. He succeeded in convincing most of Europe that they had no reason to sympathize with France. In the circumstances it would have been very difficult for Austria to fight alongside France. Most importantly, Bismarck succeeded in convincing the German public, north and south, that it was their duty to rise up against French aggression. The perfect *casus belli*, which he had often speculated might be necessary to galvanize Germany into united action, had been found. When war was already declared he caused the publication, in the London *Times*, of the plan which Benedetti had unwisely left in his hands in August 1866, that France should be compensated for Prussia's territorial acquisitions by taking over Luxemburg and Belgium. For British public opinion Belgium was a sore point and suspicions had been aroused in the previous year by a French plan to take over the Belgian railways. Napoleonic France was still in Britain and elsewhere more often seen as the disturber of the peace than Bismarck's Prussia.

*

Bismarck had succeeded for the third time in using war as an instrument of policy by limiting its extent. To keep it that way was to prove a severe struggle. He could be, more than in 1866, confident that Prussia and her allies would be victorious. The French now had a gun, the Chassepot, that was superior to the Prussian needle-gun, but French organization and logistics were much inferior to the Prussian. Even the South German contingents proved effective, in spite of the resistance there had been to the spread of Prussian military methods and organization, and their morale was high. The way the war had broken out had convinced South Germans in general that they were once more resisting the hereditary enemy that had so often in the past invaded them. It quickly became apparent that a French offensive to separate North Germany from the south was not going to materialize. Early battles in August, at Weissenburg, Wörth, Spichern, Mars-la-Tour and Gravellote, caused serious German losses, but were successful. South German contingents fought well and this raised morale further. Bismarck again followed the armies in the company of the king and of countless other royal and civil dignitaries. His private staff, Abeken, Keudell, Dr Moritz Busch, who dealt with the press, were with him.

This time both his sons, Herbert and Bill, were fighting. One evening after Mars-La-Tour, while he was with the king and Moltke, news was brought to him that Herbert was killed and Bill mortally wounded. The chancellor immediately rode out into the night in search of his sons. He found them in a village in a farmstead that was being used to house wounded men. As he entered he saw Bill, who was uninjured, but had been concussed by a fall from his horse; Herbert was lying on a straw bed, but had only a flesh wound in his thigh. To their father's great relief, neither took any further part in the fighting. By the beginning of September MacMahon's army was encircled at Sedan and had to capitulate. A hundred thousand men including Napoleon were taken prisoner. Bismarck had his famous interview with the fallen emperor, who was now afraid of being attacked by his own men, in a small weaver's cottage. 'A huge contrast to our last meeting, '67 in the Tuileries. Our conversation was difficult, if I did not wish to broach matters, which must touch him, smitten by God's mighty hand, painfully,' he wrote to Johanna.[17] God always made a more frequent appearance in his correspondence with her than elsewhere, but in the difficult weeks that followed he invoked Him more than usually. Bazaine, whom MacMahon had been sent to relieve, remained besieged in Metz until his surrender at the end of October.

To manage the political side of this war was again nerve-racking for Bismarck. Even before Sedan the demand for the annexation of Alsace-Lorraine was widely ventilated in the German press and Bismarck did nothing to discourage it. There were substantial security reasons for the annexation, the protection of south Germany against French incursions, and sometimes Bismarck emphasized these. Talking to Busch on the day after Sedan, he said: 'Metz and Strassburg, is what we need and will take – the fortresses. Alsace' – and he was obviously referring to the strong emphasis in the press on the Alsatians having been German and still speaking German – 'that is a professorial idea.'[18] That was Bismarck the cabinet politician speaking. But talking to Keudell three days after Sedan, he brought up the argument that no amount of magnanimity could stop the French desire for revenge: 'They did not forgive us Sadowa, but they will forgive our recent victories even less, however magnanimous a peace we offer.'[19] He repeated this in a dispatch to all Prussian missions a few days later. He did not resist the annexation of Alsace-Lorraine, not only because he realized that France, however leniently she was treated, would want revenge for her defeat and the loss of her semi-hegemony in Europe. The nationalist clamour in Germany for annexation was such that it would have been useless, even for Bismarck, to resist it.

The Franco-Prussian War was in fact a cabinet war that became a national war and events after Sedan, the pursuit of the war by a new French republican regime, growing French radicalism, guerrilla warfare and eventually the Paris Commune, made it ever more so. It took all of Bismarck's ingenuity to remain in control of the situation and the most bitter fight was in his own camp, with the generals. He, the saviour of the Prussian military monarchy, experienced now, even more acutely than after Königgrätz, the difficulty of making the civil power prevail over the military. The other task, which sapped his nervous energies, was the extension of the structure he had established north of the Main to the states south of it. The spirits he had raised and had so far always manipulated and controlled, militarism and nationalism, rose up to haunt him and almost slipped out of control. No wonder he was in these months that he spent in France – he did not re-enter Berlin until March 1871 – often in a highly irritable state and had to resort to his book of devotional texts to calm himself. Even so, his anger and frustration blazed forth: sometimes against the military and the general staff, the demi-gods; sometimes against the French, the civilian population that fought the invaders stubbornly, sometimes against the German princes with their petty *amour propre*. The Hohenzollern, prey to petticoat influence, as he called them, were not excluded from his anger.

The problem of bringing the fighting to a conclusion proved, after the great initial victories, difficult, and neither Bismarck nor the generals had a convincing solution. The intention of annexing Alsace-Lorraine greatly aggravated the problem. The generals had not expected the French to continue the fight when their armies had been beaten and had no plans to meet the popular resistance, by new armies and by *francs-tireurs*, that now developed. Bismarck had doubts about moving the German forces to the siege of Paris and would have preferred to leave the French to stew in their own juice and quarrel among themselves for a while. He wanted to keep the option of a Napoleonic restoration open and remained in negotiation with the ex-emperor and with Eugénie in her English exile. In his early negotiations with Jules Favre, the foreign minister of the new republican government, he used the threat of a Bonapartist restoration. The military, including Moltke, wanted the complete defeat of France in general and the end of Bonapartism in particular. In this they were at one with most of German public opinion and even with Bismarck's own family.

Then the siege of Paris moved centre stage and became the subject of bitter disputes between Bismarck and the generals. Gambetta, the radical republican war minister, left the capital by balloon and started raising new armies. The need to end the fighting became urgent and Bismarck wanted a bombardment of strong points in the city, while Moltke did not think this effective and preferred to starve the city out. Bismarck, who had moved from the Rothschild chateau at Ferrières to Versailles, wrote to his wife on 21 October: 'the gentlemen from the military make my affairs horribly difficult! they grasp them to themselves, spoil them and I am left with the responsibility!'[20] A few days later he wrote:

> I must express my indignation about newspaper reports which have reached you that it is I who is hindering the firing of our cannons on Paris and that the prolongation of the war is my fault. . . . The whole matter is enveloped by intrigue, woven by women, archbishops and professors, well known exalted influences are involved, so that the praise of the foreigners and the phrase-making should not diminish.[21]

Bismarck was clearly referring to the crown princess and the whole of what he considered English cant about the treatment of Paris and its people. But he was in fact all the time recommending a policy of the utmost severity, including hostage taking, against the resistance of the French civilian population. It brought out his streak of brutality.

Bismarck was furious at being excluded from the daily military conferences, yet he was working hard and with some success to keep foreign interference, such as any joint mediation by the powers, at bay. He was helped by the fact that the Russian government remained friendly, was alarmed by French republicanism and was chiefly concerned to use the occasion to abrogate the Black Sea clauses of the treaty of Paris, concluded in 1856 at the end of the Crimean War. The British government then concentrated its energies on getting this abrogation submitted to an international conference and Gladstone's abhorrence at the annexation of Alsace-Lorraine failed to make an impact. But the hard work Bismarck had to put into shielding his side from the adverse effects of the prolongation of the war made him all the more furious with what he considered the inadequate conduct of it. He wrote caustically to Johanna, on 16 November:

> I wasn't to begin with in favour of besieging Paris, but for other methods; but now that the great army has been tied down for 2 months while our enthusiasm evaporates and the Frenchman rearms, the siege must be carried forward; but it looks as if the 400 heavy guns and their 100,000 tons of shot are to be left here until after the peace and will then be trundled back to Berlin.[22]

Three days later he prepared his own shot, a long letter to the king, complaining about the treatment he was getting from the general staff, and demanding that he be kept informed of the intentions of the military leadership. He did not actually fire this shot until the beginning of December, in another letter demanding to be present at all military reports to the king that had political implications. The military were equally determined to keep the chancellor, 'the civilian in cuirassier's uniform', out of their decisions. Bronsart von Schellendorf, a staff officer, later Prussian war minister, wrote in his diary at this time: 'Count Bismarck begins to get ripe for the madhouse' and dreads the interference of 'a man of the ambition and lust for power of Count Bismarck'.[23] In a letter to his wife Bismarck says that except for the 'good and wise old Moltke' the general staff has been maddened by success and that he fears they might all one day be punished for their arrogant overestimate of themselves.[24] He probably had in mind the refusal of the military, as well as of German public opinion, to take the possibility of interference by the other European powers seriously. It was not until 25 January 1871 that the king came down sufficiently clearly on the side of his chancellor to enable Bismarck to conduct the final armistice and peace negotiations along his own lines. Much of what he suggested during the long siege of Paris was not militarily sound and the whole complex of military-civil relations continued to plague him for the rest of his time in office, if not in so acute a manner.

The task of bringing the southern states into some form of union with the north was no less nerve-racking than the fight with the military. One cannot but admire the mental energy which enabled Bismarck to cope simultaneously with these problems as well as with the need to negotiate an end to the war without European interference. Bismarck clung to his own solution of the German constitutional problem against all the conflicting pressures on him. What he wanted was a straightforward extension of the North German Confederation to the four southern states and the overriding reason was that it guaranteed his own power. Had he given way to the pressure for replacing the existing federation with a more unitary structure it would have opened the way to a fully parliamentary regime, which in short order would have become increasingly democratic. In the North German Confederation he had found a way of keeping these developments at bay through the elements of federalism enshrined in the Bundesrat. They were a conclusive bar to full ministerial responsibility, which he was determined to prevent. On the other hand he could not allow the petty jealousy with which at least three of the South German rulers and governments sought to preserve their sovereignty to endanger the unity of the new Reich and the supremacy of Prussia within it. Theirs was a lost cause anyway, but could still be dangerous, as it might find an ally in Saxony, the one remaining major state within North Germany other than Prussia. The pressure for a more unitary constitution came from the broad stream of German nationalism, with which the fight against France had been waged, and more specifically from the National Liberals and their allies all over Germany. It is remarkable how Bismarck managed to use this movement without allowing it any real say in the future structure of Germany. When National Liberal leaders like Lasker and Bennigsen tried to take a hand in the process, by travelling to the southern states or making proposals, he brushed it rudely aside as interference. More dangerous than mere parliamentarians was the crown prince, who also pressed for a more unitary structure.

The question was also tied up with the title which the king was to assume as head of the new Reich, the kaiser question. Bismarck and the crown prince clashed sharply over this on 16 November, an incident probably in the former's mind when he wrote to Johanna on the same day 'about princely fantasies spooking around headquarters'. The more unitary visions of the future Germany were clearly not acceptable to the southern governments, particularly those of Württemberg and Bavaria, and could only have been implemented by the use of coercion on these rulers and governments, which even the crown prince, in his impatience, was advocating. Bismarck could always use very effectively the argument that such coercion would not achieve the genuine union that was desirable. In the end he got his way completely. The key lay with the Bavarians and Bismarck was prepared to go a long way in offering them, and to a lesser extent the Württembergers, face-saving reserved powers, such as continued control over their army in peace-time and the right to maintain diplomatic representation in some foreign capitals. The Bavarians were given the chairmanship of the foreign relations committee of the Bundesrat. To some National Liberals this seemed a serious concession, possibly undermining the cohesion of the Reich, but in practice it proved virtually meaningless. Bismarck had already realized, from the experience of the previous few years, that the Bundesrat was a mechanism rather than a body exercising real power. As a mechanism it worked above all to prevent the implementation of ministerial responsibility and it did so until 1918.

The kid-glove treatment of the Bavarians and especially of their eccentric and unpredictable king, Ludwig II, helped to solve the kaiser question. King William was reluctant to accept the imperial title, which, he felt, would tarnish the glories of his Prussian kingship and he was certainly against any suggestion that it was being offered him from below, as it had been to his brother in 1849. To overcome his scruples Bismarck engineered a letter from the most senior of his royal confreres, the Bavarian king, offering his Hohenzollern cousin the title German emperor. The letter written sent by King Ludwig was almost verbatim drafted by Bismarck. In return for this service the Bavarian king, heavily in debt from building fantasy castles like Neuschwanstein, received annual payments which Bismarck drew mostly from the Guelph fund – the secret fund at Bismarck's disposal which he had obtained from the dispossession of the house of Hannover, and which he often used for bribery, especially of journalists. Thus the dispossession of one king financed the fantasies of another. Ludwig

II is often called the dream king, for he lived in a fantasy world, and later he was declared insane and unfit to rule. Count Holnstein, King Ludwig's equerry, received a commission of 10 per cent. These sordid details were shrouded in secrecy, were unknown even to the Prussian king, and not fully revealed until after 1918.

Even now King William was unsatisfied, for if he was to be kaiser at all, he had to be 'Kaiser von Deutschland' and in this he was backed by the crown prince. 'Deutscher Kaiser' sounded to him like 'temporary major' in the army, he said. This disagreement caused serious disharmony between the king and his prime minister and on the day of proclamation, 18 January 1871, they were not on speaking terms. The grand duke of Baden, who had the task of asking for cheers at the ceremony, got round the difficulty by asking the assembly to cheer Kaiser Wilhelm. Bismarck wrote to Johanna afterwards:

> This imperial birth was difficult, and kings have at such times their strange cravings, like women before they give to the world what they cannot retain. As accoucheur I frequently felt the strong urge to become a bomb and to explode so that the whole edifice should sink into ruins.[25]

The ceremony in the Hall of Mirrors at Versailles, over the dead body, as it were, of the defeated enemy, was a gesture of unrelieved military and nationalist triumphalism. Hardly a civilian was in sight, for thirty deputies of the North German Reichstag had already, a month previously, humbly besieged the king to accept the imperial title. Their speaker on that occasion was the president of the Reichstag, Eduard Simson, a converted Jew, who had also led the deputation to Frederick William IV in 1849. The circumstances were very different in 1871 and even one of the participating princes, Otto, the brother of Ludwig of Bavaria and his successor, had a sense of unease: 'I felt very hurt and pained during the ceremony. . . . It was all so cold, so proud, so splendid, so boastful and grandiose and heartless and empty.'[26] Like his brother, Otto was later declared insane and his uncle ruled as regent in his place.

All this went on when the war was not over yet. The newly raised French armies fought with valour, not least the one in the Vosges commanded by General Bourbaki, whom Bismarck had wanted to use as an intermediary between Eugénie and Bazaine, besieged in Metz. The army commander, Prince Frederick Charles, deliberately ignoring the chancellor's plan, would not let him back into Metz and he was thus free to put himself at the disposal of the republican government. It was all to no avail, for Bourbaki's army had finally, on 1 February, to cross the Swiss border into internment. On 28 January Paris fell. With the king's order of 25 January Bismarck was now in full control and he conducted the armistice negotiations with Jules Favre without any interference from the military. Favre had few cards left to play. There was a pause in the negotiations to allow elections to take place, which made the veteran Adolphe Thiers, who had so often been critical of Napoleon's policy, the effective head of the French government. Bismarck liked Thiers, in a way he often liked men who were not potential rivals, though he was occasionally irritated by his southern French loquacity.

But sympathy for Thiers and his predicament did not reduce the severity of the German terms. Bismarck still kept the option of a Napoleonic restoration open as a threat. The cession of Alsace and Lorraine was taken for granted, the French were allowed to keep Belfort, but had to agree to a German triumphal, though brief, march into Paris. Bismarck would have been prepared to forego Metz, which he thought would prove an indigestible morsel, but the generals wanted it. The war indemnity was fixed at 5 billion francs, then thought to be an enormous sum, and the German occupation was only to end when it was paid off. The calculation that this might take at least four years proved mistaken and it was in fact paid off by 1873. The preliminary peace was signed on 27 February and two days later German troops briefly entered Paris. Bismarck rode with them and was, as he told Johanna, 'everywhere recognized, a bit hooted at, but only by very small boys. No sign of any assassins.'[27] It took another couple of months before the final peace treaty was signed in Frankfurt. In the meantime the Paris Commune had broken out. It provided Bismarck with another means of bringing pressure to bear on the French negotiators. He was not above establishing contact with the communards and offering them and the Thiers government his services as a mediator. The Commune also had the effect of markedly reducing sympathies with France elsewhere in Europe. Once the Thiers government had signed the treaty of Frankfurt Bismarck facilitated the suppression of the Commune, by allowing government troops to pass through the German lines. He who had made the greatest of revolutions from above did not want any revolution from below to get out of hand.

9

IMPERIAL CHANCELLOR

Bismarck was fifty-six when he had brought about the greatest transformation in the affairs of Europe since Napoleon, but barely a third of his
time in power had passed. Nothing he could do in the future could possibly
rival what he had already achieved. A man of a different temperament might
have kept an eye open for a suitable moment to step off the stage. Threats
of resignation were part of Bismarck's stock-in-trade and the cultivation of
ill-health, real and psychosomatic, had become a habit. Nevertheless it is
impossible to discern a moment when he seriously contemplated with-
drawing. His addiction to power and his all-consuming political passion
grew with advancing age. His eventual departure was to become a fall, as
resounding and painful as any in history. Yet his great triumphs engendered
hubris only in others, not in him. On the contrary, he was plagued by
nightmares of anxiety, pessimism and dark foreboding, sometimes amounting to paranoia. It was the reverse side of the unflinching realism that made
him so formidable.

Such nightmares were aggravated by the fact that William I, aged
seventy-four when the foundation of the Reich was complete, might be
expected to depart at any moment. While he still lived it became increasingly
unthinkable that in his old age he would part company with the man who
had brought him so much glory, even if, at least until 1880, there were often
still serious differences of opinion. The long survival of the first Hohenzollern
emperor gave Bismarck one more reason, if he needed one, to stay on. He
could not abandon the old gentleman, he said, but he also complained that

with advancing age the emperor was becoming more difficult to deal with. When William I died in 1888, just short of his ninety-first birthday, the crown prince survived him by only ninety-nine days. It is impossible to know whether an earlier change of monarch would have led to the introduction of the 'English' or 'Gladstone' system that was Bismarck's nightmare. Frederick William had been useful to Bismarck at crucial moments, for example at Nikolsburg, but on the fundamental question of parliamentary government they remained divided. Behind the crown prince stood his strong-willed wife. On one occasion she said to the chancellor, half joking, that he seemed to want to become president of the German republic. He replied: 'In this country we have only royalists, who feel themselves vassals of the crown. Let the wearers of the crown beware of destroying these sentiments!'[1] In Bismarck's long sleepless nights filled with hate, Princess Vicky and her mother-in-law, the Empress Augusta, figured prominently, but he wrote in his memoirs that the older woman was even more combative and less constrained in her methods. By the 1880s liberalism was in any case much weakened and an air of resignation enveloped the crown prince, his wife and their court. The heroic founder of the Reich would have been difficult to remove against his will.

From the world in general there was no lack of recognition that the foundation of the Reich was his triumph, more than anybody else's, for all the glory that attached to the German armies and its leaders. He was now made a prince and received as a gift from the nation the Sachsenwald with Friedrichsruh, a great forested estate on the outskirts of Hamburg. He continued the lifestyle he had developed since 1866 and since the acquisition of Varzin. His quasi-dictatorship was often exercised from a distance, but he always kept his finger on the political pulse. Even before 1870 he had instituted political soirées for members of the North German Reichstag and this practice continued. He would talk freely to the deputies, at times almost making policy declarations, as he moved among his guests. His many apparent indiscretions, eagerly snapped up, were, needless to say, always carefully calculated. Even Johanna, frequently ailing and not keen on socializing, usually put in an appearance.

He kept a close grip on foreign affairs, where his mastery was universally recognized and he was rarely criticized. His reputation as a manager of foreign policy has stood the test of time better than his brooding and increasingly stultifying presence in German domestic affairs. In foreign affairs he, the great revolutionary, became strategically, but not always tactically, a supporter of the status quo. In 1866 and 1870, if he had been driven to it by circumstances, he might have tried to rouse the German-speaking subjects of the Habsburgs against their masters. But after 1870 he had no desire to pursue a pan-German agenda, though he would no doubt have played that card if the Austrians had combined with a vengeful France. But they did not, for even Beust, before his fall in November 1871, realized that a replay of 1866 was no longer on the cards. The maintenance of the Habsburg empire became a constant of Bismarck's foreign policy, though, unlike his successors, he tried to counterbalance it by maintaining close relations with Russia. It is doubtful whether his basically static approach to the European power system could have been prolonged much beyond his political life. Even in his last decade in power he found it increasingly difficult to maintain a cool, calculating cabinet policy in foreign affairs. It took him some time to accustom himself to the fact that his Germany had taken over the semi-hegemonial position previously held by France and to cope with the fear and jealousy such a position aroused.

Bismarck's prolonged stay in power has attracted much more criticism in its impact on the domestic development of the new Reich. The political system that he fashioned in its essentials after 1866 was mainly shaped by his determination to retain power, but its management came close to slipping from his hands. He only imperfectly divined whither the social forces, for the unfolding of which he had provided the framework, were taking him. His conflict with the Catholic church, the *Kulturkampf*, and his fight against socialism showed up the limits of his confrontational tactics. In diplomacy you could inflict defeats, then deal with their consequences if necessary by magnanimity, as with Austria in 1866. You could not defeat whole sections of your own population. You could not treat your domestic opponents as if they were foreign enemies.

*

The first of the major domestic confrontations, with the Catholics, began almost as soon as Bismarck returned from France and the new Reichstag for the unified country was elected. The label *Kulturkampf* was later brought into circulation by Rudolf Virchow. Bismarck did not make the Kulturkampf, but without him it would hardly have assumed the scope and bitterness that justified the label. Tensions between church and state were common in the German states in general and in Protestant Prussia in particular. Bismarck frequently inveighed against ultramontane influences, but was glad to accept some support from Catholic groups in the Prussian Landtag during the constitutional conflict. The events of 1866 divided the Catholics in Prussia, as it divided most other groups. Some clung to *grossdeutsch* ideals, others accepted the new dispensation. Among the latter was Bishop Wilhelm Ketteler of Mainz, who was also a prominent exponent of social Catholicism, the idea that the church should concern itself with problems of poverty and social harmony. On the other hand the offensive launched by Pius IX against liberalism and secularism in the Syllabus of Errors of 1864, later reinforced by the proclamation of the doctrine of papal infallibility at the Vatican Council in 1870, was seen by non-Catholics all over Europe as a declaration of war. Such fears look in retrospect exaggerated, but at the time many felt it was a war to the death between obscurantism and enlightenment. In 1869, when preparations for the Vatican Council were in train and there were signs that the pope might go on the offensive, Bismarck was not unduly alarmed. In the autumn of 1870, when Italian troops entered Rome, he was cool towards the idea that the pope might take refuge in Germany, for he did not want to offend the Italian government, but he could also see some advantages in such a move. For the same reason he reacted negatively when Ketteler appeared at Versailles in February 1871 with a petition from 56 Prussian deputies, asking the recently proclaimed emperor to help restore the pope to his sovereignty.

The chancellor was clearly taken aback when the Centre party, founded in December 1870, gained a nearly a fifth of the vote and 63 out of 387 seats in the Reichstag elections of March 1871. The party looked like a conglomerate of all those who for one reason or another were opposed to the new Reich: southern particularists, Hanoverians supporting the Guelphs, anti-Prussian Rhineland Catholics and Polish nationalists, Catholics who felt threatened by the market economy and offended by Protestant arrogance. Bismarck called them 'elements . . . that in principle fight against and negate the establishment of the German Reich.'[2] When the newly elected Reichstag debated the constitution of the new Reich, the Centre party moved an amendment that the basic citizen rights enshrined in the Prussian constitution should also be incorporated in the Reich constitution. This was widely seen not as an attempt to safeguard the liberties of all citizens, but to protect the special interests of the Catholic church. There was an impassioned debate in which the big guns on both sides took part. For the Catholics Windthorst, the diminutive Hanoverian ex-minister, was emerging as their most formidable parliamentary speaker and tactician. In the vote nearly all the other parties combined against the Centre. Immediately afterwards Bismarck wrote to Werthern, his envoy in Munich: 'the clerical faction has formed itself into a compact mass on a purely denominational basis and will sacrifice every other national and political interest to this special denominational interest.'[3] At the end of June 1871 it was decided to abolish the Catholic division in the Prussian ministry of culture. This had been formed in 1841 after a previous clash between the Prussian state and the Catholic church. It was staffed by Catholics and served as a kind of buffer between church and state. Now it was seen as a bridgehead for ultramontanism and the papacy.

Bismarck had moved on to the offensive. At the end of the year the so-called pulpit paragraph was added to the penal code. Clerics could be prosecuted for discussing, in the course of divine service, affairs of state in a manner 'liable to endanger public order'. At the beginning of 1872 Mühler, the Prussian minister of culture, who had served under Bismarck throughout the constitutional conflict, was forced to resign. For the chancellor he was not the man to conduct his offensive against the Catholic church, but before leaving his ministry he had, on Bismarck's instruction, prepared a law for the secular inspection of schools. He was succeeded by Adalbert Falk, who in the promotion of the anti-Catholic legislation fulfilled a role for Bismarck similar to Delbrück's in the economic legislation. When the Kulturkampf ended in what can only be described as failure, Bismarck in his memoirs made it out that Falk had driven him further than he wanted to go. Even he had to acknowledge that Falk was a man of great competence and serious purpose. On 30 January 1872 Bismarck himself made a speech in which he sharply attacked the Centre party and its leaders. He doubted if Windthorst, now the Centre party leader, really wanted German unity in the shape it had taken. He accused the party of 'continuous opposition in principle to the Prussian state and the German Reich'.[4] In fact he declared the Centre party members to be *Reichsfeinde* (enemies of the Reich), the tar with which he brushed all those who opposed him. He had gone out of his way to exacerbate the conflict and to give it a high profile.

As usual Bismarck had a multitude of motives for his offensive against the Catholics. His nightmares about the cohesion of the new Reich and his fear of ultramontane influences at home and abroad were genuine. To see so many of the Reich's and of his personal enemies foregather into one party was unnerving. For example Savigny, a Catholic, whom he had once marked out as Bundeskanzler before that position became so pivotal, felt himself set aside and had now become a founder member of the Centre. In his memoirs Bismarck says that he himself was motivated by anti-Polonism rather than by anti-Catholicism, but this was probably an attempt, which sounded plausible in the 1890s, to justify a failed policy. In the 1870s it was a popular policy and it made the National Liberals, the Free Conservatives and even the Progressives his natural allies. The first two were the parties with whom he now collaborated in the Reichstag, but he was under no illusion that they were his permanent friends. He wanted them to follow him, but he did not want to be dependent on them. He saw no harm in pandering to the wave of anti-Catholic feeling that swept over liberal and Protestant Germany. 'Do not worry – we will not go to Canossa,'[5] he called out to them in a famous Reichstag speech, referring to the humiliation of the medieval German emperor Henry IV by Pope Gregory VII. It signalled that he, too, saw this a struggle between darkness and light, but in fact he was not standing on the same ground as the liberals. For Bismarck the Kulturkampf was a fight against forces hostile to the state, namely to himself, and would eventually end when it was no longer required. For the liberals it was an ideological battle which could never end. The repression resulting from Kulturkampf legislation would confront the liberals with a dilemma, between anti-Catholicism and the liberal principles of freedom and toleration, which Bismarck could exploit to divide them.

He cannot have believed that the repression would be ultimately successful. Busch reports him at this time as recalling his youthful memories of the persecution of the pietists in his native eastern Pomerania by the government of Frederick William III: 'a stiff-legged gendarme, with his clanking spurs and long sabre dragging at his heels pursuing a more nimble candidate for holy orders, whom his female co-religionists were always ready to stow away in barns and cupboards'.[6] The popular response to prison sentences on Catholic clerics was at least as fierce and as often more dangerous than that of the Pomeranian pietists. Prussia was enough of a *Rechtsstaat*, a state based on the rule of law, to make the use of the law against recalcitrant bishops, priests and their flock an uncertain and hazardous procedure. Bishops and priests usually refused to pay the money penalty imposed on them; there then followed distraint of their goods, such as furniture, which met resistance from their parishioners. Finally there was imprisonment, which occasioned big popular counter-demonstrations. For example, Bishop Brinkmann of Münster was arrested in March 1875 for having filled clerical vacancies in contravention of the May laws of 1873, the most important group of laws passed during the Kulturkampf to regulate relations between church and state. Many local officials refused to act in the various proceedings against him, there was a great popular demonstration in front of the cathedral when he was arrested, and a large number of carriages from the Catholic nobility of the Münsterland accompanied him on his way to prison.[7] Bismarck claims in his memoirs that the details of Kulturkampf legislation were outside his remit, but the broad political strategy was his.

A by-product of the Kulturkampf was the further alienation between Bismarck and his erstwhile conservative friends and allies. They did not like the school inspection law, for it threatened the squire/parson control in the rural areas of east Elbian Prussia. There followed a new local government law, the details of which were the work of the interior minister Eulenburg, which was seen by Junker landowners as a further threat to their control. The change that upset them most was a more complete assimilation of the office of Landrat, usually held by a local landowner, into the official bureaucratic hierarchy. It was in fact just the sort of advance of state bureaucracy which in his earlier days Bismarck himself hated. In order to get the new Prussian local government legislation through the *Herrenhaus* (upper house), there had to be a creation of peers. Bismarck was so disgusted with what he considered the treason of the Conservative Party that he decided to give up the premiership of Prussia at the beginning of 1873 and pass it to Roon. When giving Roon notice of his intention he wrote: 'In domestic affairs I have lost the ground that is for me acceptable through the unpatriotic treason of the Conservative Party in the Catholic question.'[8] In fact many of Bismarck's old friends were now in clear opposition. Kleist-Retzow, for example, strenuously attacked the new local government law. Blanckenburg, once the husband of Marie von Thadden and nephew of Roon, did not break with Bismarck at a personal level, but withdrew from politics. Only Roon remained politically by Bismarck's side, but in his private correspondence with his nephew called Bismarck 'the great magician' who now felt comfortable 'in the role of Grand Vizier'. A few years later Roon wrote to his nephew:

> Bismarck is – though he would never admit it – in his inner being an infallible political pope. . . . To refuse due recognition to his mighty personality would only occur to a fool, who might wish to see himself on

his pedestal, but neither of us belong to the blind crowd, who deify him today and may demonize him tomorrow, and the more we are sincerely attached to him, the more deeply and painfully do we feel the ethical failings in his mighty character.[9]

Conservatives saw Bismarck and the Liberals in ever closer alliance over the whole gamut of social, economic and ideological policy. The Protestant Conservatives rejected the pretensions of the papacy, but they had much in common with the Centre party in their opposition to Manchesterism, namely the market economy, and secularism. Bismarck, who always kept all options open, realized that he might have to ally himself with the liberals permanently, especially when there was a change of monarch, and this was one reason why he gave the Kulturkampf the high emotional profile that he did in some of his speeches. The old emperor, on the other hand, was barely reconciled to his government's collaboration with the liberals. He was strongly opposed to what became an enduring part of the Kulturkampf legislation, the introduction of civil marriage, first in Prussia in 1874, and in the Reich in the following year. In his earlier years Bismarck himself was opposed to civil marriage and his former friend Ludwig von Gerlach reminded him and the world of the fact in a pamphlet. It carried on its front a quotation from a speech Bismarck had made in 1849: 'I hope to live to see the foolish fashion of our time come to grief on the rock of the Christian church.'

By stoking up the Kulturkampf Bismarck had split apart the two camps of conservatism, Protestant and Catholic, but he did not surrender to liberalism. He never gave way on what had to remain the ultimate aim of liberals, the establishment of a ministry fully responsible to parliament. At times his chief concern was to split the liberals and to highlight his hostility to their left wing, especially to Lasker. He put him on a par with Windthorst as a 'wine louse'. Throughout 1873 the renewal of military budget, temporarily renewed for three years in 1871, loomed on the horizon. Bismarck allowed the matter to drift, so that it was the next Reichstag, elected in January 1874, that had to come to a decision. The National Liberals were at their peak in terms of seats, the Conservatives were decimated, the Centre party had half as many votes and seats again as they had in 1871. The consolidation of the Centre party turned out to be the most lasting result of the Kulturkampf. It was the first of the parties to make full use of the wide Reichstag franchise introduced by Bismarck to mobilize a whole section of the population. The socialists, the second party to use universal suffrage in this way, more than doubled their vote in this election, though it was still less than seven per cent and resulted in only nine seats.

It was not the moment Bismarck would choose to separate himself from the National Liberals. Liberals had to make at least a show of rooting for an annual military budget, while Moltke and the generals wanted a permanent budget, in fact the exclusion of the Reichstag from any control over military spending. Bismarck himself was not sorry to see a compromise emerging, for a perpetual budget (*Aeternat*) would have weakened his position against the generals and made him that much less indispensable, as the only man who could manage the Reichstag. Bismarck never forgot his bitter battles with the military, but he always wore his general's uniform when he appeared in the Reichstag. In public there were all sorts of threats, that he would resign, jettison the National Liberals, make common cause with the Centre and the Conservatives, but behind the scenes it was a useful way for the chancellor to exacerbate tensions within the National Liberal party and to obtain the acceptance by the military and by the emperor of a compromise, the seven year period (*Septennat*). It still meant that a full electoral period, which at this time was three years, could pass without the Reichstag being able to vote on the military budget. Even the Lasker wing of the National Liberals had to vote for the *Septennat*, for a press campaign had whipped up feeling in favour of the generals.

A new press law was another major issue on which the government and the liberal majority in the Reichstag clashed. The governmental draft had with the agreement of Bismarck contained clauses which would allow the authorities to impose penalties on journals and editors criticizing fundamental aspects of the existing order, such as military service. Bismarck both publicly and in official consultations based his support for such provisions on the danger from the 'party of subversion', namely the socialists. It was again an issue which provoked all liberals who held their principles dear. The 1874 press law was, like the *Septennat*, a compromise between government and the liberal majority. But when in the following year Bismarck tried to strengthen further the penalties on what he called 'dangers to the state and subversive propaganda', Lasker called it a 'rubber paragraph', for it could clearly be stretched to attack almost any expression of opinion inconvenient to the government. If one of Bismarck's objectives was to drive a wedge between left and right in the National Liberal party, he was so far not successful. Nor was he for the moment willing to give up the Kulturkampf whatever his doubts about its success. In July 1874, while he was in Kissingen, a young Catholic, Kullmann, made an assassination attempt on him, which injured him slightly on one hand. He exploited it against the Centre party and it made him look to the liberals like an embattled fighter in a common cause. In his Reichstag speeches he was as confrontational towards the Centre as ever. Referring to Kullmann in a speech in December 1874 he said he claimed amid noisy scenes that the young man had been stirred by recalcitrant priests and called out to the Centre deputies: 'You may try to repudiate this murderer as much as you like, he will cling firmly to your apron strings.'[10]

*

Bismarck was aware of events in the economic sphere that were in the longer run to weaken liberalism fatally. In the summer of 1873 stock exchange collapses all over the world were heralding the end of the long mid-century boom. The Germans called it the *Gründerkrach*, the end of the euphoria of the *Gründerzeit*, the founding period. Many members of the Prussian establishment had participated in the speculative boom and were hit by its collapse. In February 1873 Lasker had already drawn attention in the Reichstag to the corrupt ramifications of the Romanian railway empire of the railway king Strousberg. Hermann Wagener, for long a close associate of the chancellor, was among those attacked by Lasker and had to resign his official position. Roon, Prussian prime minister at the time, was ineffective in defending Wagener. Bismarck was furious and it was one of the reasons why he soon decided to resume the Prussian premiership.

But the chancellor's enemies were also sucked into the financial whirlpool. In 1874 the affair of Harry von Arnim, the German ambassador in Paris, came to a head. He was one of three ambassadors who were thorns in Bismarck's flesh, but who could not easily be got rid of, because of their aristocratic connections and the favour they enjoyed in the highest royal circles. He had forced Usedom's dismissal on the king in 1869 and von der Goltz had conveniently died in the same year, but Arnim had advanced from the Vatican to Paris. Contrary to Bismarck's policy of playing ball with the Thiers government, based on the calculation that a republican France would remain isolated, Arnim advocated a monarchist restoration in France. Arnim was an arrogant intriguer who saw himself as the chancellor's successor and Bismarck's paranoia had plenty to feed on, the whole network of hostile, conservative influences, with their ultramontane sympathies and their links to the empress. He had information, through Bleichröder, about stock exchange speculations that Arnim had allegedly carried on in cahoots with the French foreign minister Decazes. Friedrich von Holstein, later the famous *éminence grise* of the German foreign office, was Arnim's subordinate in the Paris embassy and spied on his chief for Bismarck. The chancellor was not content to secure Arnim's retirement, he pursued him in the courts for the alleged purloining of official documents. To avoid imprisonment Arnim had to go into exile in Switzerland. Bismarck's remarks in his memoirs that the judicial pursuit of Arnim was excessive hardly excuses his own vindictive behaviour. His style of government aggravated the poisonous and corrupt atmosphere that surrounded the *Gründer* boom and its collapse.

It also exacerbated the bitterness of the conflict with the Prussian Conservatives that soured and irritated Bismarck so much. In June and July 1875 there appeared in the *Kreuzzeitung* a series of articles under the title 'The Era Bleichröder-Delbrück-Camphausen'. The latter was the free-trading Prussian minister of finance. The articles reflected the mood produced by the *Gründerkrach* in making international finance and bank capitalism responsible for the economic downturn. Landed property and wealth, such as that of the Junkers, was healthy and sound, finance capitalism was anti-national, parasitical and Jewish. This antithesis would continue to agitate German minds down to Hitler and would be expressed in terms that foreshadowed him. In this case the attack was clearly pointed at the chancellor. Bleichröder, in a gross overestimate of his influence, was described as the 'intellectual author' of this kind of capitalism, his opulent palace in Berlin as its centre. Bleichröder was further described as 'a wealthy fellow citizen of semitic race and Jewish faith' who had 'the ear and confidence of the leading German statesman and his ministers', who had helped the prince-chancellor build up his personal fortune 'from the time when he had to represent his sovereign in Frankfurt, St Petersburg and Paris on a modest official salary and without substantial personal wealth'.[11] Bismarck bided his time before he hit back. The heat had not yet gone out of the Kulturkampf and his dependence on the National Liberals was obvious, but also irksome. In private conversation he was talking about the need to reconstruct the party system and the loss of his former friends, which was causing him grief and sleepless nights. Ever since the estrangement between

Bismarck and the Prussian Conservatives had begun in 1866, there had been discussions about reorganizing the Conservative party to make it more loyal to him and to adapt it to the enlargement of Prussia. Hermann Wagener had floated ideas of a social conservatism that might have attraction for groups disadvantaged by the rapid spread of the market economy. But the party had remained unreconstructed, a regional party mainly based on the rural areas of the core east Elbian provinces.

At this time, at the end of 1875 and early in 1876, Bismarck made a number of important speeches in the Reichstag, where his frequent absences had been criticized. He knew how important it was to his survival that he should show himself at the same time independent of, yet capable of managing, the party situation in what was becoming, more than he originally intended, the decisive arena of national politics. His style in these speeches was an inimitable mixture of picturesque language, special pleading amounting at times to demagogy, and banal home truths. He spoke as a man who knew that he was a law unto himself and that everybody had to recognize it. Only he could have got away with such patronizing condescension and ironical contempt. In a speech on 22 November 1875 he was replying to Eugen Richter, who had become the leader of the Progressives and was to remain for the next thirty years the most consistent, not to say dogmatic, champion of liberalism in constitutional and economic affairs. The chancellor made it clear once more that he was not prepared to play the role of the head of a collegiate cabinet responsible to parliament: 'I would not under any circumstances continue to offer myself for so ungrateful a role as prime minister (*Ministerpräsident*) in a collegiate cabinet, if I was not used to obeying, from long accustomed loyalty, the wishes of my king and master; so ungrateful, so powerless, so impotent is such a role and yet so heavily responsible.'[12] Most of the rest of the speech was devoted to the subject of imperial taxation. Although he wanted no collegiate cabinet at Reich level, Bismarck wanted to develop the Reich. Ministerial responsibility would subject the Reich to trials of strength for which it was not yet ready, but better sources of revenue would make it less dependent on the separate states. Bismarck declared his preference for indirect over direct taxation and for customs duties as a means of raising money for the Reich. The need to strengthen the fiscal position of the Reich was to remain an important motive for his change of course to protection and conservatism in 1878.

*

The conduct of foreign policy was the *arcanae imperii*, the holy grail of government, which only he knew and to which he was least willing to allow others access. Yet even he had difficulty in adjusting to the changed position which the Reich now occupied in Europe. Immediately after the Franco-Prussian War Bismarck's main preoccupation was Austria. Although his disavowal of any pan-German aims was genuine enough, he could not be sure that in Vienna all desire to restore Austria's German position was dead. While France was under German occupation Austria had no potential ally on the continent. But France managed to repay the indemnity imposed in the treaty of Frankfurt more quickly than was anticipated and by 1873 the German occupation ended. It has been argued that it was this indemnity that was largely responsible for the last, frantic and somewhat inflationary phase of the German boom, but its effect may well have been exaggerated. By the time France was a relatively free agent again in European politics, a Franco-Austrian alliance was no longer likely, though the fear of it remained at the back of Bismarck's mind. Andrassy, the Hungarian who had succeeded Beust in charge of Habsburg foreign policy, became a congenial partner for Bismarck. The Austrians were doing what he had advised them to do in his conversations with Karolyi at the beginning of his premiership, they had turned their attention eastwards.

This brought another problem for Bismarck, the potential for conflict between Russia and Austria in the Balkans. Good relations with St Petersburg remained an essential requirement of German policy, but on the other hand Bismarck was not prepared to pay for ever a price of gratitude to the Russians for having abstained from impeding his policies up to 1871. Gorchakov, once a friend, was jealous of Bismarck's European pre-eminence. But the time was past for a renewal of the Holy Alliance, which been the framework for Russia's important European role earlier in the century and Bismarck was not inclined to admit a Russian influence in Central Europe which no longer had a realistic basis. What remained was some anti-revolutionary rhetoric, given resonance by events in France, but hardly sufficient to allow a return to the days of Metternich. Bismarck was prepared to reassure the Russians that he had no designs in Poland or on the Baltic provinces, where there were many Germans, though he shared the German prejudice that without this German Baltic element Russia would hardly be able to exist. A Baltic German friend reports him, in one of his frank private conversations, saying 'without German help and culture neither Russia nor Poland could govern themselves for long.'[13]

When Tsar Alexander II chose to join the meeting of the German and Austrian emperors in Berlin in September 1872, Bismarck made the best of this demonstration of monarchical solidarity, without allowing anything very concrete to emerge. Often he spoke to Odo Russell, the British ambassador in Berlin, with his legendary frankness and in this case he mocked the three monarchs as 'the three graces forming a silent but tender group to which Europe could look as a symbol of peace and confidence'. In the following year the Three Emperors' League was established but it had little substance. Bismarck wanted good relations with Russia and to prevent her from moving closer to France, but he was not prepared to take the side of Russia against Austria in the Balkans. He feared, as he told Prince Reuss, the German ambassador in St Petersburg, that France would aim for a rapprochement with Russia on the basis of common action in the Near East. Then he told the same ambassador in January 1874 that he would avoid war with France unless it was inevitable.

> We would become convinced that it was inevitable if the French Government fell prey to the domineering clericalism which we see as the born enemy of peace and order. If French policy serves the hostile aims of the Vatican towards us, we will feel ourselves threatened. . . .[14]

Bismarck saw domestic and foreign threats as one hostile amalgam and at one of his parliamentary soirées in May 1872 he said: 'My sleep is no relaxation, I go on dreaming what I am thinking awake, if I can sleep at all. Recently I saw the map of Germany in front of me, on it there appeared one decaying patch after another and peeling off . . .'[15]

The fears and problems that beset Bismarck's conduct of German foreign policy in the first few years after the establishment of the Reich came to a head in the so-called 'war in sight' crisis of April/May 1875. Moltke and the German general staff were worried by the rapid recovery of France and their alarm was given impetus by the passage in March 1875 of a new cadre law, which enabled the war strength of the French army to be raised by 144,000 men. The German alarm was scarcely justified by the facts, but there was talk of preventive war, among the military, in the press of both countries and even among diplomats. Bismarck did not believe in preventive war and was not aiming for it on this occasion, but, as so often, he favoured confrontation and provocation as a means of clearing the air. There is little doubt that he knew of the two press articles that now brought the situation to boiling point,

'New alliances' on 5 April and 'War in sight' three days later. Karolyi put it thus: 'The Prince is above all out to project the basis of his ideas into the world and to reinforce his policy through a warning . . . and this is accomplished in this way without compromising him.'

In a sense the crisis did clear the air, for it showed Bismarck that it was no longer France that was regarded as the potential disturber of the peace in Europe, but Germany. Both Britain and Russia became alarmed, offered to mediate and wanted to calm matters down. They were not prepared to see France humiliated. In the British case, opinion was alarmed by an article in *The Times*, on 6 May, by its Paris correspondent de Blowitz, under the title 'A French scare', which discussed alleged German plans for a preventive war. It had in fact been inspired by the French foreign minister Decazes, who operated skilfully in this crisis. Bismarck was particularly upset by the Russian reaction. Alexander II and Gorchakov happened to be visiting Berlin from 10 to 13 May and, while they were profuse in declarations of their concern for the maintenance of peace, Bismarck was angered by their eagerness to extinguish a fire, which he claimed had never existed. He now deeply distrusted Gorchakov and considered him motivated by jealousy of his own pre-eminent position in Europe. At all events he had to pretend that he had never wanted the crisis, but it enabled him to make a realistic assessment of where he stood in the European power game. It was also useful at a moment when the temperature of the Kulturkampf had again risen to fever pitch.

*

After the 'war in sight' crisis Bismarck spent much of the second half of 1875 at Varzin. His state of health was poor. He complained of lack of sleep, indigestion, facial neuralgia and pains in his weakened leg. Much of this was due to his intemperate eating habits, devouring whole game birds at one sitting, washing it down with champagne, wine and beer in succession. In spite of medical advice Johanna did little to discourage him. He knew himself that his habits were bad, but he also knew that his anger about the state of politics and about so many people aggravated his condition. But his giant frame could take a lot of punishment and in Varzin he soon recovered. He rose late, roamed around his extensive forests and fields, on horseback and on foot. He had a strong sense of property and was constantly adding to what he had acquired at Varzin and at Friedrichsruh. In both places he kept in touch with public affairs, particularly diplomacy, received visitors and had his confidential assistants around him, men like Bucher or Busch, and his son-in-law Count Rantzau. He was grooming his elder son Herbert for the diplomatic service and he became his eyes and ears in the government bureaucracy. When he returned to Berlin in November 1875 and made big speeches in the Reichstag, also in the Prussian Landtag, it was evident that he was reassessing the state of affairs at home and abroad.

In a Reichstag speech on 9 February 1876 he hit back in public at those of his former conservative friends who had inspired the *Kreuzzeitung* articles accusing him of corruption. He cried out bitterly,

> from such a rag one has to detach oneself, if it remains unrepentant in its falsehood; everybody, who reads and pays for it, becomes indirectly party to its lies and slanders – slanders such as the Kreuzzeitung contained last summer against the highest officials of the Reich, without a shadow of proof and in grotesque ignorance of the personalities.[16]

The immediate result was that nearly a hundred leading old conservatives, the cream of the Junker aristocracy, including the eighty-year-old father of Marie von Thadden, signed a declaration rejecting the chancellor's accusations and his 'lessons about honour and decency'. Bismarck made no secret in his inner circle of the hatred and fury to which he was roused, but he waited before hitting back, by having the names of the so-called 'declarers' published in the official gazette.

There was now a prospect of recasting the Conservative party in a form more supportive of himself and more prepared to accept current realities. A number of events occurred around this time, in some of which the chancellor was indirectly involved or of which he was at least informed, all pointing to a realignment of economic and political forces. The Central Organization of German Industrialists (*Centralverband Deutscher Industrieller*) and the Association of German Tax and Economic Reformers (*Vereinigung Deutscher Steuer-und Wirtschaftsreformer*) were founded within days of Bismarck's speech. The former was an association of industrialists, the latter of large land-owners and agrarian reformers. After three years of interrupted growth, bankruptcies, unemployment and deflationary pressures there was a crisis of confidence in the market economy. There was an inevitable growth of protectionist sentiment and the slogan 'protection of national labour' was widely heard. The big employers in the iron and steel industries were forced to dump their goods cheaply in export markets in order to keep their plants in production. Some of the bigger landowners, and the smaller ones even more so, were turning away from free trade, faced as they were with competition from the cheap commodity producers in North America and elsewhere and the loss of their traditional export markets, such as the British market, to these overseas producers. All this was bound to have political repercussions.

Some of those involved in the Centralverband and in the Vereinigung were associated with the appeal for the foundation of a new conservative party made in Frankfurt in June 1876, to be known as *Deutsch-Konservative* (German Conservatives). The majority of the signatories came from outside Prussia, but the foundation appeal was framed to build bridges to the old *Kreuzzeitung* conservatives. It also contained phrases suggesting some departure from the unfettered market of liberal theory. The new Reich was enthusiastically accepted and its authority was to be upheld against socialist subversion. Bismarck was observing these developments from the sidelines and had been consulted on the foundation of the new party. He had no intention of associating himself directly with them, any more than he had ever associated himself with the National Liberals or the Free Conservatives. When Delbrück resigned in April 1876, it was widely taken as a signal that the chancellor himself was preparing a change of front, but Bismarck went out of his way to squash any such suggestion. He made it look as if Delbrück's resignation was the result of the calumnies he had to endure in the infamous Era Bleichröder-Delbrück-Camphausen articles and the attacks he had had to suffer from the very men who were now regretting his departure. The fact was that Bismarck had increasingly criticized Delbrück behind the scenes in recent years and complained that he was getting above himself, but the timing of his departure was by no means convenient to him.

The chancellor was not going to pit himself against the National Liberals when they were still able to dominate the Reichstag. Their left wing, led by Lasker, was usually aligned with the Progressives and thus held a pivotal position. But there was a substantial shift in the elections of January 1877. The National Liberals and the Progressives together dropped from 205 to 167 seats, the Conservatives rose from 22 to 40 in their new form. The Centre lost votes, but made a slight gain of seats; the newly unified socialists now had over 9 per cent of the vote, even if it still only gave them 12 seats. In itself this shift in the Reichstag made no difference to Bismarck's hold on power, for he was determined to remain the semi-dictator operating independently of and above all other constitutional forces. Such a position would, not least in his own mind, always remain insecure and dependent on being constantly reasserted amid the shifting political currents. In September 1875, when he was still among the chancellor's confidants, Holstein had written to Bismarck's son Herbert:

> I do not think mentally he will ever quit the historical place he has hitherto occupied. To be a mere observer without the possibility of action is probably for a man of his temperament debilitating. He has moved from the company of ministers into that of the sovereigns. A sovereign never abdicates, he can only give up a part of the burden of governing as he gets older.[17]

Bismarck thus remained ever vigilant lest a rival should seek to usurp his place. Early in 1877 he saw such a rival in General von Stosch, the head of the imperial admiralty. He was a prominent member of the crown prince's camp, close to the empress and to the minister of the royal house, von Schleinitz. This was the veritable nest of vipers that was always the focus of Bismarck's hatred and paranoia. The emperor was now eighty and the accession of the crown prince could not be far distant. Bismarck suddenly lashed out against Stosch in a Reichstag speech in March 1877. Lasker and Richter, Bismarck's two *bêtes noirs*, had criticized the late presentation of the budget and once more demanded the introduction of responsible Reichministers. The chancellor, rebutting their demands, signalled his intention of linking the existing Reich offices closer to the equivalent Prussian ministries. Bismarck gratuitously revealed that Stosch had reduced the admiralty budget in response to Richter's earlier speeches, when, before the presentation of the budget to the house, the chancellor had had to fight hard to reduce the admiralty's excessive demands. 'I could not expect that the authority and persuasive powers of Herr Richter would have a greater effect on the admiralty than mine,' he declared with his usual sarcasm.[18] Thereupon Stosch as a member of the Prussian state ministry, of which Bismarck was the head, felt compelled to resign. The emperor had a high opinion of him as a general in war and resented this intrusion into his powers of command. He refused Stosch's resignation, whereupon Bismarck handed in his, on grounds of ill health. The empress was pressing her husband to accept it, but it is uncertain whether the chancellor ever gave it in writing. It was put about that the emperor refused it with a peremptory 'never'. It was hardly the moment for Bismarck to leave, for war between Russia and Turkey was about to break out. Instead Bismarck obtained another prolonged leave of absence. He was away from his post for about nine months from May 1877 to February 1878. As in his previous absences, the strategic direction of affairs abroad and at home never left his hands and certainly not his mind.

The crisis in the Balkans had come opportunely for Bismarck, as he was compelled to reconsider his strategy in foreign affairs after the 'war in sight' scare. The Balkans was an area where for the moment Germany had no major interests of her own to pursue. Bismarck expressed his view in the famous remark that the Balkans were 'not worth the healthy bones of a single Pomeranian musketeer'. His task was to maintain good relations with St Petersburg – benevolent neutrality he called it – without engaging Germany in any way positively. He did not want to give the Russians the feeling of being deserted by their traditional Prussian ally, but neither did he want to back them in the Balkans as the executant of some kind of European mission, in which he never believed anyway.

> I have always encountered the word "Europe" in the mouth of those politicians who demand something from other powers which they dare not demand in their own name. . . . In the present case Russia and England are trying in turn to hitch us as Europeans to their political wagon, which we as Germans have no call to pull.[19]

As for Austria, Bismarck's sentiments were more friendly, he now felt better about Andrassy than he did about Gorchakov, but he was inclined to advise the Austrians not to get too actively involved. The Russians were hardly strong enough, he felt, to incur Austrian hostility when they were taking on the Turks. Even when he had gone on leave in May 1877, he kept a close eye on the development of the Balkan crisis.

It was very much on his mind when on 15 June, while taking a cure at Kissingen, he dictated to his son Herbert the memorandum which has become famous as an exposition of his foreign policy principles.[20] Referring to the *cauchemar des coalitions* (the nightmare of coalitions) attributed to him in the French press, he says such a feeling would weigh upon a German minister for a long time, perhaps for ever. He would see 'as desirable outcomes for us of the oriental crisis':

1 Russian and Austrian interests and mutual rivalries should gravitate eastwards; 2 Russia's strong defensive position in the Near East and on her coasts would make her require our alliance; 3 For England and Russia a satisfactory status quo, in the maintenance of which they would have the same interest as we have; 4 Detachment of England on account of Egypt and the Mediterranean from France, which will remain hostile to us; 5 Relations between Russia and Austria, which will make it difficult for both of them to establish a common anti-German conspiracy against us, which centralizing or clerical elements in Austria might desire. If I was fully capable of working I could complete the picture that I have in mind: not that of any territorial acquisition, but of an overall situation, in which all powers except France will have need of us, and will be restrained from coalitions against us by their mutual relations.

Implicit was the concept that the other European powers would have their attention diverted to the periphery, where they might find themselves at odds with each other, while the Reich in the centre of Europe would thereby enjoy enhanced security. It was the situation that he sought to maintain as far as possible in his remaining years in power. It was the maintenance of the status quo and it gave the other European powers, in the immediate situation of disturbance and war created by the Balkans crisis, the feeling he was the anchor man of the European power system. He was under no illusion that even at this moment the tensions between the two world powers Britain and Russia could be satisfactorily resolved, as he postulated in his third point. The position of the Reich would always be exposed to danger from uncovenanted changes in the power system and demanded the constant vigilance which only he could provide.

10

TURN TO THE RIGHT

During his prolonged leave, spent mostly at Varzin, Bismarck was not only keeping a grip on the essentials of foreign policy, he was also exploring ways of dealing with the pressures of domestic politics so that his own semi-dictatorial and independent position would be preserved. To many of those who came to see him he gave the impression that he might never return to a full resumption of his duties. Central to the future of domestic political developments was the question on what support in the Reichstag the chancellor should in future base himself. Without such support the many problems requiring settlement, such as the shape of the central Reich administration after Delbrück, and the financial viability of the Reich government, could not be solved. In trying to move towards solutions Bismarck had been frequently frustrated by the National Liberals. On matters connected with creating a common judicial system for the Reich, including the law on press freedom and subversion, they had gone against the chancellor. On other issues, for example his long-running attempt to bring the railway system under the control of the Reich, even the Lasker wing had supported him. Like him they wanted to strengthen the Reich, but unlike him they also wanted to strengthen parliamentary control.

Some in his own back yard had not fully supported him and put obstacles in the way of solving all the interlocking problems. That is what he felt, for example, about Camphausen, the Prussian finance minister. He was the most important politician in financial and economic affairs after the departure of Delbrück and a convinced free trader. Articles appeared in the press, clearly inspired by the circles around Bismarck, suggesting a 'chancellor crisis': 'The need to fight for the necessary reforms piecemeal, amid misunderstandings and vexations of all kinds, perhaps without sufficient prospect of final success, this is what has induced the Prince to ask for his dismissal . . .' In another article, written by Bismarck's acolyte Moritz Busch, there was reference to a 'highly placed lady', clearly the empress, at whose court 'the dregs of the *Kreuzzeitung* society and the rooted opposition in the Upper House' come together in a Jesuitical cocktail of 'ultramontane poison from the channels of Rome with Polish and Guelph discontent'.[1]

In the face of all this Bismarck now toyed with the idea of bringing the National Liberal leader Bennigsen into the government. This would also help solve the increasing administrative burden at Reich level, by providing the chancellor with a deputy. Bismarck twice invited Bennigsen to Varzin, the second time in December 1877. In his letter of invitation he wrote:

> The current practice, brought about by the strong personality of Delbrück, produced in his time insuperable friction between the two elements [the Reich offices and the Prussian ministries] and the danger, now and later, of the Reich and Bundesrat being eroded by the separate state [*Particularstaat*] of Prussia. I am seeking the cure through an extension of the system of personal union, as it now exists in the monarch, in the chancellor, in the ministers of war and of the exterior.[2]

What he wanted was that the Prussian ministers for the various departments should also take responsibility for the equivalent Reich offices, but without establishing a collegiate cabinet over which the Reichstag might have control. He also asked Bennigsen to clarify the position of his party on tariffs and taxes, and on the railway question. These were the key constitutional and economic questions of the moment.

Bennigsen undertook extensive consultations with his colleagues, especially those on the left like Lasker. His reply to the chancellor was that he could not enter the government on his own, but had to bring at least two colleagues with him. The National Liberals were in a quandary. It might be the one chance of taking a step towards the full parliamentary system they had always sought. On the other hand Bismarck might merely be trying to involve them in the responsibility of government at a time of great economic difficulty, while through his offer also trying to widen the gulf between the right and the left wing of the party. These negotiations came to nothing. Both sides were making demands which the other side was unlikely to fulfil. Bismarck finally won game, set and match, in that in due course the National Liberals did split and became a docile governmental party, while the full parliamentary system never came and he remained the semi-dictator. But Bismarck was also in a quandary, for the way forward was not at all clear for him at the time. The emperor was aghast that he was negotiating with Bennigsen at all, without his knowledge, and a letter of reproof he wrote to the chancellor at the end of the year caused Bismarck to take to his bed once more. But the emperor was well over eighty and his successor might well install the 'Gladstone ministry' that Bismarck dreaded.

When the chancellor returned to the capital in February 1878 the domestic situation was still unresolved, but there was also a critical state of affairs abroad, with war between Britain and Russia an imminent possibility. The whale and the bear were confronting each other at Constantinople. Bismarck could, as so often before, use his barely questioned authority on foreign affairs to ride out his domestic situation. On 19 February he made one of his great foreign affairs speeches in the Reichstag. He was responding to a National Liberal interpellation, which originally he had wanted, but which then became inconvenient for him. Its central passage has become famous:

> I do not envisage the mediation of peace taking the form of playing the arbiter who declares it must be so and behind me stands the power of the German Reich, but I am thinking of a more modest role . . . that of an honest broker who is really out to see the deal done.[3]

Bismarck as the honest broker at the Congress of Berlin has entered the history books, but what he was trying to do in this speech was to dampen the triumphalist mood in Germany that saw the Reich as the arbiter of Europe. This mood had even spread to Windthorst and Liebknecht. The Centre leader argued that if Russia took Constantinople it would mean the end of Habsburg rule and the victory of the Slavs over the Germans. Windthorst's Russophobia had religious as well as racial roots, that of Liebknecht sprang from fear of Russia as the great reactionary power. Bismarck, the *Realpolitiker*, would have no truck with such ideas and rebutted Windthorst in his usual caustic manner.

Three days after this debate Bismarck suddenly showed his hand on the domestic imbroglio. Camphausen had somewhat reluctantly proposed raising the tobacco tax, as a step towards helping the Reich revenue. Without consulting him Bismarck declared that he was in favour of a tobacco monopoly and that he regarded the raising of the tax as a step towards the monopoly. Camphausen felt compelled to resign. There was now little chance that an understanding between Bismarck and Bennigsen could be reached. The chancellor was increasingly convinced that tariffs were required both for the purpose of raising revenue for the Reich and for the protection of native producers. The fact that previously free trading landowners were now also calling for protective tariffs impressed him. The widespread demand for both industrial and agricultural tariffs and the popular demand for 'the protection of national labour' might induce the parties, certainly the Conservatives, perhaps the Centre and possibly even a section of the National Liberals, to support tariffs and thus also assist financial reform. The threat of a dissolution of the Reichstag might put the parties under pressure. The parties were, however, neither able nor willing to take the responsibility for resolving the problems. Since they were in any case excluded from the citadel of executive power and Bismarck showed no intention of admitting them, it was natural for them to wait for an initiative from the government, rather than risk unpopularity and internal divisions.

Another factor had just entered the equation: the intransigent Pope Pius IX had died and his successor, Leo XIII, elected on 20 February 1878, was credited with the intention of following a more conciliatory policy towards the Reich. This opened the possibility that the Centre might support the government on some issues, especially on tariffs. Centre party voters belonged mostly to those economic groups that were calling for protection. But for the moment Bismarck had no firm prospect of carrying through the administrative and financial reforms that were clearly necessary if the Reich government was to function effectively, particularly if he as chancellor was to remain the semi-dictatorial, yet semi-detached, figure that he had hitherto been. There was naturally a widespread feeling that the Bismarckian system and its central personality had no future if they could offer no solution to pressing economic and political problems. There was a suspicion that the chancellor might attempt a constitutional coup, a *Staatsstreich*, diminishing the powers of the Reichstag, a threat which in his last decade of power from time to time figured in his political repertoire.

*

Suddenly events placed a weapon in the chancellor's hands that offered him a way out of this intractable situation. On 11 May 1878 an unemployed plumber's apprentice, Hödel, made an assassination attempt on the emperor, in which no one was hurt. Hödel had briefly belonged to the socialist party but had been expelled. Within hours Bismarck telegraphed from Friedrichsruh: 'Should we not take the opportunity to present an immediate proposal against the socialists and their press?' A hastily drafted legislative proposal was presented to the Reichstag, which no one expected to pass. Bismarck's tactics were transparent and he had tried them before. He wanted to pin on the liberal parties and all his opponents the accusation that they were soft on subversion. The law was rejected by 251 votes to 57, only the Conservatives voting for it. Bismarck looked more isolated than ever. On 2 June there was a second, more serious attempt on the emperor's life, in which he was so badly wounded that his survival, at the age of 81, was uncertain. When the news reached Bismarck at Friedrichsruh, he called out 'now we will dissolve the Reichstag', before he even inquired after the condition of the old man. These events shed a lurid light on Bismarck as a person, and are even more damaging to his reputation as a statesman. He felt at bay, surrounded by hostility and intrigue, with his inheritance already being parcelled out. The Reichstag was dissolved and in the election campaign every device of propaganda, repression and manipulation was used to frighten the voters.

It was fortunate for the chancellor that the campaign to elect the Reichstag coincided with the Congress of Berlin. For all the caution with which he had characterized his role as merely that of an honest broker, to the German public he appeared as the arbiter of Europe, the man who had transformed in little more than a decade their country from the object of great power politics into its dominant player. The very fact that the congress now took place in Berlin and was presided over by their chancellor filled the German citizenry with pride. Bismarck complained in private how strenuous the sessions were, especially as he had to conduct them in French. Little of this emerges from the lively descriptions that Disraeli, Lord Beaconsfield, the British prime minister, sent to his queen about the congress and his own meetings with the German chancellor. What particularly struck Disraeli about Bismarck was the apparently heedless indiscretions that punctuated his private conversation, which did not spare the kaiser and the Hohenzollerns in general, and the gargantuan appetite, with which he stuffed down food and drink in indiscriminate order. He and

Bismarck, both of them brilliant conversationalists and totally devoid of cant, got on famously, but the intimate smoking sessions with the German chancellor put a severe strain on Disraeli's fragile health.

The outlines of the settlement made at the congress had already been agreed in lengthy negotiations beforehand. The very fact that there was a congress and not a war between Britain and Russia meant that Russia had to disgorge some of the gains made in the treaty of San Stefano, imposed on Turkey in March after her defeat. The big Bulgaria, reaching down to the Aegean and perceived as a Russian satellite, was drastically cut in size. There were some consolation prices for Russia, Bessarabia at the western and Batum at the eastern end of the Black Sea. Austria occupied Bosnia and Hercegovina. Overall, it was a victory for the British, who kept the Russians out of the Mediterranean and acquired Cyprus. This was Bismarck's problem: not everybody could be a winner and as for being an honest broker, Bleichröder remarked that that there could be no such thing as an honest broker. The diminution of confidence in Russian-German relations that followed the 'war in sight' crisis was now aggravated and this time it was the Russians more than the Germans who felt aggrieved. They wanted gratitude for past services and felt they were not getting it. There were moments when Bismarck doubted if a congress and a settlement were in the German interest and he seems to have tossed out the suggestion to Andrassy that this might be a good moment to defeat Russia militarily. A few months later he wrote that it would be a success for German policy 'if by keeping the oriental boil festering the unity of the powers was thereby prevented and Germany's own peace assured'.[4] It was another version of the concept he had put forward in the Kissingen memorandum, that by diverting the other European powers to the periphery Germany's security would be enhanced. In the aftermath of the Berlin settlement the suspicions in the relationship with Russia caused Bismarck to move closer to Austria. The dual alliance with the Habsburg empire, concluded the following year, became a basic component of his foreign policy during his last decade of power.

The election campaign in progress while the congress was in session and the anti-socialist hysteria at its height produced a further shift away from the liberals to the conservatives, but it still left the National Liberals as the largest party, closely followed by the Centre. As for the socialists, their vote fell slightly in spite of increased electoral participation. The anti-socialist law passed in the autumn was not as stringent as Bismarck would have wished, but the National Liberals in voting for it were nevertheless reneging on the rule of law to a shameful extent. For Bismarck the rule of law, the *Rechtsstaat*, had always been an artificial concept, the dogma of jurists and professors. Fear of socialism went deep and wide and Bismarck shared it, instrumentalized it for his own purposes, but never arrived at a deeper understanding of the socialist movement. In September 1878, during the debates on the second version of the anti-socialist law in the reelected Reichstag, Bebel taunted Bismarck with his famous conversations in the early 1860s with Lassalle. After praising Lassalle as a highly interesting and intelligent man, the chancellor said his late interlocutor would have repudiated his present 'pathetic successors' with contempt.

> If Herr Bebel wants an evening's conversation with me I would not refuse, for I might hope to find out how he and his comrades envisage the future state, for which they want to prepare us by tearing down everything that exists, that is dear to us and protects us. . . . We are in the dark about it just as those attending social democratic meetings; they receive no enlightenment about it, there are promises that with less work there will be more money – nobody says where it will come from, especially where it will come from once the spoliation of the present possessors has been completed.[5]

This is how Bismarck viewed the socialists when he was about to embark on a fight with them that proved as unwinnable as his fight with the Catholics.

The socialists had been a unified party since 1875. The establishment of the Reich had rendered obsolete the bitter division between the pro-Prussian Lassalleans and the *grossdeutsch* Bebel-Liebknecht party, known as the *Eisenacher*. The Gotha programme adopted by the unified party glossed over the doctrinal differences between the two sections, which in any case mattered little to the rank and file, but it attracted scathing criticism from Marx for precisely this lack of doctrinal rigour. What mattered was that there now existed in Germany a workers' party with a radical democratic programme which could benefit from Bismarck's own innovation, universal suffrage. In the 1860s Bismarck had seen the worker question as a means of weakening the liberals. Now he saw it as a threat in itself, but he was also still using the anti-socialist hysteria as a means of stretching the liberals on the rack of their own principles. It was a painful task for Bennigsen to go back on much of what he had said on the first socialist law earlier in the year for the sake of keeping his party united. He knew that the battle over tariffs, which was already looming, would divide his party even further. Most of the amendments to the government draft came from the left wing of the National Liberals, in particular the limit of two-and-a-half years on its duration, moved by Lasker. In practice it made little difference, for it was renewed until, in 1890, the question of renewal contributed to Bismarck's fall in very different circumstances. Richter for the Progressives and Windthorst for the Centre opposed the anti-socialist law vigorously, but all the National Liberals voted for it in the end.

Under the law, associations, publications and meetings 'which through social democratic, socialist or communist intentions aim to overthrow the existing state and social order' could be suppressed. The application of such prohibitions did not rest with the judiciary, but with the police authorities. A so-called lesser state of siege could be imposed upon localities, which made it possible to expel social democratic functionaries. The one great loophole was that the social democrats were not prevented from putting up candidates for elections from the Reichstag downwards, for this would have been unconstitutional. The fighting of elections was made difficult for the socialists by the other prohibitions, but after a temporary dip the socialist vote rose relentlessly through the next decade, until on the eve of Bismarck's fall they were the largest party in terms of votes, of which they got nearly a fifth, though not in terms of seats. That was the extent of Bismarck's failure, but for the moment he was moving closer to his goal of shifting the political centre of gravity further to the right in order to underpin the continuance of his regime. But the National Liberal party had also succeeded in frustrating what he clearly wanted, namely the break with a minority of left-orientated National Liberals around Lasker. Such a split would enable the chancellor to rely on an amenable centre group made up of conservatives and right-wing National Liberals.

*

The next step was the move towards tariffs and protection. A day before the anti-socialist proposals were passed into law a protectionist association of over two hundred Reichstag deputies was formed. It included nearly all Centre party and most Conservative and Free Conservative deputies and over a quarter of the National Liberals. The way was open for Bismarck to come out unequivocally in favour of tariffs, something that had in any case become difficult to resist. His aim was not merely to give way to the protectionst clamour from industry and agriculture, but at least as much to do what he had wanted all along, to use tariffs as a means of strengthening the revenue of the Reich. But what mattered more than anything to him was his own independent position above the parties, which made him into a separate centre of power within the state, to which even the monarch had to submit, even a monarch such as the crown prince might any day become. 'A parliamentary party may support the government and thereby gain some influence over it, but if it tries to govern the government, then it forces the government to react against it,' he said.[6] It was a remarkable feature of the situation that the Centre party, which he had vilified so consistently, now supported him over tariffs. It was support at a price, for an easing of the Kulturkampf was now definitely on the agenda, though it was still to take many years to realize and to involve much manoeuvring between the Vatican and Bismarck behind Windthorst's back. It aroused a great deal of attention when at one of Bismarck's parliamentary soirées at the beginning of May 1879 Windthorst was seen in long and friendly conversation with the chancellor. Asked what had been discussed, Windthorst said with a smile 'extra centrum nulla salus' (there is no salvation outside the centre). An immediate price for the Centre's support of the tariff law was the resignation of Falk, who now felt himself to be an obstacle to the easement of the Kulturkampf.

The support of the Centre would not have been forthcoming but for a compromise over the distribution of the tariff revenues. For obvious reasons the Centre was strongly committed to the federal structure of the Reich, whereas it had been one of Bismarck's main intentions in promoting tariffs to make the Reich more independent of the Länder financially, as well as reducing the budgetary control of the Reichstag. What became known as the Franckenstein amendment, after a Bavarian Centre party deputy, laid it down that revenue from tariffs and from the tobacco tax exceeding 130 million marks was to go the Länder, though much of it would then come back again in the form of matricular contributions. Bismarck's aim of making the Reich less of a pensioner of the member states was thus at least partially frustrated. The rapprochement between Bismarck and Windthorst was by no means conclusive and the Centre party remained an opposition party. The Franckenstein amendment meant that most of the National Liberals voted against the tariff law, for the strengthening of the Reich could not now be taken seriously as one of Bismarck's aims. Any suggestion that the Kulturkampf might be written off as a failure was still anathema to most liberals.

In the debates Bismarck did his best to isolate and put in the dock the left wing of the National Liberals. To the majority, with whom he still had a hope of collaborating, he offered the tariff law as a revenue-raising measure to consolidate the Reich and played down its protectionist motives, but he ferociously attacked Lasker, the leader of the left wing. Lasker had accused him of speaking as a member of the possessing classes in his support for indirect imposts on the poor man's necessities.

> Yes I can say just as well to the deputy Lasker that he espouses the financial policy of someone without property; he is one of those gentlemen, who form the majority in the making of all our laws, of which the Bible says: 'they sow not, neither do they reap, they do not weave nor spin, and yet they are clothed' – I won't say how they are clothed [laughter]. The gentlemen whom our sun does not warm, whom our rain does not make wet, unless they happen to have gone out without an umbrella . . .[7]

It was vintage Bismarck in his most sarcastic vein.

Bennigsen tried right up to the crucial votes in July 1879 to come to an understanding with Bismarck, on the basis that the Franckenstein amendment would be dropped, in return for which the National Liberals would support the tariff laws, provided Bismarck gave certain 'constitutional guarantees' concerning the budgetary powers of the Reichstag. Yet rather than accept even such a minor concession towards the principle of parliamentarization, the chancellor preferred to accept the Franckenstein amendment. He was embarrassed when two other Prussian ministers resigned along with Falk and spoke of 'a ministerial strike'. Their replacements were men whose political orientation was much more conservative. One of them was Robert von Puttkamer as successor to Falk. He acquired a particularly reactionary reputation when he became minister of the interior two years later. But for the moment these resignations reinforced the feeling that it would prove difficult to find a dependable base to replace the collaboration with the National Liberals.

In a speech on 9 July 1879 Bismarck once more justified his position as a minister who had to remain independent of parties and could not agree to become a parliamentary minister.[8] He accused the liberals of undermining the cohesion of the Reich just as much as the Social Democrats, a provocative remark which aroused a storm of protest among the deputies on the left. If the National Liberals had a majority, and, as he pointed out, they only had a quarter of the seats, and they collaborated with him, they might have more influence over his policy, provided 'they don't demand from me that the drop of democratic oil required to anoint the German kaiser should become a bucketful'. There was a veiled threat. He was accused of siding with reaction, but this accusation might induce a minister 'to fight the hostility, which the suspicion of reaction brings . . . by seeking the support of those who for the moment are less hostile'. Bismarck was executing a conservative turn, but he put the blame for it on the liberals, who were not cooperating with him on the only terms he considered acceptable. He now blamed men like Richter and Lasker and their followers for attacking him when he was introducing reforms vital to the Reich. Yet it was he, he reminded them, who had, against the inclination of his older conservative friends, insisted on continuing the constitutional system in 1866. He was not in love with the constitutional system as such, he said, but considered it the only possible form of government to achieve German unity. He had then had to fight the Kulturkampf, 'in fact because of the connection between the Polish question and church affairs', and this had 'robbed [me] of the natural support of the conservative party' and 'the ways I had to go, in order to develop the Reich's constitution and give it a guarantee of durability – these ways would probably have been different if the conservative party had not deserted me.'

Bismarck's conservative turn has been interpreted in much recent historiography as amounting to a new foundation of the Reich, almost as important as that of 1871. He would not have it seen that way, but as usual his reading of history was self-justificatory rather than accurate. He claimed that he had been forced, step by step and through developing circumstances, into a revision of the collaboration with the national-liberal movement, into which he had entered in 1866, and there was even a suggestion in the speech of 9 July 1879 that at some time in the future he might get together again with his former 'comrades-in arms'. But the Prussian constitutional system which he had perpetuated in 1866, when after the success of Königgrätz, as he put it, he might have gone with colours flying into a bold policy of reaction, was not liberal and fell far short of realizing the aspirations of German liberalism. It was the tragedy of those who still cherished these aspirations, men like Richter, Lasker or Bamberger, that it was now too late to realize them.

Many of the developments that now pushed the centre of political gravity further away from liberalism were not of Bismarck's making. He was not responsible for the economic slump after 1873, which so radically changed all expectations. Indeed, had governments of that age been held responsible for the economic weather and been deemed capable of changing it, he might have been swept from power. He had, however, to respond to what was occurring: loss of faith in the market, the call for the protection of national labour, the rise of interest groups and lobbies articulating the dissatisfaction of their clientele with the state of the economy and advocating specific remedies to suit their separate and often incompatible needs. The parties could not offer remedies, for they had no means of implementing policy. The chancellor thus had an opportunity of by-passing the parties and finding a way forward mainly designed to safeguard his own independent position of power. In this he was not as successful as he had hoped. In his last decade of power a secure right-of-centre rally, or *Sammlung*, as it came to be called, never emerged. The solidarity of the elites, agrarian-aristocratic and industrial-bourgeois, was real enough against the socialist threat, but limited in economic matters. Nevertheless, if Bismarck's repackaging of the political forces in 1866 had shifted the centre of gravity well to the right of what was previously expected, the revamp of 1879 nudged it further in that direction. Exclusive and strident nationalism was given an even more favourable framework in which to operate, while the counterforces were severely handicapped. In these developments Bismarck played a central role and used to the full the heroic, mythical stature he had acquired in the eyes of the German public. It was a form of Bonapartism.

11

POWER PROLONGED

In changing course and allies and in fighting elections, to the Reichstag in 1878 and to the Prussian Landtag in 1879, Bismarck had not only used his myth, but also what appeared to be his standing as the arbiter of Europe at the Congress of Berlin. It was less obvious to the public that the aftermath of the congress had left Bismarck's foreign policy dangerously exposed. Mutual suspicion between Berlin and St Petersburg, evident since at least the 'war in sight' crisis, had multiplied. The Russians blamed Bismarck for the setback that they had suffered at the congress; there were renewed efforts to strengthen Russia's relations with France and Russian troop concentrations on the Polish border with Germany. The Russians were also annoyed by the new German tariff policy, which might restrict their agricultural exports to the German market. German veterinary regulations, which impeded the import of cattle even more than the tariffs, were another Russian grievance. There were other pinpricks that the Russians could interpret as provocations. Under a clause in the treaty of Prague of 1866 Prussia agreed to hold a plebiscite in the areas of North Schleswig inhabited by a large number of Danes. Russia attached importance to this clause, because of her dynastic ties to and strategic interest in Denmark. Bismarck chose this moment to make public the fact that Austria had agreed to this clause being dropped. Alarm bells began to ring when on 15 August 1879 William received a letter of complaint from his nephew the tsar, which in spite of professions of friendship and familial devotion, was judged to have a threatening undertone. It became known as 'the box on the ear' letter.

Bismarck had left Berlin soon after the passage of the tariff law to take cures at Kissingen and Gastein. The tsar's letter confirmed him in the view that it was time to seek a closer alliance with Austria, the pressure of which might in due course induce the Russians to resume a meaningful place in the Three Emperors' League. Bismarck had long regarded the survival of the Habsburg empire as a vital German interest and this had motivated his restraint after Königgrätz. He now had in mind a far-reaching alliance, which would almost amount to a reversion to the German Confederation. He knew that a closer alignment with Austria would be popular in Germany as an assertion of the German presence against the pressure of the Slavs in eastern Europe. At Gastein at the end of September Bismarck met Andrassy, who was about to resign as Austrian foreign minister. Bismarck suggested a far-reaching defensive alliance, to be ratified by the parliamentary institutions of both empires, which might also be extended to a customs union. Andrassy was not prepared to go so far and the dual alliance signed on 7 October 1879, initially for five years, was in form an old-fashioned piece of cabinet diplomacy. The actual terms, though not its existence, remained secret till 1888.

In retrospect the dual alliance looks like the first step in the division of Europe into blocs and the beginning of the process by which Germany, the rising power, tied herself fatally to a weaker and declining partner. At the time Austria was still a major power and Bismarck argued strongly that if this opportunity of an alliance was rejected, the Habsburg empire might turn to the French alliance that had so often seemed a possibility before and after Königgrätz. This might then lead to a dangerous tripartite pact between Russia, Austria and France. He used this argument in his clash with his own master, the emperor, who strongly opposed the Austrian alliance. William was still entirely committed to the traditional close relationship with Russia based on conservative solidarity and dynastic ties. His reaction to the 'box on the ear' letter was much less forceful than Bismarck would have liked and the chancellor was less than delighted when the two emperors met in Poland at the beginning of September. Only Manteuffel was present, the man usually employed when Berlin wanted to make itself pleasant to St Petersburg: Bismarck felt that this was not the time to make oneself pleasant. The chancellor was evidently not prepared to interrupt his cure at Gastein or judged it impolitic to appear at the side of his master at this moment. William might even think, if he saw him, that he did not look as ill as he made out and that his threat to resign was not genuine.

Instead Bismarck went on to Vienna to negotiate the details of the Austrian alliance. To get William finally to sign it required all the subtlety and brinkmanship Bismarck was capable of. What particularly upset the emperor was that the alliance treaty appeared to impose unequal obligations: Germany had to support Austria if she was attacked by Russia, but Austria was only required to remain neutral if Germany was attacked by France. This did not bother Bismarck, since an attack by France without the help of Russia was very unlikely. The chancellor threatened to resign unless the treaty was signed, William threatened to abdicate, the chancellor mobilized a collective threat of resignation by the Prussian state ministry, before the emperor finally gave way. It was the last great clash between the ageing emperor and his chancellor. With his well-calculated frankness Bismarck put it about that the great fund of 'royalist sentiment and veneration towards the king', with which he had entered upon his office was now nearly exhausted. In a conversation with Scholz, the state secretary of the treasury and later Prussian finance minister, he went through all the great occasions, the intended abdication in 1862, support for Augustenburg in 1864, the intention to march on Vienna in 1866, the refusal to take the imperial title in 1870, when he had had to wrestle with the king:

> If someone had to write the inside history of the last few years they would find that my chief merit lay in my being the shield of the country against its own master and in preserving him from fatal deeds or omissions . . . but this always corrosive struggle has brought me low.[1]

The clashes with the king no doubt cost him even more nervous energy than the battles with his many other opponents, but if his health had deteriorated his immoderate habits and lifestyle were as much to blame as the volcanic passions he found so difficult to control.

His diplomacy remained as coolly calculating as ever and he was under no illusion, whatever he may have argued, that the dual alliance solved Germany's security problem. To some extent Germany was now carrying the burden of containing Russia in the Balkans that Britain had so often taken on, most recently at the end of the Russo-Turkish war. A tentative enquiry in London in the summer of 1879 about the British attitude in case Germany had to continue resisting Russian provocations evoked only a non-committal reply from Disraeli. One purpose of the closer link with Austria had always been, in Bismarck's argument, that it would eventually force Russia to come to heel. In the next twenty months Bismarck used events and personalities with his usual skill to breathe fresh life into the Three Emperors' League. He was helped by the departure of Gorchakov and the appointment of the more pro-German Giers as Russian foreign minister.

When the Liberals won the British general election of 1880 and Gladstone replaced Disraeli as prime minister, Bismarck exploited the Liberal leader as a bogeyman to frighten the Russian leadership. He depicted him not only as a radical, but claimed that England could not be far from becoming a republic. Bismarck was well aware of the internal weaknesses of Russia and the turbulent state of her domestic politics, which makes it unlikely that he believed that a Russian attack on Austria or Germany or both was a realistic threat. The assassination of Alexander II in March 1881 was further grist to the Bismarckian propaganda mill in highlighting the dangers of an international anarchist-socialist conspiracy. Bismarck had almost more difficulty in persuading Vienna than St Petersburg that a renewal of the Three Emperors' League was desirable. Haymerle, Andrassy's successor, was intensely suspicious of Russian intentions and there remained many bones of contention between Austria and Russia in the Balkans.

The signature of a new Three Emperors' League on 18 June 1881 was therefore a considerable triumph for Bismarck, a high point of his diplomatic achievement and eloquent testimony to the powerful position Germany and he personally enjoyed in Europe. The treaty enabled him to apply the brakes on both Russian and Austrian expansionist ambitions in the Balkans. He could claim that there was now less cause for his nightmares about hostile coalitions and that he had struck a blow for peace and stability. He knew that it was a limited stability, for there were many dynamic tendencies – pan-Slavism in Russia, the aspirations of the Balkans nationalities, and the Austrian need to combat these aggressively – that made the treaty precarious. It was implicit in the fact that it was limited to three years and that it had to be kept secret. Bismarck, with his congenital pessimism, had no unrealistic expectations. The clash of interests was such that

> we could not expect mutual friendship and love, but we can be glad if we succeed in living in peace with a neighbour, with whom war would not only be an evil like all wars, but without any desirable prize in case of victory.

The 'probability of such a war' with Russia was at least reduced.[2]

In the following year, 1882, a further brick was cemented into Bismarck's alliance system of the 1880s, the conclusion of the Triple Alliance between Italy, Austria and Germany. Italy had taken the initiative, for she now felt more threatened by France and her imperial foray into Tunisia than concerned about her remaining irredentist claims against the Habsburg empire in Trieste and the south Tyrol. It was Bismarck himself who had encouraged the French interest in Tunisia, to divert her from pursuing her revanchist aspirations against Germany, and also to set her at odds with Italy and Britain. It was part of the Triple Alliance that it was intended to give Austria additional security against a possible Russian attack, by securing her on the Italian flank. There was thus an implicit incompatibility with the Three Emperors' League, but both treaties were secret. It was accompanied by declarations, insisted on by Italy, that nothing in the treaty was directed against Britain. Bismarck was thus the spider at the centre of a diplomatic network of great complexity, the spinning of which was a masterpiece of cabinet diplomacy. In an age when popular pressures and ideologies were of increasing importance, it was bound to be precarious.

*

The basis of Bismarck's domestic policy after the changes of 1878/9 also rested, like his system of foreign alliances, on alignments that were by no means dependable. The concessions Bismarck was prepared to make in the Kulturkampf legislation were designed to keep control firmly in the hands of the Prussian state, while reducing the sense of grievance among ordinary Catholics. 'We will not treat with Rome, we won't go to Canossa, we are trying, independently, on our own to make peace with the Prussian Catholics,' he told Moritz Busch in May 1880.[3] To the crown prince, who in common with the liberals, was reluctant to see a retreat over the Kulturkampf, he wrote on 23 August 1881:

> We have regained through the May laws, in the main, the strong points, which we surrendered in 1840 and 48, but now it is a matter of allowing the external manifestations of the Kulturkampf to disappear, while carefully maintaining our arsenal of weapons, so that the Catholic voters can see nothing that can made to appear as an oppression of the Church.[4]

Bismarck thus wanted to avoid any impression of retreat, while at the same time outflanking Windthorst and the parliamentary leaders of the Centre party. One way to do this was to appease the ordinary Catholic voter, the other was to negotiate directly with the Vatican, where there was a strong desire to bury the hatchet with Germany. Neither of these outflanking manoeuvres could be rapidly effective. The Centre party voted for the tariff law, but it remained otherwise an opposition party.

As for the National Liberals, a small number of right-wing deputies had left the party when it voted against the tariff law. This was followed by elections to the Prussian chamber of deputies, in which the National Liberals dropped from 169 to 104. Bismarck had the satisfaction of seeing Lasker lose his Prussian seat. Lasker left the party in March 1880 and later in the year other prominent figures, Bamberger, Forckenbeck and Stauffenberg, followed. The last two were the men Bennigsen had wanted Bismarck to include in his government two years earlier. This split known as the Secession came over the relaxation of some of the Kulturkampf laws, which was judged by the Secessionists to be a better issue on which to seek detachment from Bismarck than the renewal of the septennial military budget. The Secessionists felt that any further collaboration with Bismarck would damage the long-term future of liberalism. They looked to a time when the overmighty chancellor was gone and the crown prince was on the throne. Bismarck had therefore obtained one of his aims, to split the National Liberals. As he saw it, the secessionists were those who clung obstinately to the old liberal dogma of parliamentary control, rather than concentrating on the interests of their constituents. But the liberal split was a negative success for the chancellor, for no new basis for a reliable majority had emerged. Even the passage of the septennial military budget brought further problems, for it raised expenditure when the Reich's revenue problem remained as intractable as ever. Bismarck had to get further taxes through the Reichstag, otherwise he would again face the stagnation that threatened his hold on power.

There was another strategy that Bismarck pursued in seeking to cut free from his dependence on the Reichstag. It was to bypass the political parties altogether by establishing a direct link between the government and the interest groups and lobbies that had brought protection on to the agenda. In October 1880 Bismarck personally took over the Prussian ministry of trade and caused a proposal for a Prussian economic council to be worked out. It was to consist of representatives of chambers of commerce, trade and agricultural associations and thirty nominated members, half of them workers and artisans. It was to work with government departments in the drafting of economic regulations. What Bismarck would really have liked was such a council at Reich level, but it was immediately recognized in the Reichstag that this was an attempt to form an alternative or even counter-parliament. Suspicion of what was now commonly called the 'chancellor dictatorship' was widespread. Therefore only the Prussian council could be established on the basis of the greater support the government enjoyed in the Prussian Landtag as opposed to the Reichstag. In fact even the Prussian council was almost entirely stillborn, for it met only rarely. Bismarck also toyed with more direct ways of 'drying out' the Reichstag, for example by lengthening the period for which budget allocations were made, and thus reducing the need for the Reichstag to be called into session. In all these initiatives he used the argument which he had always used against the left liberals: these parliamentarians were theorizing bureaucrats and professors who impeded the measures dealing with the real needs of the people.

Whatever he did Bismarck could neither reduce the powers of the Reichstag nor make it less important. In fact the rise of state interventionism, the reverse side of declining *laissez-faire* liberalism, made legislation ever more important and new laws could not be made without the Reichstag. There remained only one further option for Bismarck, a constitutional coup to reduce the powers of the Reichstag and curtail universal suffrage. At the height of the hysteria over the assassination attempt on the emperor in 1878, he told the wife of the Württemberg envoy in Berlin, Baroness von Spitzemberg, with whom he was friendly, that everybody around him, especially his colleagues in the Prussian state ministry, were so spineless that he had constantly to wave the big stick of a constitutional coup. The constitution was a compact between twenty-five sovereigns, could be revoked by them and it might be within the chancellor's capacity to persuade the Bundesrat to agree to such a constitutional revision. For this process Bismarck coined the verb *staatsstreichern*, from the German *Staatsreich*, a *coup d'état*, and this was what he kept hinting at every so often during his last decade in power. In conversation with Frau von Spitzemberg '*staatsstreichern*' was said in his ironical manner, with half a smile.[5] But he could threaten it more seriously, as in his speech of June 1882, when the Reichstag had turned down one of his favourite financial proposals, the tobacco monopoly.

> If I became convinced that absolutism and patriotism coincided, if German nationhood could only find protection and honour with the ruling houses, principally with my own master, if I had to opt between

the fatherland and a parliamentary majority, there could be no doubt about my choice.[6]

Staatsstreichern never went beyond a threat, but when he came closest to carrying it out, in 1890, it helped to bring him down.

*

Such was the miasma of distrust that now surrounded the chancellor, at least among the political classes, that even the constructive initiatives he took were treated with suspicion. This was the case with the social insurance schemes that he brought to fruition in the 1880s. He had toyed ever since he came to power with the idea of doing something about what was broadly termed the social question. He believed in the loyalty of the masses to the monarchical order provided they were not misled by self-interested agitators. His predominant motive was often, as in his talks with Lassalle and in his adoption of universal suffrage, to outflank the liberals. When the fight against socialism became a major preoccupation he did not entirely lose sight of the need for amelioration in the living conditions of the worker. In his speeches on the anti-socialist laws of 1878 he stressed that the fight against social democracy needed to be complemented with measures to improve the situation of the workers. He had, however, set his face against an extension of factory legislation, measures to limit hours of work and conditions of employment particularly for women and children. In this respect he concurred with the usual argument of employers that such measures would damage competitivenes. He was infuriated when a factory inspector criticized the conditions in a paper factory on his Varzin estate. Here he displayed all the hostility to bureaucracy characteristic of the Junkers as a class.

This left insurance against accidents and sickness and pensions as the area in which he felt improvements in the conditions of the worker should be made. He saw it as a means of tying the working classes to the state, in contradistinction to liberal *laissez-faire*, which would leave them to their own devices. His preference was therefore for insurance schemes administered by the state; he regarded the state pension scheme that was introduced in 1889 in the last of the three major measures of this period as the most effective in giving the worker a stake in the existing order. As was so often the case with Bismarck what mattered most to him was less the substance of these policies than their impact on the immediate political situation. They were meant to take the wind out of the sails of the socialists and, in so far as they were opposed by the liberals, as they were bound to be, they gave Bismarck a chance to attack them as narrow adherents of Manchesterism. In his first major speech on the accident insurance proposals he flung at Richter such gibes as: 'let each man see how he gets on and where he gets to' which rhymed in German; 'to him who hath shall be given, from him who hath not shall be taken.' He attacked Bamberger, who had shown concern for the private insurance companies: 'That these noble souls had sacrificed themselves for the sake of the workers by establishing their joint stock companies I have never believed,' which earned the chancellor a shout of approval from Bebel 'very good'. Bismarck claimed that his aim was 'practical Christianity', adding with a thinly veiled anti-Semitic dig at Bamberger that he appeared to have taken no exception to the word 'Christian'. The reference to 'practical Christianity' was also an appeal for support to the Centre party.[7]

Bismarck was speaking on the proposals for accident insurance that had originally been prepared for him by an official in the trade ministry, Theodor Lohmann, whose interest in social policy was guided by Christian motives and a concern for the dignity of the worker. Another draft came from a Ruhr mining and steel industrialist Louis Baare, who, while prepared to extend employer liability for accident through compulsory insurance, wanted to protect industry from having to meet the cost. Bismarck himself ensured that a Reich insurance institute was put at the centre of the official draft, with the cost being divided equally between employer, employee and the state. It may now seem short-sighted on the part of the liberals that they opposed these proposals so strenuously, but behind anything coming from the chancellor ulterior motives were suspected. State socialism, an authoritarian regime fortified by plebiscites, Bonapartism reinforced by bread and circuses in the style of ancient Rome, these were the devices which were widely attributed to Bismarck to shore up his chancellor-dictatorship. He in turn blamed the parties for looking at everything from the point of view of party tactics, 'from the feeling "away with Bismarck" and the like. I would wish, as soon as possible, another in my place, if he would only continue this work, I would gladly say: "Son, here is my spear", even if he wasn't my own son [laughter].'[8] There were already fears of a Bismarck dynasty. The government proposals were mauled in the Reichstag committee set up to examine them. The liberals saw the state subsidy as 'state socialism'; the Centre, always out to stress the federal nature of the

Reich, turned against the Reich institute and substitued Land institutes. When the Reichstag accepted the draft in this modified form, without state subsidy and Reich institute, Bismarck withdrew the proposals.

It required two more bites at the cherry, in 1883 and finally in 1884, before accident insurance could pass into law. Bismarck had by this time given up the idea of having a Reich institute of insurance and a Reich subsidy and had thereby met the objections of the Centre party. He had gone for corporative organizations, each comprising a branch of industrial activity, to administer the insurance scheme, part of his many plans to 'dry out' the Reichstag by devising alternative methods of interest representation. By this time the less contentious scheme of health insurance had been passed into law and both schemes gave an opening to worker representation in their administration. In due course this helped to turn the Social Democratic Party into a reformist rather than a self-professed party of revolution. In his speech on the introduction of the third accident insurance proposal in March 1884 he strongly counterattacked those who accused him of state socialism. 'If you accuse me of socialism, I am not deterred. Where is the permissible limit of state socialism? Without it we cannot carry on. Every kind of poor law is socialism,' he said. To those like Bamberger, who accused him of curtailing liberty by establishing compulsory state insurance he said:

> Freedom is a vague term; no one can use the freedom to starve . . . in my experience everybody means by freedom only freedom for himself and not for others . . . what they mean by freedom is really dominion; 'freedom of speech' means 'dominion of the speaker', 'freedom of the press' means the predominant influence of editors and newspapers.[9]

Always he made the distinction between the professional agitators who run the socialist parties and need a discontented working class to do their business, and the real workers who would benefit from his social policies. In 1889 the old age and invalidity insurance bill was introduced as the last of the three social insurance schemes and the Social Democrats again opposed it. In what turned out to be his last speech to the Reichstag, on 18 May 1889, he said: 'The masses which are dissatisfied with something, which even the Social Democrats could not remedy, vote at elections for the Social Democrats, because they want to express their dissatisfaction by voting against the government. Completely different is the position of the gentlemen, whose power rests on the fact the masses which they lead or mislead, should remain dissatisfied.'[10]

*

If Bismarck had hoped that the original accident insurance proposal would help the governmental parties in the Reichstag elections of October 1881 he was to be disappointed. In spite of a massive press campaign, direct pressure on state employees and outright persecution of socialists through the imposition of the lesser state of siege in many cities, the elections produced a definite defeat for Bismarck. The Secessionists won as many seats as the National Liberals, who had tried to maintain their link with the chancellor, and the Progressives nearly doubled their vote and more than doubled their seats. It was not possible, it seemed, to mobilize the German middle classes behind Reich and chancellor and against those who had been classified as *Reichsfeinde*, be they liberals, Catholics or even socialists. Even among conservatives there were problems. The Christian-Social Party of the court preacher Adolf Stoecker had become attached to the German-Conservatives. Stoecker sought to woo the working classes away from socialism, and anti-Semitism figured prominently in his demagogic repertoire. Bismarck often exhibited the instinctive anti-Semitism of the Prussian Junker, but was no dogmatic, let alone racial anti-Semite. He once said that the not uncommon marital alliances between Prussian aristocrats and Jewish heiresses produced a very positive mix and he employed Jews, like Bleichröder or his Friedrichsruh doctor, in his confidential service. But that so many of his hated enemies, Lasker, Bamberger, Sonnemann, the editor of the *Frankfurter Zeitung*, were Jews and could be attacked as such did not escape him. Stoecker was useful as another stick to beat the liberals with, for 'he is an active, fearless steadfast man, with a mouth one can't kill', but he did not wish to be associated with him personally.

Bismarck's second son Wilhelm was campaigning in Berlin and his father instructed him to support Stoecker

> because his opponent is a Progressive; but identification with Stoecker is not convenient for the government, and no one will believe that you express anything other than government opinion. Stoecker's election is very desirable, because it means defeat for his opponent, then because he is an extraordinary, fighting, useful battle companion, but as soon as one supports him, one endorses everything he has said in the past,

as well as all other anti-semites, and this cannot be countersigned by me en bloc.[11]

When Richter accused him of having given a friendly reply to a telegramme from Stoecker supporters, he hit back by accusing him, Lasker and Bamberger of fomenting class war against the aristocracy, but also remarked 'If it gives anyone pleasure to paint me as a member of the anti-Semitic associations, let him have that pleasure. I have kept my distance, as my official position requires, from all these movements, which to me are undesirable.' Stoecker did not win a seat, but Wilhelm, who had sat as a Free Conservative, lost his. For liberals like Bamberger and Richter Bismarck's tolerant attitude to Stoecker was one more proof that all the chancellor's works, including his social policy, were part and parcel of his Caesarism.

Wilhelm's political career was modest, but it was Herbert, the elder son, who had really been marked out as the standard bearer of the dynasty. He had for a long time wanted to marry Princess Carolath-Beuthen, who was unhappily married. She divorced her husband in April 1881 and the way was open for her marriage to Herbert von Bismarck. The prospect threw his father into a virtual nervous breakdown. According to Philipp von Eulenburg, Herbert's close friend and later the man whose close friendship with William II brought scandal to the monarch, the mighty chancellor broke down in tears, said he could not go on living and predicted that the shock would kill Johanna. How much of this was play-acting is difficult to tell, but the threats were backed up with more concrete action. Permission to marry, required for a member of the diplomatic corps like Herbert, was refused. Bismarck got the emperor to change the rules governing entailed estates, so that Herbert could be disinherited. This kind of pressure was too much for Herbert and he abandoned Elisabeth von Carolath. The betrayal had a corrosive effect on his personality and he became brutal and misanthropic. The main reason for Bismarck's attitude, apart from the public pressures that surrounded him at this time, was probably the princess's family connection with Schleinitz, the minister of the royal house and twenty years earlier Bismarck's predecessor as foreign minister, whose wife Mimi was Elisabeth's step sister.

This circle around the Empress Augusta was the focus of Bismarck's fiercest and most persistent hatred and to them he attributed the undermining of his health, worn down by his unending struggle against their nefarious intrigues. He regarded Augusta as one of those Germans who admired everything foreign and held their own nation in low regard. In many of his speeches this picture of the German propensity to be impressed by all things foreign, particularly French and English, kept on making an appearance and he liked to apply it to his domestic enemies, especially the Progressives. Augusta did in fact write in French rather than German and William had been compelled to marry her, because the lady of his choice, a Princess Radziwill, was disapproved of by his father Frederick William III. Elisabeth von Carolath might not have fitted well into the Bismarck household, for she was a grand dame accustomed to follow her own whims, whereas Otto and Johanna in their domesticity never moved from their modest Pomeranian Junker roots. Bismarck demanded and received total devotion from Herbert and found him increasingly indispensable in the transaction of business. The second son, Wilhelm, kept his distance rather more. He wrote to his brother: 'Believe me, life with Papa and continuous responsible work with him, is, for someone who loves him and wants to keep troubles away from him, enormously wearing.'[12]

Around this time, in the spring and summer of 1881, a deterioration in Bismarck's health was widely remarked upon. He suffered more than ever from facial neuralgia and could not shave. The white beard that now marked his appearance made him look very old. He was persuaded by his son Wilhelm, who also suffered bad health, to put himself in the hands of a Dr Schweninger, a swarthy Bavarian. By sheer force of will his 'black tyrant', as he jocularly called Schweninger, succeeded where others had failed in imposing a more sensible regime upon his patient. Bismarck worked more regular hours, took some exercise during the day, above all gave up his immoderate eating habits, though Johanna could not resist occasionally smuggling him treats that Schweninger had strictly forbidden. As a result he recovered remarkably and within a year, certainly by the end of 1883, enjoyed better health than he had done for a long time. Improved physical health could not disguise a mental hardening of the arteries. The same tunes kept recurring in Bismarck's private and public pronouncements. Often he liked to go over the past, how in face of the opposition of those, like the Progressives, who were still opposing him, he had conquered all, had always been right when they were wrong.

In March 1885 a Centre party deputy had flung back at him a term he had used, 'the spring of the nation' (*Völkerfrühling*), when after years of economic depression it was clearly no longer spring. He replied:

What I imagined as our nation's spring was that we had reconquered the German border lands, had founded the unity of the Reich, had assembled a German Reichstag around us, had seen a German emperor rise again. But then came . . . the old German rooted habit, the party spirit . . . and we arrived in a condition of our public life . . . in which in the German Reichstag the shield of unity, which I had hoped to find there, has vanished and the spirit of party strangles us . . . this spirit I accuse before God if the splendid work of 1866 and 1870 disintegrates again and if, here, the pen ruins what the sword has created. . . .[13]

In other words, the splendour of achievement was his, the misery of the present was the work of his enemies. Like all those who exercise very great power over a very long period, he was surrounded by subservience and increasingly isolated. His lifestyle, prolonged absence on his now very large estates of Varzin and Friedrichsruh, added to the isolation. 'I am tired of driving swine,' Herbert reports him as saying. Only the German word *Schweine* conveys the full flavour of misanthropy. There was little joy in the life of the Bismarcks now, laughter only at the expense of others, a greater moral insensitivity than ever.

But even when so much had turned against him and frustrated him, as it did in domestic German politics in the early 1880s, he never would really have given up or confined himself to conducting foreign policy. In fact nothing invigorated him more than hitting back hard against the opposition and for all the complaints about his health his long speeches in the Reichstag and the Prussian Landtag were as forceful as ever. He would have liked to 'dry out' the Reichstag, but nothing kept it alive as the central arena of German politics as much as his own appearances there. When he spoke, the chamber and the public galleries were full and there were crowds in the street outside. As the dictatorial chancellor he may have been Bonapartist or Caesarist, but he lacked the dimension of a popular platform orator. His influence over the public imagination was that of the legendary founder of the Reich, not that of a leader of a mass movement. He could not emulate men like Gambetta or the Gladstone of the Midlothian campaign. It may have been one more reason why he never tired of denigrating the British liberal leader. To the emperor he wrote in October 1883:

Our task would be easier [of maintaining the peace of Europe], if in England the race of great statesmen of times past, who understood

> European politics, had not apparently died out completely. With a
> politician as incompetent as Gladstone, who is nothing but a great
> demagogue, one cannot conduct policy which requires England to be
> securely taken into account.

He went on to say that if Gladstone remained in power a few years longer,
Queen Victoria might live to see the abolition of the monarchy, as everybody
was already getting used to the abolition of the House of Lords. 'May the Lord
protect our Fatherland from ministers like Gladstone.'[14] Bismarck, feeling
that communion with the masses in the manner of Gladstone was not
his style, invoked the kaiser's imperial majesty itself to give charisma to his
pronouncements. Important steps, such as the second version of the accident
insurance proposals in November 1881, were made known to the Reichstag
through an imperial message.

*

Bismarck's distrust of England under Gladstone was one of the reasons why
he embarked upon a policy of colonial expansion in 1884, when previously
he had always set his face against it. Germany's entry into the arena
of colonial rivalry was in contradiction to his foreign policy principle of
encouraging the other major powers to engage themselves on the periphery
to take the pressure off Germany as the power in the centre. In the early
1880s he had encouraged French penetration in Tunisia and had carefully
refrained from putting any obstacles in the way of the growing British
involvement in Egypt. It suited him well that France and Britain drifted into
antagonism over Egypt, a situation aggravated by the incompetent way in
which, in his view, the Gladstone government handled the aftermath of the
British occupation of the country. In his instructions to German missions
abroad he was adamant that there must be no German involvement.

In the meantime interest in colonial activity had grown in Germany,
partly as a result of the move away from free trade. It was also seen as means
of easing the social pressures caused by economic recession and the rise of
the Social Democrats. In 1880 there had been a proposal for state aid to
an ailing German trading company in Samoa, but the liberal groups in
the Reichstag, including many National Liberals, had turned it down.
In the following years pressure for German participation in the colonial
race grew and the *Deutsche Kolonialgesellschaft* (German Colonial Association), founded in 1882, became the most influential among a number of

organizations promoting the colonial cause. Right-wing National Liberals, those who after the Secession still stuck to Bismarck, now supported the acquisition of colonies. This gave the chancellor a domestic political reason, ahead of the next Reichstag elections due in the autumn of 1884, to associate himself with the colonial cause.

This social-imperialist motive might not have been strong enough in itself, but in 1884 Bismarck saw a window of opportunity for throwing the weight of the government behind colonial activity without imposing any penalty on his conduct of foreign policy. In addition to the friction between Britain and France over Egypt, tension had also developed in 1883 between the two western colonial powers over West Africa and the mouth of the Congo. The Gladstone government had dealt with German enquiries about the position in Angra Pequena, which later became German South-West Africa, in a dilatory manner. A colourful but rather shady German merchant adventurer, Adolf Lüderitz, had built up an interest there. Bismarck saw an opportunity to associate himself with France in a protest against an Anglo-Portuguese treaty of February 1884, which looked like an attempt to pre-empt the ownership of large parts of West Africa for Britain. It was the beginning of a Franco-German colonial entente, which lasted for about a year. Bismarck hoped that it would help to bring about a thaw in Franco-German relations, might divert French attention further from revenge and in the longer run even force Britain into a closer understanding with Germany. In March 1884 a letter of protection was issued to Lüderitz and others followed in West Africa. It was not yet a full territorial acquisition, but rather reluctantly the Bismarck government was soon forced to send out administrators. The chancellor himself always had a low opinion of the German capacity to act as colonial administrators. His preference would have been for an informal empire, of the kind that the British had established successfully in many parts of the globe. Speaking in the Reichstag in March 1885, when his foray into colonial expansion had almost run its course, he made it clear that he did not see colonies as places where Germans would settle in large numbers, as the British had done overseas, but as trading assets and sources of raw materials.

From November 1884 to February 1885 an Africa conference of the powers met in Berlin, under Bismarck's nominal chairmanship, to work out common guidelines for African development, including the humanitarian treatment of the native populations. Little came of the Congo agreements that were agreed at this conference and particularly the Congo itself, the private domain of the Belgian king Leopold II, became a byword for cruelty and exploitation. The Franco-German colonial understanding also proved short-lived, for the government of Jules Ferry that had shown interest in imperial development fell in March 1885. Bismarck reverted to the policy of reaching an understanding with Britain over German colonial acquisitions in Africa and the Far East. In these negotiations his son Herbert played a leading part. He had been in the London embassy from 1882 to 1884, became undersecretary in the German foreign office in 1885 and was a friend of Lord Rosebery. The result was that for the time being the German acquisition of colonies did not become a major disturbing factor in Anglo-German relations. An active colonial policy no longer fitted into Bismarck's foreign policy after 1885 and he found other, more effective means of mobilizing German nationalism for electoral purposes. When in December 1888 a German colonial enthusiast came to see him, he made, to his visitor's consternation, the often quoted remark: 'Your map of Africa looks very fine, but my map of Africa lies in Europe. Here is Russia and there, pointing to the left, lies France, and we are in the middle; that is my map of Africa.'[15] He could not, however, undo the fact that there were now widely scattered German footholds in Africa and the Far East, which came to haunt his successors.

*

In spite of the many checks that Bismarck's policies encountered in the Reichstag elected in 1881, gradually a more favourable party constellation came about and enabled him to build up defences against the accession of the crown prince. Changes in the alignment of the liberal groups eventually turned out in his favour. In 1884 the Secession merged with Richter's Progressives to form the *Deutsche Freisinnige Partei*, for short *Freisinn*. It looked like the revival of a bigger liberal party, but it was not. Lasker had died in January 1884 while on a journey in the United States and Bismarck had refused to pass on to the Reichstag a resolution by the US House of Representatives expressing regret at the death of so distinguished a parliamentarian. The chancellor defended his action, even by his standards flagrant in its lack of magnanimity, in a confrontational speech in the Reichstag. He saw in the American resolution praising Lasker's work as beneficial for Germany an attack on himself: 'If Lasker was right, if his policy had really brought Germany the benefit that is alleged in these words, then the policy of the emperor and myself was wrong, for I did not receive from Lasker any support for my policy, only opposition from the beginning.'[16] And he went over the whole ground of his conflict with Lasker again. He conveniently forgot that it was men like Lasker who played a leading role in creating, in collaboration with Bismarck and Delbrück, the legal framework of a united Germany. But he had long been boasting of his own initiative in bringing free trade, the Delbrück disease he called it, to an end.

Days before he delivered his crushing verdict on the dead Lasker the fusion programme of the Freisinn was published. Two days after the Lasker speech, the chancellor, speaking on the third version of the accident insurance draft bill, and after his remarks, quoted earlier, about freedom applying only to oneself and meaning dominion over others, said:

> Therefore I have become suspicious whenever I see the word 'free' in front of another adjective, and that includes the word 'free thinking' – thinking, that may be [laughter], but free thinking is really equivalent to lust for power or narrowness or intolerance. In short I do not trust the word [laughter].[17]

The reunion of the liberal factions had alarmed him. A few days later the formation of the Freisinn brought about a countermovement among the National Liberals. Bennigsen had tired of keeping his party together and resigned in June 1883. His successor was Johannes Miquel, a 1848 revolutionary who had turned to the right and was now mayor of Frankfurt. The way was open for him to turn the National Liberals into a party very similar to the Free Conservatives, a Bismarck party *sans phrase*. In the Heidelberg declaration, issued only a fortnight after the formation of the Freisinn in March 1884, a group of mainly South German National Liberals endorsed most of the current Bismarck policies, tariffs, financial strengthening of the Reich through indirect taxes such as the duty on spirits, the social insurance legislation and strong defence, buttressed by the septennial budget, and support for colonial development. When this programme was adopted by the party in May 1884 the National Liberals had become a centre-right party, able to join in a block with the Conservatives. It was what Bismarck had long hoped for, but it remained to be seen whether the voters would support it.

What was working in favour of such an alignment was precisely what would eventually prove to be the most serious of Bismarck's domestic failures, the inability to suppress the socialists. When it came to the renewal of the anti-socialist law in May 1884, Bismarck painted the revolutionary danger in the most lurid colours and did his best to link the Freisinn with support for terrorism and subversion. He confronted the Reichstag with the choice of either passing the law or facing a premature dissolution. Both for the new Freisinn and for the Centre it became a game of poker, to vote so that the law passed without receiving their full endorsement, while not giving Bismarck a chance to dissolve upon this issue. As for the Centre, the chancellor had not succeeded in undermining the position of Windthorst and his colleagues through the modification of the Kulturkampf negotiated behind their backs with the Vatican. Windthorst stuck to his strongly constitutional stance and continued to oppose the anti-socialist law, but a considerable number of Centre deputies voted for it or abstained. Undoubtedly there were now many in the Centre party for whom the government's social policy was attractive and the party did in fact vote for the third version of the accident insurance law in June 1884. It was becoming obvious that there was an ideological affinity between the Conservatives and many of the diverse social groups included in the Centre.

When the elections took place without a premature dissolution in October 1884, the Freisinn only obtained 67 seats, when the Progressives and the Secession together had held 106 in 1881. The spectre of a centre-left coalition that might form the basis for a 'Gladstone' ministry in the next reign was no longer there to plague the chancellor. When in the spring of 1885 the old emperor, now eighty-eight, became seriously ill, Bismarck engaged in one of his carefully controlled musings with his journalistic acolyte Moritz Busch. He felt like a husband whose wife was about to die and who had been asked to say whether he would remarry:

> It looks as if the crown prince wants to keep me, but I will think about remaining . . . it may not get that bad; if I stay, I could advise against, prevent or weaken many things. But if I did not have a free hand, with colleagues like Forckenbeck and Georg Bunsen [both leaders of the Freisinn, the former mayor of Berlin, the latter the son of the well-known Prussian envoy in London], and endless discord with them, when the old gentleman let me do latterly what I thought for the best, choose the ministers or replace them. And then the co-regency of the crown princess, who influences and completely dominates him.[18]

And he launched into a long disquisition how only he was trusted by the rulers of Europe, how the crown princess had always remained an Englishwoman and how the crown prince would be guided by his predeliction for England and regard for Queen Victoria. In some ways it was banal stuff that could be read in countless newspaper articles, but there did not seem much disposition to give up and retire.

*

Bismarck thus had reasons satisfactory to himself for prolonging his hold on power, but contemporaries as well as subseqent gènerations have wondered what was the point of it. A better case can be made for the benefit derived from Bismarck's conduct of foreign policy in these last few years than for his continuing formidable impact on Germany's internal affairs. Domestic and foreign affairs formed in his mind an inextricable whole, but in neither sphere could he hope to have the creative ability to shape the future that he once had. In the affairs of Europe, for all the ever more complicated devices he had to employ, at least he kept the peace and safeguarded the security of his own country. At home he perpetuated a system increasingly ill-adapted to a country in rapid transformation and he held out no prospect of change and made no preparation for his succession. Abroad he had succeeded in renewing for another three years from 1884 the alliance of the three emperors, which still constituted the basis of his system. It was, however, progressively eroded by the recrudescence of rivalry between Austria and Russia in the Balkans. In the middle 1880s Bulgaria became the focus of renewed crisis. It was a case of role-reversal, for the Russians had become disillusioned with what at the Congress of Berlin had been regarded as their satellite. Alexander of Battenberg, the nephew of Tsar Alexander II, had been installed as prince of Bulgaria and was initially regarded as virtually a Russian viceroy. The country had become increasingly dissatisfied with Russian influence and Prince Alexander encouraged this trend. It was his only choice if he was to stay in power. When in September 1885 the Bulgarians took over Eastern Rumelia, the Russians, in a reversal of their stand of 1878 for a larger Bulgaria, opposed the enlargement. Bismarck was anxious that his two allies, Russia and Austria, should reach agreement over this matter.

There was a sub-plot: Alexander of Battenberg and Princess Viktoria, daughter of the Prussian crown prince, known as Moretta, wanted to get married. It was a marriage strongly opposed by Bismarck as likely to involve Germany in the Bulgarian entanglement in opposition to Russia. It was, however, fervently supported by the crown princess and her mother Queen Victoria, but opposed by the girl's grandfather, the emperor, which gave Bismarck a good cover for his own opposition. The Battenbergs were descended from a morganatic marriage in the house of Hesse-Darmstadt and the Hohenzollerns did not consider them of adequate royal status. When Alexander of Battenberg visited Berlin in 1884 Bismarck told him in no uncertain terms that there could be no marriage and that he should get on with the Russians as best he could. The chancellor's efforts to keep his two eastern allies from each other's throats nearly came to grief when Serbia, then regarded as an Austrian satellite, invaded Bulgaria in November 1885, was badly beaten and had to be rescued by the Austrians. The amalgamation of Bulgaria with Eastern Rumelia was internationally accepted by the device of appointing Alexander of Battenberg as Turkish governor-general of Eastern Rumelia in April 1886, but in August he was overthrown by a Russian-engineered coup. Bismarck looked at the Balkan imbroglio entirely from the point of view of its impact on great power relationships. The survival of the Habsburg monarchy was a vital German interest, but Germany could not underwrite Austrian ambitions in the Balkans. Nor could she take upon herself the burden of containing Russian ambitions in the Balkans, a task that must be left to Austria and Britain. As for Russia, Bismarck wanted to keep the door open and give no encouragement to those elements in Russian opinion in favour of an alliance with France. He refused to contemplate a preventive war against Russia, advocated by some in the German military establishment and in German public opinion. Talking to the Austrian crown prince Archduke Rudolf in March 1887 he said: 'They want to urge me into war, and I want peace; it would be frivolous to start a war; we are not a pirate state, which makes war, because it suits a few.'[19] Even a victorious war against Russia would have no positive results for Germany. Maintaining the link with St Petersburg would exert a restraining influence on Vienna and vice versa.

When it proved impossible to renew the Three Emperors' League again in 1887, Bismarck concluded the secret reinsurance treaty with Russia of 18 June. The two countries promised each other neutrality, but not if Germany attacked France or Russia attacked Austria. Germany promised diplomatic support to Russia over Bulgaria and the straits. In themselves these undertakings did not mean much. Within the German foreign policy establishment many, including Holstein, felt this treaty created an over-complicated situation. They feared it gave the Russians a means of blackmailing Germany by making it public. In a memorandum the chancellor dictated a few weeks after the signature, he argued that it would not matter if Francis Joseph learnt of the existence of the treaty. Relations between Germany and Austria were so close and so firmly grounded in public opinion that such a disclosure could only temporarily damage them, whereas relations with Russia were more tenuous. The Austrians would realize that the purpose of the reinsurance treaty was to prevent a Franco-Russian alliance at least for the time being. The reinsurance treaty was made public by Bismarck himself in his resentful retirement in 1896, as a stick to beat his successors with, because they had not renewed it after his fall. The treaty later assumed an importance in the German view of their progressive diplomatic isolation which initially it did not have.

It remained a burden on Bismarck's system that no rapprochement with France was possible. He had tried to bring it about by the colonial route, through Egypt and West Africa, but after 1885 revanchism came to the fore again in French public opinion. All Bismarck could do was to exploit this in dealing with German public opinion and the Reichstag parties. An understanding with Britain would have been useful as a backstop to his system and he encouraged Austria to have such an understanding. It was realized in a fashion in the Mediterranean agreement between Austria, Britain and Italy in February 1887 and in December 1887 by the Near Eastern agreement between these powers. These arrangements did sit rather uneasily with the clauses regarding Bulgaria and the straits in the reinsurance treaty, had these become public. But Bismarck was not going to pull British chestnuts out of the fire in the Balkans or the Black Sea, or get himself into any dependence on Britain, any more than he wanted to be dependent on Russia or Austria. He placed little trust in agreements with parliamentary states, though he was more disposed to deal with Salisbury, who had succeeded Gladstone in the summer of 1886. The growing criticism of Bismarck's foreign policy system in Germany sprang in part from the justified perception that it was still a product of cabinet diplomacy in the style of Metternich. It was under constant threat not only from the traditional ambitions of the great powers, but also from the growing pressure of public opinion. Even in autocratic Russia there was the powerful current of pan-Slavism among the educated classes, as well as the constant threat of revolution. He knew how precarious the situation was in the Habsburg empire and had his doubts if the Slav and Greek Orthodox subjects of Francis Joseph could really be relied on. It is evident from Bismarck's many dispatches and letters on foreign policy that he realized the fragility of his system, but he was less willing to admit that the ground under his own feet was also shaky. At least he could argue that for the moment no better system was possible, even if it did not endure long into the future. War might mean revolution all round and an end to the conservative order which was the basis of his own existence.

*

To survive in power the chancellor had to remain in control in domestic as well as foreign affairs and here he was on less firm ground. The Reichstag elected in 1884 was more favourable to him than that of 1881, the spectre of a large liberal party forming the basis for a 'Gladstone ministry' in a new reign was largely banished, but he still had no reliable party basis. The various schemes to bypass the Reichstag, reduce its sittings, curtail its budgetary powers, limit the suffrage, had all come to nothing. No preparations were ever made for the constitutional coup he sometimes threatened and it is unlikely that he would have wanted to weaken the Reichstag too drastically. It would have exposed him unaided to the monarch and to the Conservatives, from both of whom he had had plenty of trouble in the past and might well have again in the future. But the parties he regarded as hostile, the Freisinn, the Centre, and most obviously the Social Democrats, continued to give him trouble, while the Conservatives and the reformed National Liberals were not always docile. The possibility of appealing to the powerful emotion of German nationalism and directing it against internal enemies, *Reichsfeinde*, remained. Bismarck used it with considerable effect on the Polish question. Raising the alarm about the Polish threat had the added advantage that it really corresponded with his own long and strongly held Prussian convictions, whereas he had referred to the colonial question privately as a 'swindle', just as he had so often done with the German national movement in the past. In the eastern Prussian provinces, where there lived more than 2 million Poles, Polish and German nationalism clashed more fiercely than before. One factor was the Kulturkampf, which had repressed the Catholic Poles and their language in schools and elsewhere. Against this German nationalism had been aroused by evidence that the Polish population was rising faster than the German in Prussia's border provinces, fuelled by a higher birth rate and a lower rate of westward migration. It was the age when the ideas of Darwin, as understood by the popular mind, were creating a sense of alarm about racial degeneration.

In February 1885 Bismarck initiated a policy of expelling Poles and Jews of Russian nationality from the eastern provinces. Many of them had migrated there to replace the indigenous Poles who had moved further west. It was an early example of ethnic cleansing and what makes it in retrospect look even worse was that Bismarck exploited it ruthlessly and deliberately to stir up national feeling against his domestic opponents. He had always regarded Polish nationalism, the sense of Polish identity and nostalgia for the resurrection of a Polish state, as a direct threat to Prussia and one of the ties that bound Prussia and Russia together. His view of Polish national consciousness was old-fashioned: he thought the carriers of it were the aristocracy and the priests. Without them the peasants would be receptive to the blessings of superior German civilization, would learn the German language and only use Polish as a local dialect. He ignored the rise of a democratic national movement, roused by measures against the Polish identity, such as those imposed in the schools as a result of the Kulturkampf. The expulsions would deprive the great Polish estate owners of their labour force. Polish deputies raised the issue of expulsions in the Reichstag at the end of 1885. Bismarck denied that the Reichstag had any competence in a matter of purely Prussian concern and he and his Prussian ministerial colleagues ostentatiously left the chamber. Leaders of the Freisinn and the Centre, including Windthorst, managed, however, to reintroduce the matter in the Reichstag.

Bismarck then made a major speech on the Polish question in the Prussian chamber of deputies on 28 January 1886.[20] He went over the whole history of the Polish question in his highly tendentious way, justifying his own policy at the time of the Polish rebellion in 1863, on the other hand playing down his own role in the Kulturkampf. He pulled no punches in presenting the current situation as a defence of German nationality against the Polish flood. Quoting in dialect a rhyming proverb from his time as Elbe dyke supervisor at Schönhausen he said: 'Was nicht will deichen, das muss weichen' (those who will not help to build dykes must get out); those who will not cooperate with the state for its protection do not belong to the state, have no rights in the state, should get out of the state. He linked the Polish danger unblushingly with his internal opponents. The constitution of the Reich had given them (the Poles) strong support from parties which were prepared to fight the government under all circumstances, which were unable to govern positively but came together in negation. Again he attacked Windthorst personally as a man whose sympathies were with the liberals, who was prepared to defend the Poles more vigorously than the Germans and who would sit as a member of the Freisinn if he was not a leader of the Centre. It was these two parties who fought most strongly against the chancellor's illiberal policies, on the Polish question as on the renewal of the anti-socialist law later in 1886.

Bismarck was still relentlessly pursuing his tactics of driving a wedge between the Vatican and the Centre party. Within the Centre party he was trying to divide Windthorst together with most of his parliamentary colleagues from those other groups in the party who wanted to make peace with the government and pursue an alliance with the Conservatives. He had gone out of his way to flatter the pope, for example by accepting his arbitration as an independent sovereign between Germany and Spain in a dispute over the Caroline Islands in the South Pacific. Even as he clashed with the Centre in the Reichstag and the Prussian chamber of deputies, he had succeeded in getting the Vatican to propose a German for the vacant archbishopric of Posen. In spite of the resistance of most German bishops, the pope had conceded the right of the civil authorities to be advised of clerical appointments, the *Anzeigepflicht*. A number of so-called 'state Catholics' were appointed to bishoprics. Windthorst had to step warily, but so did Bismarck, for the National Liberals looked askance at anything which seemed too much like a retreat in the Kulturkampf. Speaking on the first of the so-called peace laws in the Prussian upper house in April 1886,[21] Bismarck said that he was not now going to Canossa, nor was it incompatible with Prussian honour to seek peace with the Catholic church, when the pope himself was seeking it. He again emphasized the connection between the Kulturkampf and the Polish question. With reference to the further measures he was taking to buy out Polish landowners and support the German purchase of land he said: 'If we succeed in combating Polonism by our more recently proposed measures, then this provides a substitute for our ecclesiastical fight.' Again he made the link between the Centre as a political force and the left liberals and painted them both as obstacles to the development of the Reich.

*

Even more than the Poles the socialists lent themselves to the role of bogy-men whom the chancellor could use to sort out his enemies from his friends. There was no sign that the policy of repression enshrined in the anti-socialist law was successful, but neither were the Social Democrats sufficiently numerous either in the electorate or in the Reichstag to cause someone of Bismarck's temperament much immediate alarm. When the Freisinn and the Centre proposed in 1886 that the anti-socialist law should only be extended for two years and not for five, as the government demanded, he had no difficulty in weaving sideswipes against Richter and Windthorst into his diatribe against Bebel, as a man who condoned political assassination. Puttkamer, the reactionary Prussian minister of the interior, tightened the enforcement of the anti-socialist law again in 1886, on Bismarck's instructions, after a period when it had been applied more leniently. But it was the military budget which Bismarck envisaged as the most appropriate issue for rallying the centre-right behind him and isolating the left as *Reichsfeinde*. There was a sense of international crisis in the air, as a result mainly of events in the Balkans. Some aspects of it, the hostility to Russia and the enthusiasm for Alexander of Battenberg, did not suit the chancellor, combined as they now often were with public criticism of his foreign policy. He was aware that there was opposition to his benevolent attitude towards Russia within the political and military establishment. His paranoia was aroused by the fact that the Battenberg prince, after his overthrow and return to Germany, was seen in some quarters as a potential chancellor in the impending new reign. It suited Bismarck much better that public hostility to Russia was combined with alarm about the rise of a new revanchism in France, personified in the colourful figure of General Boulanger, the French minister of war appointed at the end of 1885. Bismarck and his son Herbert, who became state secretary for foreign affairs in May 1886, played up the threat posed by Boulanger and linked it with the threat of revolution that might spread from a radical France. Waldersee, Moltke's deputy as chief of staff and a man with his own political ambitions, thought the French threat as portrayed by Bismarck was a 'comedy', but he was among those toying with the idea of a preventive war against Russia.

A new military budget would have to be agreed in 1887, for the septennial grant ran out at the beginning of 1888. International tension was the justification for the introduction, in November 1886, of proposals providing for an increase of about 10 per cent, 40,000 men, in the strength of the army. There would have been no difficulty about getting the Reichstag's agreement, but the government's demand that there should be a renewal of the septennial grant became the real bone of contention. Under Windthorst's leadership the Centre party, along with the Freisinn and Social Democrats, insisted that the grant should this time be limited to three years in order to safeguard the budgetary rights of the Reichstag for every three year legislative period. The pope had pressed the Centre party leaders to agree to the seven-year grant, for he wanted the remains of the Kulturkampf liquidated and would have liked to see the Centre take its place in a conservative, anti-socialist front. Bismarck went out of his way to exacerbate the confrontation in order to have an effective cry on which to dissolve the Reichstag. He played down any threat from Russia, 'we live with Russia in the same friendly relationship as under the late emperor [Alexander II] and these relations will not be disturbed by me,' he said.[22] He entirely rejected the notion of preventive war and made the frequently quoted remark: 'I can't look into the cards held by providence.' But 'if we have encouraged French tendencies to aggression, then I attribute to the gentlemen [Richter, Windthorst and the socialists], by delaying us for so long, a large measure of the responsibility for the calamity of an outbreak of war.' The septennial grant was reduced to a triennal grant by 186 votes to 154. Centre and Freisinn formed the majority, Conservatives, Free Conservatives and National Liberals the minority, while the Social Democrats, opposed to increased military spending, abstained. Bismarck had his excuse for a dissolution of the Reichstag and a theme for the election campaign.

These elections of January 1887 became known as the cartel elections and on the face of it gave Bismarck what he had long aimed for. The three parties of the right formed a cartel, or *Sammlung*, and made agreements for the run-off ballots. The deliberately fomented hysteria about the alleged dangers which threatened the Reich from its external and internal enemies meant that there was a greatly increased electoral participation, 77.5 per cent as against a previous peak of 63.4 per cent in 1878. Among the cartel parties the Conservatives held their votes and seats, the Free Conservatives considerably increased both votes and seats, but, most striking of all, the National Liberals greatly increased votes and nearly doubled seats. They were back to where they had been in 1878. The Centre held its ground, the Social Democrats got more than 10 per cent of the vote, but, because the electoral system was so stacked against them, got only 11 seats, less than half their 1884 result. The cartel parties had 220 out 397 seats, a clear majority.

But the cartel did not prove very cohesive and did not provide Bismarck with a reliable majority. The semi-parliamentary system, which he had established and strenuously defended, worked against him. It failed to force the parties to work together in coalitions, as they would have had to do if they had had to provide the executive government. Even within parties the basis for tight party discipline did not exist. After the elections and under pressure from the Vatican the majority of the Centre party deputies abstained on the septennial grant of the military budget. A further peace law to liquidate the Kulturkampf was passed in the Prussian Landtag. There was a tendency for Centre and Conservatives to come together in support, while most National Liberals and a lot of Free Conservatives were in opposition; even though Bismarck again stressed that he was not retreating on the principles of church–state relations. It also proved difficult to keep the cartel parties together on financial policy. The increases in defence spending made the Reich's financial position more acute than ever and most of Bismarck's proposals for dealing with it, such as the tobacco and spirit monopolies, had come to grief. In 1887 the cartel parties did unite behind a tax on the production of alcoholic spirits, but their unity broke down again over the revision of tariffs. They were raised steeply in December 1887, something most National Liberals, with their constituencies of mainly urban consumers, could not support, while it appealed to many of the Catholic farming community as well as to the Conservatives with their east Elbian base. Putting so much of the burden of defence spending on the consumer was flagrant class egotism. It played into the hands of the social democrats and was one reason for their big leap forward in the next Reichstag elections of 1890.

12

FALL AND RESENTFUL RETIREMENT

Bismarck entered the year of the three emperors, 1888, with his dominance at home and abroad outwardly undiminished, but many were wondering if he was merely clinging on to power for its own sake. Among the political elite doubts and intrigues were rampant, labyrinthine and poisonous. Holstein, the influential counsellor in the foreign office, had been a close friend of the Bismarck family, had tried to act as an intermediary between the chancellor and the crown princess, but was now alienated, for personal and political reasons. Collaboration with Herbert, the chancellor's son, was very difficult. He treated his subordinates badly, drank too much and owed his rapid promotion to his father. Waldersee, who succeeded Moltke as chief of staff in 1888, was an anti-Bismarck frondeur. He had links with Stoecker and there was a widely noticed meeting at his house in November 1887, to support Stoecker's Berlin mission, which was attended by prominent Conservatives and by Prince William, the future kaiser, and his wife.

A few weeks later Bismarck wrote Prince William a letter, which showed his undiminished skill in appealing to the prejudices of its recipient. The prince had sent him the draft of an accession proclamation, to be sent to his German fellow rulers, but had also in a letter justified his attendance at the Waldersee soirée.

> We would have succumbed to a parliamentary rule in the past 17 years, if the princes had not stood firmly by the Reich . . . *Acheronta movebunt* [that favourite tag of Bismarck's again: they, the princes and their

governments, will turn to the devil]; the opposition in parliament would be much reinforced if the present solidarity of the Bundesrat came to an end and Bavarians and Saxons made common cause with Richter and Windthorst. It is therefore the right policy for your highness to address yourself in the first place to your princely cousins. But I would humbly suggest, that you do so with an assurance that the new emperor would respect and protect 'the contractual rights of his allied princes' as conscientiously as his predecessors.[1]

He advised him to burn the draft proclamation and warned against associating himself with so sectarian a group as the Stoecker mission.

By this time everybody knew that Frederick William was mortally ill and that Prince William's accession could not be long delayed. Bismarck had known about the seriousness of the illness since the previous May and had then advised against an operation on the crown prince's larynx. This was probably the right advice, for the success rate for such operations was very small and, even if successful, would leave the patient terribly mutilated. There was then a tremendous hue and cry against the Scottish doctor Sir Morrell Mackenzie for having advised against an operation, allegedly on the basis of a misdiagnosis that the diseased larynx was not cancerous. The campaign against Mackenzie had as its main target the crown princess, for preferring for reasons of her own the advice of an English doctor to that of the German doctors. Bismarck did nothing to counter this vicious campaign.

As for Prince William, Bismarck had said years earlier, speculating that a short-lived ruler would follow upon a long-lived one:

The one whose turn will then come, is quite different, he will want to govern himself, he is energetic and decisive, has no time for parliamentary co-rulers, a pure guards officer. . . . He dislikes the way his father consorts with professors, with Mommsen, Virchow and Forckenbeck, and perhaps he will develop into that *rocher de bronze* which we need.[2]

As a reading of the prince's character, it was both true and false. He was like a guards officer, but he was no hard rock. Bismarck's misreading of William II's character was among the causes of his downfall. The correspondence between Bismarck and the prince about the Stoecker affair closed with a letter from the prince assuring the chancellor of his continuing deep devotion. In reprinting this letter in his memoirs Bismarck remarked that it contained just a hint of what the prince later said in a speech, after he had ascended the throne: 'I will smash him who opposes me.' He added ruefully that in retrospect he recognized that as 'emperor he had only with difficulty suppressed the desire to get rid of his inherited mentor, until it exploded . . . and forced a separation in a sudden and for me hurtful manner.'[3] Stoecker himself revealed in a letter to the editor of the *Kreuzzeitung* in August 1888, when William was already kaiser, that the prince had said 'I will let the old man catch his breath for six months and then I will govern myself.'[4]

Prince William's ambivalence about Bismarck was in many ways typical for his contemporaries of the younger generation. The massive figure of the Reich's founder, who was still through his personal presence giving Germany a dominance in Europe that she had scarcely enjoyed in a thousand years, seemed irreplaceable. Even liberal intellectuals not susceptible to the appeal of power were impressed by the sheer brilliance, the self-evident superiority that lifted him head and shoulders above all other public men. And yet the faults were also self-evident and loomed ever larger with the passage of time, the sheer greed for power and the petty tenacity in holding on to it, the terrifying vindictiveness in the pursuit of even minor enemies and above all the lack of anything forward-looking. It had been one of Bismarck's strengths that he could concentrate a blinding light of realism on the immediate problem without allowing himself to be distracted by imprecise visions of the future. But then he was aligned with many of the trends that pointed most clearly to the future and now he no longer was. Theodor Fontane, one of the leading literary portrayers of the Prussian scene, put it thus: 'His genius, which springs forth from his every sentence, delights me again and again, and demolishes all my reservations, but when I look at it calmly the reservations return. One cannot wholly trust him in any respect.'[5]

Among the younger generation there were those who were strongly engaged in what might broadly be called the social question and felt stifled by the conventions of bourgeois society. They might still feel enthusiasm for the sheer genius of Bismarck while feeling oppressed by the negativity of his repressive policies. Others were enthused by the prospect of Germany as the most dynamic power on the world scene and felt hemmed in by Bismarck's emphasis on the international status quo. Much of what was criticized in German society was hardly the work of the chancellor on his own, but few doubted that he had used and manipulated everything and everybody with the aim of ensuring his own dominance. Across the board there was a feeling that Bismarck had unified the nation in its outer form, but had divided it in its inner being. In these later years it seemed that he was treading water and reacting in a manner which looked increasingly out of touch. During his long absences in Friedrichsruh or Varzin he had the air of a man detached from the society over which he still held sway.

The rapid passage of the crown through three generations in 1888, and the lamentable and ugly intrigues that accompanied it, highlighted the obsolescence of the Bismarck regime. William I died on 9 March; on 15 June Frederick III died and William II ascended the throne. On the face of it the fatal illness of Frederick III relieved the chancellor of the nightmare that had haunted him for years, but nothing was certain and rumours of Bismarck's resignation or dismissal filled the air during the fourteen weeks of the reign. Ill-advisedly the empress wanted to revive the Battenberg marriage, even though Alexander, having fallen in love with an actress, was no longer interested. Bismarck breathed fire and slaughter and Vicky finally desisted. The imperial couple managed to achieve one step of symbolic significance, the dismissal of the reactionary Prussian minister of the interior, Puttkamer. He was responsible for carrying out in practice the policy enshrined in the notorious *Beamtenerlass* (civil service regulation) of 1882, requiring loyalty of public servants to the emperor. It was used to enforce a conservative recruitment policy to the public service, required public servants to support the government at election times and made the position of officials and judges sympathizing with the opposition parties, the *Reichsfeinde*, difficult. Puttkamer was also responsible for the rigorous enforcement of the anti-socialist law. Bismarck's part in Puttkamer's dismissal was murky in the extreme, hunting with the hounds and running with the hares. Ludwig Bamberger was secretly advising the empress, but could not show his face openly in the imperial palace. Writing to another stalwart of the Progressive party and now the Freisinn, the Bavarian Stauffenberg, he compared Germany to a doghouse.

Events after the accession of William II reinforced the impression that politics under Bismarck was a vipers' nest. The new kaiser had his parents' palace surrounded by troops, to prevent incriminating papers being removed by his mother to England. William II later blamed such incidents on the chancellor and it was certainly the case that Bismarck was concerned only to aggravate the tensions between the young sovereign and his mother. When in the autumn of 1888 extracts from the dead emperor's war diaries during the Franco-Prussian campaign were published Bismarck made public his report to the new emperor that these extracts were a forgery, when everybody knew that they were genuine. He then had the editor of the extracts, a Professor Geffcken, arrested and put on trial for endangering the state. Even the German public, accustomed to accepting what was handed down from on high, reacted negatively to these shameless perversions of the judicial process. The affair misfired badly for Bismarck. Not only was Geffcken released by the *Reichsgericht*, the highest court, but the emperor, concerned for his popularity, changed tack and felt he had been misled by the chancellor.

Bismarck was beginning to learn the truth of what Johanna had written to her younger son Bill on the day of William's accession:

> God give dear Papa the strength to carry through the probably not easy matters, which will now come, and fortify the young emperor with wisdom, clarity and above all calm. I am terribly afraid of his hot-headedness and of his great inner immaturity, which is greater than his years. May God not desert us![6]

Was Bismarck simply losing his touch with old age, had years of imposing his will deprived him of the ability to gauge the reaction of others, had the habit of confrontation become ingrained? Elements of calculation, of the kind Bismarck had always employed, were probably still at work. From the extracts of the crown prince's war diary it was clear that Frederick William had, in November 1870, strongly argued the case for a unitary Reich based on liberal principles, against Bismarck's policy of conciliating the German princes and thereby building a bulwark against the spread of parliamentarism. Making public this fact was inconvenient for the chancellor and it was also an attack on what was to him the holy grail of his way of founding the Reich. He wanted to tie the young emperor to himself by pushing him further along the route of blackening the reputation of his father.

It was all to no avail. It was a moment when Bismarck's indispensability in the management of foreign affairs counted for less than it had done in the past. Public opinion was not in tune with his policy of maintaining Russian friendship and it had powerful enemies within the establishment, Holstein, Waldersee and others with access to the emperor. The clash of opinions became very public when Bismarck favoured the placement of Russian railway bonds on the Berlin stock exchange in May 1889, while the kaiser, probably influenced by Waldersee, tried to persuade the chancellor to use his influence against the placement. Bismarck was not impressed by the military argument that to facilitate Russian railway building was to open the way to a rapid mobilization of forces on Russia's western border. The chancellor saw no reason at this time to add to the trade and financial difficulties in Russian-German relations. In November 1887 he had agreed to the so-called Lombard stop, the refusal of the Reichsbank to discount Russian state securities. This and the constantly rising German grain tariffs were a major Russian grievance. The way was open to a greater Russian reliance on French capital and this became an element in the development of closer political relations between Paris and St Petersburg. Bismarck's one major foreign policy initiative in 1889 was a formal proposal of an alliance with Britain, to be notified to the parliaments on both sides. He cannot have believed that it would get anywhere and Salisbury could do no more than leave it 'lying on the table' for future reference. Bismarck did not want colonial complications to get in the way of his pursuit of better relations with London, but his coolness towards colonial development at this time displeased many, including some of his National Liberal allies.

*

In domestic affairs it was plain for all to see that the cartel Reichstag was not accomplishing much and that Bismarck's majority in it was not reliable. The one major achievement, the enactment of old age pensions, was accompanied by the most acute social conflict of Bismarck's last decade, a big miners' strike in the Ruhr, which spread to other parts of country and led to bloody clashes. The chancellor's approach was that one should not be too hasty in using strong-arm methods against it. He would regard it as 'politically useful if the settlement of the strike and of its sad consequences did not occur too quickly and should be felt by the liberal bourgeoisie,' he said in a meeting of the Prussian ministry. He was already looking ahead to the renewal of the anti-socialist law, due early in the next year. The kaiser wanted conciliation and shied away from seeing bloodshed at the beginning of his reign. But Bismarck saw clearly enough that he would equally shy away from a real realignment of forces, from governing with a coalition in which the Freisinn and even the social democrats would need to take their place. It would be capitulating to the ghost of his father and bowing the knee to his mother. The other alternative would be that either the cartel parties would rally behind Bismarck and a strengthened anti-socialist law, or else there would be a crisis, repeated dissolutions of the Reichstag, finally a constitutional coup, a situation only he could master and which would make it impossible for the young monarch to do without him. Bismarck was aware that his relationship with the kaiser was becoming uneasy and removed himself from personal contact by absenting himself from Berlin almost without a break from late May 1889 to late January 1890. He relied on his son Herbert to keep an eye on developments and on the kaiser, with whom Herbert had been on friendly terms before his accession.

In October he was briefly in Berlin for a meeting with Tsar Alexander III. Afterwards he said: 'Strange, he [the tsar] seemed to assume that I would not remain in office much longer. I am not clear who could have suggested that to him . . .'[7] In the meantime the kaiser, influenced by those around him, including his old tutor Hinzpeter, thought the way forward lay in factory legislation, what is in German called protection of the worker, such as restricted hours of work especially for women and children. It would take the sting out of the social confrontation, something that Bismarck's social policy had so far failed to do. Bismarck had always been opposed to factory legislation and, moreover, he had now ordered the preparation of an uncompromising version of the anti-socialist law, which was to remain in force without a time limit. It became clear that even the National Liberals wanted it to be modified, especially the clause under which it was possible to expel Social Democrats from their place of residence. This had had the effect of dispersing Social Democratic activists from their strongholds to other parts of the country, where they often gave a fillip to the rise of new Social Democratic centres of strength.

Matters came to a head at a crown council on 24 January 1890. The kaiser had called it and the chancellor had to inconvenience himself by leaving Friedrichsruh to attend it. At the meeting Bismarck pushed the kaiser's factory legislation to one side and insisted on the anti-socialist law being passed unamended. His ministerial colleagues backed the chancellor, but with evident lack of enthusiasm; the kaiser left the meeting saying he had been trapped. As a result the National Liberal version of the law, without the expulsion clause, was on the following day rejected in the Reichstag, by a strange coalition of the Conservatives with the real opposition of Centre, Freisinn and Social Democrats. The cartel was now openly split and it seemed only too obvious that the chancellor was banking on a crisis that would allow him to appear as the saviour of the nation. He then made some concessions to the kaiser's intention to promote factory legislation, but it is not clear whether in the next few weeks of desperate manoeuvrings he really thought he could cling to power or whether he was trying to execute a dignified retreat from at least the domestic part of his responsibilities. He could have been in no doubt that the kaiser wanted to get rid of him. When during an audience on 8 February the chancellor said: 'I fear I stand in Your Majesty's way,' he was met with silence. About his ministerial colleagues Bismarck remarked bitterly to his son: 'At the thought of getting rid of me, they all say *Ouf!*, relieved and satisfied.'[8]

The possibility of a severe crisis became obvious with the result of the Reichstag elections of 20 February 1890. The three cartel parties, who in the eyes of the ordinary voter had done little but raise the cost of living, saw their seats reduced from 220 to 135, while the Freisinn more than doubled theirs from 32 to 66. The real shock was that the Social Democrats became the largest party in terms of votes, with over 19 per cent, though the electoral system only gave them 35 seats. For a moment the kaiser seemed to lose confidence and seek a common way forward with his chancellor. But he soon changed his mind again. It was becoming clear that from top to bottom, from the grand duke of Baden down to the liberal press, almost everybody was moving against the chancellor and his played out tactics of confrontation, and that most were pinning their hopes on a more conciliatory and forward-looking future under the young emperor. The volatile monarch did not need much persuading that it was his duty to respond to that mood and to dismiss the chancellor whose desperate remedies would drag dynasty and state into the abyss.

The actual reasons for the dismissal were almost a side-issue. There was Bismarck's reminder to his colleagues to observe the cabinet order of 1852, under which the prime minister had to be kept informed of all official contacts between individual ministers and the monarch, with the exception of the minister of war. Then there was the chancellor's interview with Windthorst, a last desperate attempt to construct a coalition with the Centre. Afterwards Windthorst said: 'I have come from the political deathbed of a great man.' The kaiser claimed that he should have been informed of this meeting and, since it had been arranged through Bleichröder, remarked that Jews and Jesuits always stuck together. Finally there was the kaiser's complaint that reports from the German consul in Kiev about Russian troop movements had been withheld from him. These accusations were flung at

Bismarck when the kaiser appeared at Herbert's official residence early in the morning and had the old man woken up. At the end of a stormy interview Bismarck hit back by mentioning reports he had received about the tsar's visit to London. He refused to read out the report, but when the kaiser demanded, as Bismarck no doubt anticipated, to see the document, he could himself read Alexander III's wounding remark about his German cousin, 'c'est un garçon mal élevé et de mauvaise foi.'

*

Bismarck's exit was as bitter as could be, but with his letter of resignation, published immediately after his death eight years later, he laid the basis for a historic counterattack.[9] His version of the reasons for his resignation soon established themselves deeply in the German consciousness. He gave the impression that the kaiser's demand for the withdrawal of the cabinet order of 1852 was pointing towards a new absolutism. It soon became widely accepted that the kaiser had tried in the subsequent decade to establish a personal regime, which proved a fiasco and was responsible for many of Germany's ills. Bismarck then gave the reasons why it was not possible for him to remain as chancellor and Prussian foreign minister, giving up the Prussian premiership, as had been under discussion in the previous few weeks. He cited the kaiser's complaints about not having seen the reports from Kiev about Russian troop movements and argued that he could no longer be responsible for the conduct of foreign policy when the friendly relations with Russia, which he had always maintained and which the Russian ambassador had just reasserted, were being undermined. This part of the resignation letter became the basis for the opinion, again widely held in Germany, that the non-renewal of the reinsurance treaty with Russia, which followed immediately upon Bismarck's departure, was the beginning of the fatal deterioration in Germany's international position. This became evident even in the 1890s and eventually led to her defeat in the First World War. In 1896 Bismarck reinforced this view by making the reinsurance treaty public.

Bismarck's resignation, followed within days by that of his son, was greeted by the official world with a sigh of relief, but a large and enthusiastic crowd cheered him on his way from his official residence to the station. Outwardly, the decencies were preserved by the conferment of the title duke of Lauenburg, a title he never used and of which he said it might come in useful when travelling incognito. He was also promoted to colonel-general.

But without politics his life would have become meaningless and even without power and the sources of information that went with it he remained as passionately committed as ever. Resentment was the driving force, but not the only one. Mixed with the contempt in which he held his former collaborators and present successors, many of whom he accused of having betrayed him, was real anxiety for the future of the Reich. The circumstances of Bismarck's fall were profoundly ambivalent and so was the continuing influence on the fate of Germany which he exercised in his retirement. Nobody could say the programme through which he attempted to cling to power, the unleashing of a crisis near to civil war, would have been anything other than highly and unnecessarily destructive, but those who toppled him, above all the kaiser himself, had no recipe for the future either. Within a few years this became abundantly obvious. Bismarck proposed to suppress social democracy and was prepared to change the constitution and emasculate or abolish the Reichstag in order to do so. Soon the kaiser gave up all idea of reconciling Social Democrats and the workers with the state, as Bismarck had predicted, and threatened to shoot them, but he never actually got round to doing so, for it was not practical politics.

Bismarck in his retirement in the Sachsenwald had thus plenty of scope for attacking the regime that succeeded him. He immediately acquired the means of attack, by receiving countless journalists from all over the world. In particular he developed a close relationship with a newspaper appearing in neighbouring Hamburg, the *Hamburger Nachrichten*. He also fostered close links with Maximilian Harden and his weekly *Die Zukunft*. Harden was the most influential investigative and muck-raking journalist of Wilhelmine Germany, in due course responsible for heaping massive discredit on the kaiser and his court. Bismarck was quite willing to employ in his own cause this left-liberal, Jewish writer, who often sailed close to the wind. Another propaganda platform developed by Bismarck was authorized biography and autobiography, though the latter could only be published after his death. Soon after leaving office he started work, mainly with the help of Lothar Bucher, on his *Erinnerung und Gedanke* (Memory and Thought), eventually better known as *Gedanken und Erinnerungen* (Reflections and Recollections, probably an adaptation of an English title). It was difficult to get him to work systematically and Bucher died in October 1892, before the work was finished, though Bismarck made many subsequent changes. It became a German classic, but in its treatment of history it is like one of Bismarck's highly polemical speeches in the Reichstag. It is not an effort to establish the truth, but a highly coloured plea for the defence. Another way in which Bismarck was kept in the public mind was through the many group visits to Friedrichsruh and through the crowds that cheered him whenever he appeared in public. He courted publicity, more than was ever the case during his years of power.

There was no real reconciliation between the retired chancellor and the kaiser. Relations became particularly bad with the official world when his son Herbert married the Hungarian Countess Marguerite von Hoyos in 1892 in Vienna. The kaiser and his ministers were sent into a panic by the fear that the occasion and Bismarck's journey there, via Dresden on the way out and Munich on the way back, would become a public demonstration for the 'Bismarck dynasty'. Caprivi, Bismarck's successor, instructed the German ambassador in Vienna not to attend the wedding and the kaiser wrote a letter to Francis Joseph asking him not to receive the rebellious subject who was making life difficult for him. These ham-fisted interventions turned the journey of the Bismarcks into a royal progress. The rift became so damaging for the reputation of the monarchy and the whole political establishment that efforts were made to achieve at least an outward show of reconciliation. In January 1894 Bismarck paid a ceremonial visit to the kaiser in Berlin, but returned to Friedrichsruh before the day was out. No one was really deceived and subsequent visits of the kaiser to Friedrichsruh were embarrassing occasions. But matters were no better with the former *Reichsfeinde*. When it was proposed to send Bismarck the Reichstag's congratulation on his eightieth birthday in 1895, a majority composed of Centre, Freisinn and Social Democrats refused. Thereupon the kaiser immediately jumped on the anti-parliamentary bandwagon of outrage and expressed his 'deepest indignation' at this gulf between the parliamentary representatives and the real feelings of the nation.

The fact was that Bismarck had no political future and his opposition to all his successors did had no consistent theme and exhausted itself in negativity. He stood as a National Liberal candidate in a by-election in Hanover in 1891. In what had been in the past a safe seat for the party held by Bennigsen, he won only on the second ballot and never took up his seat. Now that his career had been ended by the emperor, behind the authority of whose grandfather he had always sheltered, he declared that he had in the past been too concerned to limit the power of the Reichstag. What was required was a balance between the elements in the constitution. In a speech in Jena in 1892 he said:

Perhaps I myself contributed unconsciously to the result that the influence of parliament has reached its present low level, but I do not wish it to remain so in perpetuity. . . . Without a Reichstag, harbouring a constant majority, which is thereby enabled to criticize, control, warn the government . . . without such a Reichstag I am concerned for the durability and solidity of our national institutions.[10]

But then, as his hostility to the Caprivi government rose, he allowed his name to be used by organizations like the *Bund der Landwirte* (Agrarian League) and the *Alldeutscher Verband* (Pan-German League). The agrarians, led by the Junkers, were fighting bitterly against Caprivi's sensible steps of mitigating the high tariff policy in the interests of the consumers. Bismarck now seemed to associate himself with narrow agrarian interest politics, oblivious of the fact that Germany was rapidly turning into an industrial country. Caprivi's trade treaties were also designed to soften some of the international friction caused by high German tariffs, particularly with Russia. Yet Bismarck never tired of accusing his successors of having 'cut the wire to St Petersburg'. When this culminated in his publication of the reinsurance treaty in October 1896, it unleashed a veritable storm of protest and there was talk of 'high treason'. Even the right-wingers who had been taking his name in vain were embarrassed. As for the Pan-German League, it had originated in the protests against the agreement of August 1890, under which Heligoland was ceded to Germany by Britain in return for the German surrender of claims to Zanzibar and other territory in East Africa. This agreement had already been in the pipeline while Bismarck was still in office and was exactly in accordance with his policy of not allowing colonial excursions to get in the way of European power relations, yet he attacked Caprivi for it.

Thus the powerful Bismarck myth was used by all and sundry for their own purposes and had passed out of the control of the old man in the Sachsenwald. The only thing he could achieve was insecurity among his successors and he probably contributed to Caprivi's decision to resign in October 1894. For some years the thought that he might stage a comeback inspired panic in such as Holstein, who had turned from friend into bitter enemy. Bismarck sensed the danger that the hubris of increasing power was pushing the Reich into dangerous directions, but if anything his own activities were adding to, rather than reducing that danger. Anyway, time was running out for him. Johanna, with all her limitations the essential centre of his existence, died at Varzin in November 1894. His religious faith had already weakened in his latter years in office. When his old friend Alexander Keyserling visited him soon after his resignation and asked how it stood with his faith in Christ he replied that he no longer counted himself among the believers. 'In the struggles of the last few decades he had become more distant from the Lord – especially in the difficult times he was living through he felt this distance painfully,' he said.[11] He died on 30 July 1898, ten weeks after his great antagonist Gladstone.

CONCLUSION

BISMARCK AND THE GERMAN QUEST FOR WORLD POWER

In the last few years of his life, after his fall, Bismarck remained a powerful but ambiguous presence in Germany's public life. Many objected to his continued political activity and particularly to his use of the press. He referred to journalists as reptiles and as 'a debased category of humans . . . prepared to write for modest sums in favour of those who pay',[1] but even in his days of power his relations with newspapers had been scarcely restrained by either a sense of responsibility or of decency. Now he claimed that he saw his life's work endangered by the mistakes of his successors and that he could not remain silent. The press became his main outlet. 'Should I allow myself to be muzzled? I have dealt with affairs for nearly thirty years passably well and acquired some experience. Should I not be allowed to use it for the benefit of the Reich?' he said to Arthur von Brauer, a foreign office official whom he trusted.[2] But which part of his experience did he want posterity to benefit from? On the one hand he seemed to give his blessing to the widespread yearning for *Weltpolitik*, the idea that the time had come for Germany to play a role in the world commensurate with her strength and the value of her culture. It was a sentiment that found expression in the most diverse ways and among many different groups. The building of an ocean-going fleet, taken in hand by Tirpitz and strongly backed by the kaiser, was a fateful step, which Bismarck, in the year before his death, cautiously endorsed. Perhaps he was no longer able to gauge its full implications.

Max Weber's inaugural address at Heidelberg in 1895 was another, quite different manifestation of the rising sentiment for world power. Weber was a liberal imperialist, but also in favour of the full parliamentarization of Germany. He said:

> We have to grasp that Germany's unification was a youthful escapade which the nation undertook against its old age and which, because of its costliness, would have been better left undone, if it was to be the end rather than the beginning of a policy of world power.[3]

Bismarck himself had said in the Reichstag in 1888: 'We Germans fear God but nothing else in this world; but it is fear of God that lets us love and cherish peace.'[4] All those many Germans who wanted to see their country assert its strength, remembered the first part of Bismarck's sentence and forgot the second. After his fall he counterbalanced his encouragement for *Weltpolitik* with occasional warnings to his countrymen against overreaching themselves. The Reich should not behave like someone who has suddenly come into money and then offended everybody by pointing to the coins in his pocket, he said.[5] But the Bismarck cult encouraged hubris rather than moderation.

BISMARCK'S LEGACY IN DOMESTIC GERMAN POLITICS

There was also a deep yearning among Germans that their show of international power should be buttressed by internal unity. They were aware that Bismarck had not succeeded in unifying Germany internally as fully as he had done externally. He had gone out of his way to seek confrontations, to exacerbate conflicts and conducted himself in the German political arena as if it was a foreign battlefield. He had fallen because it was too obvious that mere repression of the Social Democrats led nowhere. In his last years he never moved beyond his view that the Social Democrats did not really represent the workers, but were demagogues whose influence would come to an end when they were put in prison. Talking to Brauer he said: 'I do not believe in the future of social democracy. Their utopias cannot be realized, as long as man prefers freedom to prison.' With his usual contempt for the rule of law he said that if pedantic bureaucrats and jurists had not stopped him, he would have put the loudest agitators behind bars and that would have served its purpose. Rather more prophetically he said that princes had more to fear from socialism than the possessing classes. A radical republic might come, but the abolition of property, which even the little man did not want, would not.[6]

With this prediction Bismarck proved right in the long run, but immediately the most serious fault-line in the political system he had devised was the exclusion of the ever-growing Social Democratic Party from any share in power. It was the most obvious sign that the Bismarck constitution was becoming an anachronism. It was a system that allowed the old powers, monarchy and aristocracy, to survive in far greater strength than was appropriate for a country that was industrializing and modernizing as fast as Germany. Bismarck himself, in the bitterness after his fall, had reason to reflect that the monarch, whose power he had preserved, had used it to bring him down. That is probably why he told Brauer, no doubt with an air of grim satisfaction, that it would be princes who would be the chief sufferers from a rise of socialism. The kaiser had not acceded to his chancellor's demand for the continued repression of social democracy, because he did not want to begin his reign by shedding the blood of his subjects. But as Bismarck foresaw, attempts at conciliating the workers were far too slow in bearing fruit to satisfy the erratic kaiser. Before a year was out, the monarch was telling his troops that if he gave the order, they would have to fire on their brothers.

The signals that came from Bismarck about Germany's domestic problems were as mixed and open to competing interpretations as his pronouncements on her international situation. On the question of the workers and social democracy he had not in fact confined himself to repression. His social policies of the 1880s, which would never have become law without his powerful pressure, were forward-looking and creative. He did not even mention them in his memoirs, which suggests that he attached no great importance to them. His policies did not stop the rise of the social democratic party, but in the longer run they helped to turn them from the party of revolution, which they claimed to be, into a party of reform. When war came in 1914, the German working class did not lag behind other sections of society in coming to the defence of the fatherland. On the broader issue of the constitutional system Bismarck remained utterly determined not to move an inch towards parliamentary government. He bent every effort to maintain his independence of parties, to remain their manipulator but not their instrument.

Perhaps the most serious consequence of his long reign was that large sections of the German middle classes became convinced that Bismarck's semi-authoritarian system represented the acme of political wisdom. Parliamentary talking shops, monkey houses as the kaiser called them, were looked down upon. For many the ideal was the state above politics, administered by a non-political bureaucracy. The good citizen had no need to involve himself in the dirty trade of politics; the strong state protected him and left him free to follow his superior cultural pursuits. This was the consequence of the exclusion of the German bourgeoisie from the inner citadel of power, the work of Bismarck, and of the blow he administered to their self-esteem. The generation of the Virchows and Forckenbecks, forthright defenders of liberal principles, who waited in vain for the end of the Bismarck regime, had no successors. Their kind of liberalism was dead, *Realpolitik* was in.

Nevertheless, Bismarck's domestic legacy was mixed and not only backward-looking. The settlement of 1866 was a compromise and in providing a national parliament elected by universal male suffrage created a platform for further advance. It made possible the rapid growth of the Social Democrats and also the development of an increasingly powerful national state. Bismarck revolved endless and fruitless schemes to 'dry out' the Reichstag, but it was most alive when he appeared and spoke there. His brilliance and his towering stature became most evident to the general public in his parliamentary performances; and his enjoyment and zest were obvious when he assailed his opponents with the poisoned darts of his sarcasm. He despised parliaments, but was nevertheless a great parliamentarian. There was then another respect in which his legacy for parliamentarism was profoundly ambivalent. He laid the foundations for the interventionist state, but such a state required legislation and a legislature. Right-wingers in the post-Bismarck era, from the kaiser down, might echo the great chancellor's threat of a *coup d'état* to abolish the Reichstag, but such talk was increasingly unrealistic. It would have risked civil war.

There was another side to Bismarck's ambivalent legacy in the internal affairs of the Reich. It was the survival of the age-old German particularism, the separate identity of its component states and tribes. The most important of these particularisms was that of Prussia and the relationship between Prussia and the Reich was crucial to Germany's development. Bismarck was Prussian to the core and everything he had done was done for the preservation of Prussia. But many of his peer group, the Prussian Junkers, and at times even his own king, felt that he had buried the old Prussia. The almost impenetrable, interlocking constitutional relationships he had established between Prussia and the Reich left him as the linchpin of the whole system. As chancellor after 1870 he had used the language of the new German nationalism to uphold his semi-dictatorial rule. It was the ideological cement for the various cartels of the patriotic, *staatserhaltenden*, conformist classes and parties which he tried to rally to sustain him. But when it suited him he used the various Prussian institutions, the pre-eminent Prussian position in the Bundesrat, the Prussian chamber of deputies elected by the three-tier franchise, the Prussian state ministry, over which he presided, to get his way. After his fall there was a further rapid erosion of particularism, including that of Prussia. Reich patriotism rose mightily and it was the wave on which the chauvinism and imperialism of Wilhelmine Germany moved forward. What was left of Prussia were features and devices that enhanced the anachronistic nature of the German political system. There was the exceptional position of monarch and court and the privileged foothold that it continued to give the Prussian aristocracy. Connected with it was the power of the military. Bismarck had fought it fiercely whenever it threatened his own power, but he had never attacked the principle of the royal power of command. The result was that the military occupied an even more privileged position in the decision-making process when he was no longer there to control them. The Schlieffen plan, to attack France through Belgium, was devised at the turn of the century by the chief of staff, but Bismarck's successors as chancellors never had a chance of questioning its political implications.

Most important of all was the survival of the Prussian three-tier franchise. It was basically a plutocratic franchise and therefore Bismarck introduced the universal franchise for the Reichstag. It was a far-sighted move, but also a misjudgment, which he often came to regret. Farsighted, because eventually the masses had much more to lose than their chains and did not use the vote to dispossess the owners of property. A misjudgment, because Bismarck thought of the masses as peasants loyal to their king, whereas they came to be mainly composed of industrial workers. In the industrial and urbanized Germany of the early twentieth century the universal manhood suffrage of the Reichstag enabled the Social Democrats to become the greatest socialist party in Europe. It left the Prussian franchise as a crying anomaly. Its flagrant injustice became an obvious target for attack, while Bismarck's former peer group, the Prussian Junkers, clung to it tenaciously.

BISMARCK'S FOUNDATION OF THE REICH AND GERMANY'S FATE IN THE TWENTIETH CENTURY

Bismarck's legacy was largely predetermined by the achievements of his heroic period, the years between 1862 and 1870. He was called to power by the Prussian king who felt himself threatened. Prussia was an army with a state and not a state with an army. William I was not prepared to surrender what he considered the essence of the legacy handed on to him by his Hohenzollern ancestors. The army was also the ultimate bulwark against revolution and had proved so again twelve years earlier. Bismarck saved the king from surrender, but did so by taking over a large part of the aims of the opposition. The opposition were the liberals, who were also the principal protagonists of German nationalism. Bismarck accomplished a trick of such dazzling virtuosity that most of his liberal opponents became his devoted followers. The essentials of the constitutional framework for a united Germany were Bismarck's handiwork. It was a compromise, for even so powerful a man as the iron chancellor could only operate on the materials that lay to hand. The German bourgeoisie could not be shoved aside, it had to be coopted. Industrialization and urbanization made a more unified political structure in central Europe all but inevitable, but the process was so dynamic that even Bismarck's structures could scarcely contain it. His long years in office after 1870 were increasingly pervaded by an air of stagnation. The perpetuation of power became an end in itself, the methods reeked of despotism. When he fell in 1890, Bamberger wrote: 'it is unfortunate that his departure is fortunate.'[7]

ALTERNATIVES TO BISMARCK'S MODEL OF GERMAN UNIFICATION

In interpreting Bismarck's role the question arises whether there were alternative ways of reorganizing Central Europe to his method of blood and iron. What seemed most real to Bismarck's contemporaries was the establishment of Grossdeutschland, a Germany that included Austria. Even in the 1860s it seemed not so much an alternative to the creation of a Prussian-led Germany excluding Austria, but still the most natural solution to any conceivable reform of the German Confederation. In retrospect the multi-national Habsburg empire evokes nostalgia, because it looks much preferable to the ethnic conflicts, let alone the brutal fascist or communist empires that followed. Contemporaries often called it 'the prison of nationalities' and saw no future for it. Yet even Bismarck kept open the alternative of an accommodation with Austria, almost until the eve of the war of 1866. The obstacles were formidable, as the events of 1848 had shown. The majority of the Frankfurt parliament would have wanted Grossdeutschland, but they could not get it. Either there would be virtually no advance on the loosely constructed Confederation, or else the Habsburg empire would have to be broken up. The failure of Austria to join the Zollverein in the 1850s showed how difficult the achievement of an economically effective union was. In the Europe of the twenty-first century the jury is still out about the question how close a political union is necessary for an economic union to be viable. Bismarck's Kleindeutschland did provide the political framework for a dynamic market economy. It was the outcome of the cooperation that Bismarck entered into with the national-liberal movement, but in which the Prussian monarchical state remained unequivocally the senior partner.

Another conceivable alternative to Bismarck's unification was the possibility of a revolution from below. It was what the democrats of 1848 had hoped for and some of them or their successors were still around in the 1860s. Such a revolution was still the great fear, the *grande peur*, which terrified monarchs and governments and which Bismarck was called to power to ward off. What gave Bismarck a sinister air in the eyes of conservatives and even of his own king was his willingness to use the threat of revolution, to make a pact with the devil, the *acheronta movebo* of which he sometimes spoke. It is hard to believe that a popular uprising with the double aim of democracy and national unity was really on the cards in the 1860s; Bismarck was doing no more than using it as a spectre to cause alarm when that suited his tactics. The obstacles to a far-reaching reform of Central Europe were so great that the use of force might well be required to remove them. If it was unlikely to be force from below, it was going to be war between states. In his many letters and memoranda written when he was a diplomat in Frankfurt, St Petersburg and Paris Bismarck regarded war as a probability in resolving the problems of Central Europe. It was his view that Prussia was a country that had always flourished when the weather was stormy. Nevertheless, it might have been possible to create by peaceful means a Germany sufficiently cohesive to meet economic pressures and ideological aspirations. In 1866, the hinge of fate of his career, he was forcing the pace towards war. His survival in power was increasingly dependent on a resolution of the differences with Austria by war. A slower, negotiated solution, perhaps based on the 'trias' model, the two big powers and a third Germany of the smaller states, might have had a chance. Its development might have been less dynamic than that of the Bismarckian Reich, but it might have carried a lesser burden of external hostility and domestic tension.

Alternatives to the course taken under Bismarck's prolonged dominance can be more plausibly envisaged once he had achieved German unity. In cooperating with the chancellor in the years up to 1879 many National Liberals were buoyed up by the hope that soon there would be a time after Bismarck when their aspirations for a fully parliamentary system could be realized. In the meantime they were, with Bismarck and more immediately with Delbrück, carrying forward the economic unification of Germany. Even in this phase the nature of the liberal movement had changed. Earlier liberals had defined themselves by ideas and seen themselves as the 'general estate' representing the progressive aspirations of society as a whole. Now they had become more of a class and interest-bound movement, seeing themselves as the representatives of the economic middle class, the class that was in the van of modernizing society. This change of self-image had made it easier for them to switch from opposition to Bismarck, the head of a regime of repression, into support for Bismarck, the unifier of Germany. The Kulturkampf created another bond between them and the chancellor. But many of them, certainly those on the left around Lasker and even the centre around Bennigsen, did not delude themselves that they were in full harmony with Bismarck. The change of course in 1879 was not so much a refoundation of the Reich as a reinforcement of the existing liberal deficit.

The hour when after Bismarck the liberals would enter into their inheritance never came. Liberalism was fatally weakened by the great depression, by the rise of doubts about free trade and the free market. Fear of the workers and of socialism pushed the once liberal middle classes to the right. A defensive solidarity developed between the old privileged classes and the entrepreneurial classes recently risen to wealth. Bismarck manipulated these developments so that he remained an independent power in the state. After the turn of 1879 the liberal alternative to the chancellor regime became less plausible, but it did not vanish. Had a fully parliamentary system been in place, German society might have become less polarized. Compromises attempted by some of Bismarck's successors might have had more of a chance. Caprivi might have prevailed with his return to freer trade and regard for the consumer. Later Bethmann Hollweg attempted a 'policy of the diagonal', an accommodation between those clinging to the Prussian three-tier law and the demands of the Social Democrats. The Bismarckian system frustrated him. Bismarck himself continued to be plagued by nightmares of a 'Gladstone ministry' following the accession of the crown prince and it was only after 1884 that he slept more easily. But right up to the moment of his fall the fear never completely left him that an alternative policy, to him abhorrent and destructive to his life's work, might come to prevail.

It is more difficult to know, even with hindsight, how different matters would then have turned out. Chauvinism, intolerance, conformity, servility, militarism, and many other unattractive characteristics of imperial German society, were not made by Bismarck. They were facilitated by the way the Reich, largely through him, came into being and then aggravated by his style of ruling. Contemporary critics, ranging from intellectuals like the historian Jakob Burckhardt and the philosopher Friedrich Nietzsche, to perceptive politicians like Ludwig Bamberger, targeted the 'success German', made arrogant, blinded and seduced by Bismarck's wizardry. Nietzsche warned in 1873 against the delusion in German public opinion that the victory of 1870 was a victory for German culture: 'This delusion is most pernicious . . . because it is capable of turning our victory into total defeat: into the defeat, even the extinction of the German spirit in favour of the German Reich.'[8]

Great men like Bismarck can only do their work because they know how to use the circumstances and pressures of their time. Prussia, the Zollverein, the national-liberal movement, industrialism and other historical factors lay to hand, but the way Bismarck used them was not predetermined. The impermanence of Bismarck's Reich, and the disasters to which it gave rise, have made critics argue that it was founded against the grain of history. Bismarck shored up monarchical power and inhibited parliamentarization, when moves towards constitutional monarchy and parliamentary government would have been much more in line with the secular trend. The semi-constitutional system became the accepted German political system during Bismarck's long tenure of power and was not in essentials modified until the collapse of the German empire in 1918. At the same time the economic unification of the Reich promoted under Bismarck's aegis gave rise to a dramatic upsurge of industrialization, urbanization and modernization. Even by the end of Bismarck's period in office his political system appeared to be out of phase with the development of German society and this accounts for the sense of relief with which his departure was greeted in many quarters. The iron chancellor's dominance, continually reasserted through his unique charisma as the Reich's founder, left little room for political growth. The institutions were caught in the gridlock he had deliberately created and his overpowering presence had inhibited the rise of an independent political class. The population at large had become accustomed to having their affairs ordered by a Caesaristic figure, while the system required a supreme coordinator to give it direction. The kaiser attempted to fill the vacant role, but his performance was a farce. In his retirement Bismarck spoke of him as 'the stupid boy' and turned the five-mark coins that carried the kaiser's image face down.

BISMARCK AND THE QUEST FOR A SAVIOUR

Bismarck felt after his fall that a Germany that did not need him was doomed. 'It may be that what God has in store for Germany is a second period of disintegration, followed by a new time of glory, on the new basis of a republic, but it will not touch us any more,' he wrote. It was his tragedy that much of the decline he foresaw in his resentment was of his own making. In March 1867 in recommending the constitution to the constituent Reichstag of the North German Confederation he had said: 'Gentlemen, let us work quickly! Let us, so to speak, lift Germany into the saddle! She will be able to ride.'[9] Bismarck never allowed his Germany to ride. Another riding metaphor he often used was that he would not allow anyone to throw the leading rein over his head, but he went on doing just that to everyone else. Parliamentary government, parties capable of taking responsibility for executive government, many aspects of public life and of the political culture as a whole, were prevented from developing or at least distorted by Bismarck's style of governing. 'Bismarck made Germany great but the Germans small,' said the liberal Georg von Bunsen.

Perhaps the most serious consequence was that there continued to be in Germany a yearning for the great, the Caesaristic figure that would brush all dissent aside and lead the way forward. The posthumous Bismarck cult is a manifestation of the void left by the iron chancellor. Those who came along to fill the void, Hindenburg in the First World War, not to speak of Hitler, were harbingers of catastrophe. With each catastrophe Germans looked back to Bismarck with nostalgia. When war broke out in 1914 there was an upsurge of national enthusiasm. German society, previously deeply divided, leapt like one man to the defence of the Fatherland. At least that is what conservative, nationalist right-wing Germans wanted to believe. The 'spirit of August 1914' was elevated into a myth and kept burnished by right-wingers throughout the Weimar period. The Nazis rekindled it in 1933 by calling their take-over a 'national uprising', a reincarnation of the spirit of 1914. In all this the ghost of Bismarck was never absent. The patriotic mobs baying for war in Berlin in July 1914 spontaneously turned to the Bismarck statue in front of the Reichstag.[10] When the conservative, nationalist elites that helped Hitler into power lost control of him, they liked to contrast Hitler, the reckless gambler threatening Germany's ruin, with Bismarck, the careful, moderate cabinet politician. In 1944, when Germany's total defeat was imminent, Ulrich von Hassell, son-in-law of Tirpitz and at one time German ambassador in Rome, was staying at Friedrichsruh. He was soon to be executed as a participant in the assassination plot against Hitler. He wrote of Bismarck:

> Hardly to be borne, I am constantly near to tears at the thought of what has been destroyed. . . . It is regrettable, the false picture of him we have put around, as the man of violence in military boots, in our childish joy, that at last someone has given Germany respect. He uniquely knew how to create trust in the world, the opposite of what we now have. In truth the highest diplomacy and a sense of restraint were his great gifts.[11]

It was true, but it was not the whole truth about Bismarck. He had also stunted the capacity for self-government in Germany and made the people look for a saviour.

NOTES

ABBREVIATIONS

W = Bismarck. *Die gesammelten Werke (Friedrichsruher Ausgabe)*, edited by Gerhard Ritter, Rudolf Stadelmann, 15 vols, Berlin, 1924–35

AW = Otto von Bismarck, *Werke in Auswahl*, edited by G.A. Rein, Wilhelm Schüssler, Albert Milatz and Rudolf Buchner, 8 vols., Stuttgart, 1962–81

Gedanken = Otto Fürst von Bismarck, *Gedanken und Erinnerungen, Taschenausgabe*, Stuttgart and Berlin, 1926

A.P.P. = *Die auswärtige Politik Preußens 1858–1871*, 10 vols, Oldenburg, 1933–41

Grosse Politik = *Die grosse Politik der europäischen Kabinette von 1871–1914*, edited by J. Lepsius, A. Mendelssohn-Bartholdy and F. Thimme, 40 vols, Berlin 1922–7

Keudell = Robert von Keudell, *Fürst und Fürstin Bismarck, Erinnerungen von 1846 bis 1872*, Berlin-Stuttgart, 1901

Engelberg = Ernst Engelberg, *Bismarck*, vol. I: *Urpreuße und Reichsgründer*, Berlin, 1986; vol. II: *Das Reich in der Mitte Europas*, Berlin, 1990

Eyck = Erich Eyck, *Bismarck. Leben und Werk*, 3 vols, Erlenbach-Zürich, 1941–4

Gall = Lothar Gall, *Bismarck. Der weisse Revolutionär*, Frankfurt am Main, 1980

INTRODUCTION

1 Michael Stürmer (ed.), *Bismarck und die preußisch-deutsche Politik, 1871–90*, Munich, 1970, p. 130, Robert von Benda to Rudolf von Bennigsen

2 W.J. Mommsen, *Imperial Germany 1867–1918. Politics, Culture and Society in an Authoritarian State*, London, 1995

3 J. Heyderhoff and P. Wentzke, *Deutscher Liberalismus im Zeitalter Bismarcks: Eine politische Briefsammlung*, Bonn and Leipzig, 1925–6, vol. 1, p. 494

4 F. Meinecke, 'Bismarck und das neue Deutschland', in *Preußen und Deutschland im 19. und 20. Jahrhundert*, München and Berlin, 1918, pp. 510–31

5 J. Ziekursch, *Politische Geschichte des neuen deutschen Kaiserreiches*, 3 vols, Frankfurt am Main, 1925–30; a good selection of Kehr's work in English is Eckart Kehr, *Economic Interest, Militarism and Foreign Policy: Essays on German History*, Berkeley, 1977

6 W.L. Shirer, *The Rise and Fall of the Third Reich*, London, 1960; A.J.P. Taylor, *Bismarck: The Man and the Statesman*, London, 1955

7 E. Crankshaw, *Bismarck*, London, 1981, p. 414; E. Eyck, *Bismarck and the German Empire*, London, 1950, is an abridged translation

8 See also, H.-U. Wehler, *The German Empire 1871–1918*, Leamington Spa, 1984

9 L. Gall, *Bismarck: The White Revolutionary*, 2 vols, 1986 (English translation); T. Nipperdey, *Deutsche Geschichte 1800–1866*, Munich, 1983, *Deutsche Geschichte 1866–1918*, 2 vols, Munich, 1992; Michael Stürmer, *Das Ruhelose Reich. Deutschland 1866–1918*, Berlin, 1983

1 EARLY DAYS

1 Engelberg I, 119
2 Gall, 45
3 Engelberg I, 139, 3/12/1836
4 W.14l, 30, 9/1/1845
5 Engelberg I, 146, 21/10/1837
6 Gall, 43
7 W.14l, 25, to Scharlach, 4/8/1844
8 E. Marcks, *Bismarcks Jugend 1815–1848*, Stuttgart, 1909, p. 244

2 ENTRY INTO POLITICS

1 Horst Kohl, *Die politischen Reden des Fürsten Bismarck, 1847–1897*, Stuttgart, 1892–1905, vol. 1, p. 21, 15/6/1847
2 Gall, 75
3 Gedanken, 48
4 W.10, 38
5 Eyck I, 147
6 W.14l, 179, 7/11/1850
7 W.10, 105
8 Gedanken, 74
9 W.14l, 211, 14/5/1851
10 AW.I, 421, 4/7/1851

3 DIPLOMAT WITH A DIFFERENCE

1 Engelberg I, 371
2 W.14l, 213, 18/5/1851
3 W.14l, 336, 22/12/1853, to his sister
4 W.14l, 217, 5/6/1851
5 W.1, 471, 25/7/1854
6 W.1, 104, late November 1851
7 W.14l, 354, 21/4/1854
8 W.14l, 227, 26/6/1851
9 W.1, 61, 29/9/1851
10 W.14l, 352, 13/4/1854

11 W.1, 425, 15/2/1854
12 W.14I, 352, 13/4/1854
13 W.14I, 376, 6/1/1855
14 W.14I, 374, 12/12/1854
15 W.1, 513, 8–9/12/1854
16 Engelberg I, 433
17 W.2, 138
18 Gedanken, 150–82
19 AW.II, 6, 22/2/1854, to Alexander von Below-Hohendorf
20 W.14I, 439, 8/4/1856
21 W.11, 301, 30/3//1858
22 W.14I, 493, 12/11/1858
23 W.14I, 528, 25/6/1859
24 W.3, 67, 19/12/1859
25 Eyck I, 311f.
26 W.14I, 524, 4/6/1859
27 AW.II, 273
28 W.3, 35, 12/5/1859
29 W.14I, 515, 1/5/1859
30 Gall, 191

4   MINISTER IN WAITING

1   W.14I, 552, 12/5/1860
2   W.14I, 548, 2–4/5/1860
3   W.14I, 558, 3/8/1860
4   W.3, 147, 10/12/1860
5   Eyck I, 357
6   Gedanken, 230f.
7   W.3, 266, July 1861
8   W.14I, 578, 18/9/1861
9   Gall, 211
10 W.14I, 58, 17/1/1862
11 Gall, 225
12 Engelberg I, 515
13 W.3, 384, 8/7/1862
14 E. Feuchtwanger, *Disraeli*, London, 2000, 123
15 Engelberg I, 518
16 W.14.II, 600, 15/7/1862
17 W.14.II, 605, 29/7/1862
18 W.14.II, 611–13, 14/8/1862, 19/8/1862, 20/8/1862
19 AW.III, 166, 16/9/1863
20 W.14.II, 619, 12/9/1862
21 Gedanken, 255
22 Gedanken, 256f.
23 Eyck I, 418

5 PRIME MINISTER

1 W.14.II, 621, 24/9/1862
2 W.10, 138, 30/9/1862
3 W.7, 59, 1/10/1862
4 Gedanken, 272f.
5 W.7, 69, 4/12/1862
6 A.P.P.3, 154, 5/1/63
7 W.14.II, 639, 17/4/1863
8 W.10, 152, 27/1/1863
9 W.14.II, 637, 17/2/1863
10 W.4, 57, 11/2/1863
11 W.7, 93; also Reichstag speech of 17/9/78, W.11, 602
12 Gedanken, 306
13 Ibid., 323

6 FIRST TRIUMPH

1 W.14I, 460, 11/4/1857
2 W.3, 208, 7/4/1861
3 W.4, 240, 20/12/1863
4 W.14.II, 658, 24/12/1863
5 Gall, 305, 31/12/63
6 Keudell, 140f.
7 W.10, 208, 22/1/1864
8 W.10. 164, 21/1/1864
9 W.14.II, 661, 21/1/64
10 Eyck I, 594
11 A.P.P.5, 119
12 W.14.II, 672, 20/7/1864
13 W.14.II, 673, 27/7/1864
14 W.14.II, 675, 20/8/1864
15 W.4, 551, 8/9/1864
16 Eyck I, 648
17 W.14.II, 683, 16/10/1864

7 FRATRICIDAL WAR

1 W.10, 235, 1/6/1865
2 AW.III, 437, 20/1/1865
3 AW.III, 506, 8/4/1865
4 A.P.P.6, 174f., 29/5/1865
5 W.5, 285, 1/9/1865
6 Keudell, 227f.
7 W.5, 354, 13/1/1866
8 W.14.II, 709, 26/12/1865, to Andrae Roman

9 W.5, 368, 26/1/1866
10 Gall, 345
11 W.10, 258, 3/2/1866
12 A.P.P.6, 611f., 28/2/1866
13 W.14.II, 710, 7/4/1866
14 W.14.II, 709, 11/3/1866
15 W.5, 390, 8/3/1866, to Reuss
16 Engelberg I, 575
17 Eyck II, 188
18 AW.III, 692, 26/4/1866
19 Eyck II, 220/1
20 Engelberg I, 588/9
21 Eyck II, 195
22 W.14.II, 717, 9/7/1866
23 Ibid.
24 Gall, 368
25 Keudell, 297
26 Gedanken, 395f.
27 W.6, 120

8   HIGH NOON

1 Keudell, 292
2 W.7. 139, 8/7/1866
3 W.14.II, 719, 3/8/1866
4 Eyck II, 305
5 Eyck II, 304
6 Preussische Jahrbücher, vol. 18
7 W.6, 167ff.
8 W. 7, 213, to von Wilmowski
9 W.6, 158, 7/9/1866
10 W. 7, 186, March 1867
11 W.7, 243, 2/2/1868
12 W.11, 98, 24/2/1870
13 W.6b, 266
14 W.14.II, 776, 13/5/1870
15 D.G. Williamson, *Bismarck and Germany 1862–1890*, 2nd edn, 1998, pp. 104–5
16 Gedanken, 447
17 W.14.II, 789, 3/9/1870
18 W.7, 337, 4/9/1870
19 Keudell, 457
20 W.14.II, 796, 20–21/10/1870
21 W.14.II, 797, 28–19/10/1870
22 W.14.II, 800, 16/11/1870
23 Engelberg I, 744

24 Eyck II, 503
25 W.14.II, 810, 21/1/1871
26 Gall, 450
27 W.14.II, 816, 5/3/1871

9 IMPERIAL CHANCELLOR

1 W.8, 170, 19/4/1876, to Lucius v.Ballhausen
2 W.14.II, 819, 19/6/1871, to v.Frankenberg
3 W.6c, 3, 17/4/71, to v.Werthern
4 W.11, 224
5 W.11, 269, 14/5/1872
6 See also Gedanken, 487
7 M.Scholle, *Die preussische Strafjustiz im Kulturkampf 1873–1880*, Marburg 1974, pp. 118–61
8 W.14.II, 844, 13/12/1872
9 Engelberg II, 62
10 W.11, 374, 4/12/1874
11 Gall, 545
12 W.11, 405, 22/11/1875
13 AW.V, 260, late 1872, to von Oettingen
14 Grosse Politik 1, 235, Nr. 147
15 AW.V, 186
16 W.11, 425
17 Engelberg II, 264–5
18 W.11, 487, 10/3/1877
19 Grosse Politik 2, 87, 9/11/1876
20 Grosse Politik 2, 153

10 TURN TO THE RIGHT

1 Engelberg II, 266
2 W.14.II, 890, 17/12/77
3 W.11, 520
4 Engelberg II, 282
5 W.11, 602, 17/9/1878
6 W.12, 117, 9/7/1879
7 W.12, 69, 8/5/1879
8 W.12, 117

11 POWER PROLONGED

1 W.8, 331, 3/10/1879
2 Grosse Politik 3, 152
3 W.8, 363, 11/5/1880

4 W.6c, 222
5 *Das Tagebuch der Baronin Spitzemberg geb. Freiin von Varnbüler* (ed. Rudolf Vierhaus), Göttingen, 1960, p. 172, 13/6/1878
6 W.12, 366, 14/6/1882
7 W.12, 236, 2/4/1881
8 ibid.
9 W.12, 416, 15/3/1884
10 W.13, 395
11 Engelberg II, 329. See also Fritz Stern, *Gold and Iron*, London, 1977, chapter 18
12 Engelberg II, 359
13 W.13, 9, 12/3/1885
14 W.6c, 282, 22/10/1883
15 Gall, 623
16 W.12, 406, 13/3/1884
17 W.12, 416, 15/3/1884
18 Moritz Busch, *Tagebuchblätter*, Leipzig, 1899, vol. III, p. 190, 31/5/1885
19 W.8, 557, 17/3/1887
20 W.13, 144
21 W.13, 181, 12/4/ 1886
22 W.13, 207, 11/1/1887

12 FALL AND RESENTFUL RETIREMENT

1 W.6c, 382, 6/1/1888
2 Moritz Busch, *Tagebuchblätter*, Leipzig, 1899, vol. III, p. 84, 9/6/1882
3 Gedanken, 679
4 Gall, 683
5 Engelberg II, 5/8/1893, to August von Heyden
6 Engelberg II, 526
7 W.8, 665, 11/10/1889, to Arthur von Brauer
8 Gedanken, 722 and 724
9 W.6c, 435, 18/3/1890
10 W.13, 474, 31/7/1892
11 Engelberg II, 599

CONCLUSION

1 W.5, 325, 26/11/1865, to Robert von der Goltz
2 A. von Brauer, 'Bismarck', in *Meister der Politik*, Stuttgart, 1921, vol. 2, p. 606
3 T. Nipperdey, *Deutsche Geschichte 1866–1918*, Munich, 1992, vol. 2, p. 629
4 W.13, 326, 6/2/1888

5   Engelberg II, 643
6   Brauer, loc. cit.
7   Bruce Waller, *Bismarck*, 2nd edn. Oxford, 1997, p. 110
8   M. Stürmer, *Das ruhelose Reich. Deutschland 1866–1918*, Berlin, 1983, p. 122
9   W.10, 320, 11/3/1867
10 J. Verhey, *The Spirit of 1914: Militarism, Myth and Mobilization in Germany*, Cambridge, 2000, p. 30
11 U.von Hassell, *Vom andern Deutschland. Aus den nachgelassenen Tagebüchern 1938–1944*, Frankfurt am Main, 1964, p. 319

FURTHER READING

There are many good biographies of Bismarck in English. The most recently published is the second edition of Bruce Waller, *Bismarck* (Blackwell, 1997), a short, but comprehensive assessment in the Historical Association Studies series, intended primarily for students. Older biographies include Edward Crankshaw, *Bismarck* (Macmillan, 1981), written by someone with a wide and distinguished background in European history. It is on the whole condemnatory of Bismarck's methods and their long-term results. Alan Palmer, another well-known biographer and historian, published a more neutral, but also very readable biography in 1976, Bismarck (Weidenfeld & Nicolson). W.N. Medlicott, *Bismarck and Modern Germany* (Athlone Press, 1965) is particularly good on foreign policy. George O. Kent, *Bismarck and His Times* (South Illinois University Press, 1978) is short and analytical. A.J.P. Taylor, *Bismarck: The Man and the Statesman* (Hamish Hamilton, 1955) is interesting and worth reading, but some of its interpretations are now difficult to accept.

The fullest treatment of the life and times of Bismarck in English are the three volumes of Otto Pflanze, *Bismarck and the Development of Germany*, vol. I: *The Period of Unification, 1815–1871*; vol. II: *The Period of Consolidation, 1871–1880*; vol. III: *The Period of Fortification, 1880–1898* (Princeton University Press, 1973–90).

Two major German Bismarck biographies of recent years are available in English: Lothar Gall, *Bismarck: The White Revolutionary*, 2 vols (Allen & Unwin, 1986); and Erich Eyck, *Bismarck after Fifty Years* (Allen & Unwin, 1950), an abridged version of the German work. Eyck's book is easier to read and more lively; it is written by a committed liberal, who condemns much of what Bismarck did. Gall gives sophisticated and balanced answers to the historiographical problems presented by Bismarck's life and work. The reader who comes new to the subject may find Gall's arguments sometimes difficult to follow. There is also a translation of Werner Richter, *Bismarck* (Macdonald, 1964), a popular German biography.

There is an English translation of the first two volumes of Bismarck's reminiscences, *Bismarck, the Man and Statesman, being the reflections and reminiscences of Otto Prince von Bismarck* (translated by A.J. Butler, Smith Elder, 1898). The third volume, published only after the fall of the German empire and giving Bismarck's version of his own fall, has not been translated. Much of the documentation relevant to Bismarck, particularly that concerned with foreign policy, can be found in translation in the many collections of documents available on German history. They include D. Hargreaves (ed.), *Bismarck and German Unification* (Macmillan, 1991); David Welch, *Modern European History 1871–2000: A Documentary Reader* (2nd edn, Routledge, 1999); W.N. Medlicott and D.K. Coveney (eds), *Bismarck and Europe* (Edward Arnold, 1971); J.C.G. Roehl (ed.), *From Bismarck to Hitler: The Problem of Continuity in German History* (Longman, 1970); N. Rich and M. Fischer (eds), *The Holstein Papers*, 4 vols (Cambridge University Press, 1955–63).

There is a large literature on German history in general and on the Bismarck period and imperial Germany in particular. General histories which give an overview of the period include the two relevant volumes in the Oxford History of Modern Europe: James J. Sheehan, *German History, 1770–1866* (1989) and Gordon A. Craig, *Germany 1866–1945* (1978). William Carr, *A History of Germany 1815–1990* (Edward Arnold, 1991) and Edgar Feuchtwanger, *Imperial Germany 1850–1918* (Routledge, 2001) provide more succinct surveys. Volker Berghahn, *Imperial Germany 1871–1914: Economy, Society, Culture and Politics* (Berg, 1994) is slanted towards the economic and social background. T.S. Hamerow's three volumes, *Restoration, Revolution, Reaction: Economics and Politics in Germany, 1815–1871* (1958), *The Social Foundations of German Unification, 1858–1871*, vol. 1: *Ideas and Institutions* (1969), vol. 2: *Struggles and Accomplishments* (1972), all published by Princeton University Press, give a thorough coverage of the background for the period up to 1871. Hans-Ulrich Wehler, *The German Empire 1871–1918* (Berg, 1984), published in German in 1973, is very succinct, but the most influential post-1960s revisionist work. Wolfgang J. Mommsen, *Imperial Germany 1867–1918. Politics, Culture and Society in an Authoritarian State* (Edward Arnold, 1995) is a collection of essays published in the 1970s and 1980s, which deal with the principal historiographical problems.

Much has been written on foreign policy, diplomacy, nationalism and militarism. A.J.P. Taylor, *The Struggle for Mastery in Europe, 1848–1918* (Oxford University Press, 1954) is readable as well as useful as a work of reference. Peter Alter, The *German Question and Europe* (Edward Arnold, 2000) is a thoughtful survey of Germany's place in Europe. John Breuilly, *The Formation of the First German Nation State, 1800–1871* (Macmillan, 1996) is an excellent analysis of the rise of German nationalism. Werner E. Mosse, *The European Powers and the German Question 1848–1871* (Cambridge University Press, 1958) remains the classic modern account of the diplomacy around German unification. William Carr, *The Origins of the German Wars of Unification* (Longman, 1991) is partic-ularly useful on the Schleswig-Holstein question. The campaigns of 1866 and 1870 are well described in Gordon A. Craig, *The Battle of Königgrätz* (Weidenfeld & Nicolson, 1965) and Michael Howard, *The Franco-Prussian War* (Rupert Hart Davis, 1962). The classic post-1945 conservative-nationalist German view of

Bismarck and Prussian militarism is put forward by Gerhard Ritter in *The Sword and the Sceptre: The Problem of Militarism in Germany*, 4 vols (University of Miami Press, 1969). E.J. Feuchtwanger, *Prussia: Myth and Reality* (Oswald Wolff, 1970) deals with the background to Prussia and its ethos. Two books by W.N. Medlicott remain indispensable for foreign policy after 1870, *Bismarck, Gladstone and the Concert of Europe* (Athlone Press, 1956) and *The Congress of Berlin and After* (Methuen, 1938). For Bismarck's excursion into colonial policy, there is S. Förster, W.J. Mommsen and R. Robinson (eds), *Bismarck, Europe and Africa: The Berlin Africa Conference 1884–1885 and the onset of Partition* (Oxford University Press, 1988). A good survey for the period up to 1914 is Immanuel Geiss, *German Foreign Policy, 1871–1914* (Routledge, 1976)

There is also a copious literature on the issues and personalities surrounding Bismarck and his activitities. For the period of Bismarck's rise to prominence David E.Barclay, *Frederick William IV and the Prussian Monarchy, 1840–1861* (Clarendon Press, Oxford, 1995) gives a valuable insight into the Prussian background. James J. Sheehan, *German Liberalism in the Nineteenth Century* (Methuen, 1982) is wide-ranging and indispensable. Very important to an assessment of the role of the German bourgeoisie and the theory of the *Sonderweg* is Geoff Eley and David Blackbourn, *The Peculiarities of German History: Bourgeois Society and Politics in Nineteenth-Century Germany* (Oxford University Press, 1984). Dan S. White, *The Splintered Party: National Liberalism in Hessen and the Reich, 1867–1918* (Harvard University Press, 1976) is a useful study of the transformation of the National Liberals during the Bismarck years. Stanley Zucker, *Ludwig Bamberger: German Liberal Politician and Social Critic, 1823–1899* (Pittsburgh University Press, 1975) portrays one of Bismarck's principal opponents; another great opponent, as well as the Catholic political spectrum, are depicted in Margaret L. Anderson, *Windthorst: A Political Biography* (Clarendon Press, 1981) and in Ellen L. Evans, *The Center Party 1870–1933: A Study in Political Catholicism* (Illinois University Press, 1981). A Bismarck opponent of a different kind is portrayed in Hannah Pakula, *An Uncommon Woman: The Empress Frederick* (Weidenfeld & Nicolson, 1996), readable, but somewhat amateurish on the political side. Her son, who brought Bismarck down, is reassessed in John C.G. Röhl and Nicolaus Sombart, *Kaiser Wilhelm II: New Interpretations* (Cambridge University Press, 1982). Helga Grebing, *History of the German Labour Movement. A Survey* (Berg, 1985) is a good general introduction to the German socialist movement, while Vernon L. Lidtke, *The Outlawed Party: Social Democracy 1878–1890* (Princeton University Press, 1966) deals with the period during Bismarck's anti-socialist law. A wide-ranging series of essays, David E. Barclay and Eric D. Weitz, *Reform and Revolution: German Socialism and Communism from 1840 to 1990* (Oxford, 1998) puts the subject into a larger context. Anti-Semitism and its background are examined in Peter Pulzer, *The Rise of Political Anti-Semitism in Germany and Austria* (John Wiley, 1964) and in Shulamit Volkov, *The Rise of Popular Antimodernism in Germany: The Urban Master Artisans, 1873–1896* (Princeton University Press, 1978). Also illuminating on this subject is Fritz Stern, *Gold and Iron: Bismarck, Bleichröder, and the Building of the German Empire* (Allen & Unwin, 1977) but Bismarck was not quite as much influenced by his banker as the author claims. For the Conservatives, James N. Retallack, *Notables of the Right: The Conservative Party and Political Mobilization in Germany, 1876–1918* (Unwin Hyman, 1988) and Larry E. Jones and James N. Retallack (eds), *Between Reform, Reaction, and Resistance: Studies in the History of German Conservatism from 1789 to 1945* (Berg, 1993) provide good overviews. For the period after Bismarck's fall, J.C.G. Röhl, *Germany without Bismarck: The Crisis in Government in the Second Reich 1890–1900* (University of California Press, 1967) was a ground-breaking study.

Articles are sometimes more accessible than books and here are a few on a variety of aspects which may be found useful: Hans Rosenberg, 'Political and social consequences of the Great Depression of 1873–1896 in Central Europe', *Economic History Review*, xiii, 1943, pp. 58–73; see also 'Hans Rosenberg and the Great Depression, 1873–96', in Geoff Eley, *From Unification to Nazism: Reinterpreting the German Past* (Allen & Unwin, 1986); James C. Hunt, 'Peasants, grain tariffs and meat quotas: imperial German protectionism reexamined', *Central European History*, vii, 4, December 1974, pp. 311–31; Gordon R. Mork, 'Bismarck and the "capitulation" of German liberalism', *Journal of Modern History*, xliii, 1, March 1971, pp. 59–75; Allan Mitchell, 'Bonapartism as a model for Bismarckian politics', *Journal of Modern History*, xlix, 2, June 1977, pp. 181–209; John C.G. Röhl, 'The disintegration of the Kartell and the politics of Bismarck's fall from power, 1887–1890', *Historical Journal*, ix, 1, 1966, pp. 60–89.

INDEX